D0395691

PRAISE FOR *The War Against Parents*

"Cornel West thinks like a sage, acts like a warrior, and writes like a poetical prophet. His recent book *The War Against Parents,* with Sylvia Ann Hewlett, is a brave, wonderful effort." — **Maya Angelou**

"What a marvelous alliance of two wise and gifted advocates and authors! The narratives of their divergent lives are stirring, vivid, and emotionally loaded, and they serve as the prologue to an eloquent agenda for the future of the family and the dignity of parents in our social order. This is an important book, nicely balanced, superbly presented, and tremendously convincing. I hope it gets an early reading in the White House and from members of the Congress. Parents everywhere will find it healing and restorative." — **Jonathan Kozol**, author of *Amazing Grace: The Lives of Children and the Conscience of a Nation*

"*The War Against Parents* is a powerful book on one of the central questions of our time—how can society do more to help overworked, overburdened parents do a better job of raising their children? It shows how mothers and fathers have been damaged by an economy and a culture that increasingly devalue the role of parents. But it also contains important ideas for reform. Hewlett and West propose a Parents' Bill of Rights to bolster economic security, ease the time crunch on parents, and strengthen marriage. The authors spent three years listening to mothers and fathers around the country. The voices of these typical representatives of America's 62 million parents give special power and legitimacy to the authors' far-reaching policy solutions." — **Senator Edward M. Kennedy**

"This is a brave book by two of America's best thinkers. Hewlett and West cut through the dead wood of political ideology and the underbrush of media hyperbole to enter a fresh new place in our discussion of families. The complex and compassionate stories they tell refute simple sanctimonious solutions by either the left or the right. The solutions they offer as alternatives are both workable and inspired. This book is enormously useful and important. It will become the modern parents' best friend." — **Mary Pipher**, author of *Reviving Ophelia: Saving the Selves of Adolescent Girls*

"*The War Against Parents* presents an insightful social analysis that examines the parent's role in American society and how it vastly affects our children. This important discourse creates a powerful case for uniting parents and healing the nation across the racial divide." — **Kweisi Mfume**, president and CEO, NAACP

"Our nation faces an enormous problem with so many children growing up with inadequate parental guidance. This book is both vivid and compelling. Using stories as well as analysis, *The War Against Parents* goes to the heart of the matter—what our society must do to support mothers and fathers so they can come through for their children." — **Michael Goldstein**, CEO, Toys "R" Us

"The stock market is soaring, yet schools are falling apart. American CEOs earn more than in any other industrialized nation, yet most American children don't have quality child care, and tens of millions go without health care. Unemployment is low, yet one out of three working couples with young children work split shifts because they can't afford child care. There *is* a "war against parents," and Hewlett and West have written a timely battle plan to start fighting back." — **Karen Nussbaum**, director, AFL-CIO Working Women's Department

BOOKS BY SYLVIA ANN HEWLETT

Child Neglect in Rich Nations

When the Bough Breaks

A Lesser Life

Family and Work: Bridging the Gap
(EDITED WITH ALICE ILCHMAN AND JOHN SWEENEY)

The Global Repercussions of U.S. Monetary and Fiscal Policy
(EDITED WITH HENRY KAUFMAN)

The Political Economy of Brazil and Mexico
(EDITED WITH RICHARD S. WEINERT)

The Cruel Dilemma of Development

BOOKS BY CORNEL WEST

Restoring Hope

Struggles in the Promised Land
(EDITED WITH JACK SALZMAN)

The Future of the Race
(WITH HENRY LOUIS GATES, JR.)

Jews and Blacks
(WITH MICHAEL LERNER)

Race Matters

Keeping Faith: Philosophy and Race in America

Prophetic Thought in Postmodern Times

Prophetic Reflections

Breaking Bread
(WITH BELL HOOKS)

The Ethical Dimensions of Marxist Thought

The American Evasion of Philosophy

Prophetic Fragments

Post-Analytic Philosophy
(EDITED WITH JOHN RAJCHMAN)

Prophesy Deliverance! An Afro-American
Revolutionary Christianity

The War Against Parents

WHAT WE CAN DO FOR AMERICA'S BELEAGUERED MOMS AND DADS

Sylvia Ann Hewlett
and Cornel West

HOUGHTON MIFFLIN COMPANY   *Boston • New York*

Library of Congress Cataloging-in-Publication Data
Hewlett, Sylvia Ann, date.
The War against parents : what we can do for America's be-
leaguered moms and dads / Sylvia Ann Hewlett and Cornel West.
p.   cm.
Includes index.
ISBN 0-395-89169-8
1. Parenting — United States. 2. Family policy — United States.
3. Child welfare — United States. I. West, Cornel. II. Title.
HQ755.8.H49   1998
649'.1'0973 — dc21   98-5779 CIP

Printed in the United States of America

Book design by Robert Overholtzer

QUM 10 9 8 7 6 5 4 3 2

FOR JEAN AND VERNON HEWLETT
IRENE AND CLIFTON WEST

*and all the other nameless heroes
who have fought these wars
with such courage
and dignity*

Acknowledgments

For both of us this book represents a coming together of our private and public lives. It therefore gives us particular pleasure to acknowledge the extensive help we have received from family, friends, and colleagues.

Our greatest debt is to our spouses, Richard S. Weinert and Elleni Gebre Amlak. Their generous love has buoyed our spirits and replenished our energies at critical junctures over the last five years. We also owe much to our wonderful children, Shira, Clifton, Lisa, David, Adam, Kalen, and Emma, who are living reminders of the splendors of this project.

We are indebted to many others. Peggy Shiller has given extraordinary energy to the research and organizational effort that undergirds this book; she and Nancy Rankin coordinated our Task Force on Parent Empowerment and spearheaded our national poll and focus group interviews. We are deeply grateful.

Our agents, Molly Friedrich and Gloria Loomis, saw this book through its birth pangs with skill and judgment; our editor, Steve Fraser, devoted large chunks of his precious time to shape the bones of this book; while our publisher, Wendy Strothman, gave us her unstinting support and wise counsel. We thank them all. Eric Chinski, Wendy Holt, and Lisa Weinert contributed valuable editorial and logistical help; Nicole Campbell, Elizabeth George, Jessica Greenbaum, Andrea Hetling, Lisa Jacobs, Elizabeth Leff, Geoffrey Rodkey, Laura Sedlock, Adam Weinert, and David Weinert assisted with the research and fact-checking; and Marthe Abraham, Ada Domenech, David Kim, and Andrea Parker played critical roles on the home and office front. Few authors receive such loyal support, and we are extremely appreciative.

We would like to thank the foundations that lent generous support to the research that underlies the book and the jacket art: American Express Foundation, Bodman Foundation, Aaron Diamond Foundation, Robert

Wood Johnson Foundation, McKnight Foundation, Charles Stewart Mott Foundation, Scholastic Inc., Surdna Foundation, Toys "R" Us, and the Unitarian Universalist Veatch Program at Shelter Rock.

We are extremely grateful to the scholars, analysts, and activists who participated so wholeheartedly in our Task Force on Parent Empowerment and its outreach programs around the nation: Enola Aird, Charles Ballard, Dick Bartlett, Derrick Bell, Andrew Billingsley, David Blankenhorn, Don S. Browning, John A. Buehrens, Sara Moores Campbell, Geoffrey Canada, Allan C. Carlson, Susan Carlson, John Mack Carter, Craig Charney, Renée Cherow-O'Leary, Forrest Church, Judy Comeau-Hart, James D. Cox, Francine Diamond, Gardner Dunnan, David Elkind, Jean Bethke Elshstain, Amitai Etzioni, Judy Farrell, Sandra Feldman, Roxanna Foster, Hyman Frankel, Lucy N. Friedman, Maggie Gallagher, William A. Galston, John A. Gherty, Carol Gilligan, Michael Goldstein, David Harris, Peter Herbst, Fran Hesch, Jody Heymann, Betty Holmes, Lou Iacovelli, Ann Jackson, Philip W. Johnston, Barbara M. Jones, Carol Kamin, Julia Kristeller, Joyce S. Lapenn, James Levine, Dana Mack, Judith Martin, Jake Mascotte, Mark Mauer, Sarah McLanahan, Benita Melton, Hope Melton, Frank Moretti, Catherine O'Neill, Essie D. Owens, Samuel P. Peabody, Hugh Pearson, Susan D. Phillips, Edward Pitt, David Putnam, Wornie L. Reed, James Renier, David G. Richardson, Richard Robinson, Esmerelda Santiago, Juliet Schor, Raymond Seidelman, Jack Sheinkman, Robert Sherman, Theda Skocpol, Ralph Smith, Giovanna Stark, James P. Steyer, Sonia Taitz, Carl Taylor, Martha A. Taylor, Ruy Teixeira, Stanley Turecki, Amanda Vaill, Judith S. Wallerstein, David Walsh, Peter Winn, Edward N. Wolff, Ira Wolfman, and Ruth Wooden.

Bill Acosta, Carlos and Daryl Benaim, Raina Sachs Blankenhorn, Ellen Chessler, John Eatwell, Katherine El Salahi, Al and Franni Franken, Flavia and Barden Gale, RoseLee Goldberg, Sue Gronewold, Abby Hirsch, Anne Howe, Dakota Jackson, Enid Jones, Helen Knight, Greta Knowles, Kay and Peter Leslie, Helen Levine, Kathy Lord, Matt Mallow, Mary and Roger Mulvihill, Silu and Marcello Olarte, Ursala Oppens, Ruth and Tom Sedlock, Ruth Spellman, Sandra Stingle, Margot Waddell, Christine P. Wasserstein, Thelma Weinert, and Marcia Welles gave generous amounts of support, advice, and affection. We thank them all.

We are also grateful to the scholars, teachers, parents, and children who contributed to the success of our "Images of Mothers and Fathers" art project. In particular we would like to thank Jakia Bland, Robert Coles, Joan Davidson, Maria Friedrich, Diana Mercado, Ruth Messinger, Juan Padilla, Debra Prothrow-Smith, Dominique Theronier, Angela Williams, and Su Li Zheng.

Most of all, we want to thank the parents and children we interviewed. Throughout the lifespan of our Task Force on Parent Empowerment, we crisscrossed the country from the South Bronx to Santa Barbara, from St. Paul to Sacramento, talking to families on the front lines, trying to understand their most urgent needs and yearnings. In a profound sense, these interviews made this book possible, and we are extremely grateful to the courageous parents and children who allowed us into their lives. Hundreds of moms, dads, and kids contributed their voices to this book. We cannot thank them all in person, but we would like to make mention of Linda DeCarlo, Theodore Fisher, Michelle Gittings, Tracy and Marcus Glover, Andrew Haimes, Marcus Harris, Fran Hesch, JoAnn Luehring, Jeff Metzer, Michael Motta, Jim Papathomas, Vanessa Sims, Taino Soba, Maria Torres, and Burley Leon Whitten.

Contents

IV. Reweaving the Web of Care

Prologue

OURS IS A special partnership.

A black man and a white woman come together to confront our nation's war against parents and our consequent inability to cherish our children. Such a collaboration is rare and precious. Given the sharp segregation that scars late-twentieth-century American life, it is hard to find examples of sustained projects that rest on a black-white partnership. And our work together is not merely some cloistered, scholarly endeavor but involves high-stakes political action. It requires nothing less than the launching of a new political movement.

Our partnership is particularly significant given that the issues we deal with are among the deepest and most intractable in our society. They are also ones typically exacerbated by race and gender. For thirty years the problems associated with absentee parents and out-of-control kids have inspired impassioned and bitter debate between blacks and whites, men and women.

Given this backdrop, one of the achievements of our work together is that we have constructed a vision and a movement with the power to heal. By giving moral heft to the art and practice of parenting and by crafting a political agenda capable of delivering new and substantial support to parents, we have found a repository of comfort and strength that has the potential to bridge the deep divides of race, gender, and class.

As parents ourselves, we are hungry for this healing. For two decades we have been on the front lines, wrestling with the enormous challenge of trying to be a good mother and a good father in this parent-hurting society. Much of this painful struggle has been unnecessarily lonely, for the fact is, our "blackness" and our "femaleness" pale in the light of an even more fundamental identity: that of being a parent. After all, we share the bedrock stuff: we are crazy about our kids. This may not be obvious every hour of every day, because our children are capable of being as exasperating and challenging as any other youngsters, but when push comes to shove, we know we would give our lives for them. There is not a whole lot in life that can compete with this commitment. When God asked Abraham for the ultimate sacrifice as a test of his faith, he did not ask Abraham to lay down his own life; rather, he asked him to take the life of his son, Isaac. This is one of the great stories of all time, shared across many religions, and for at least two millennia it has provoked anguished reflection in men and women, because it transgresses our most elemental emotion: the love of a parent for a child.

We also share a load of impotence and guilt—and mounting rage—with other parents. We know firsthand the agony of the impossible pressures and choices our society thrusts upon moms and dads. How do you bond with an infant if you are constrained to be back at work ten days after birth? How do you enforce a curfew or insist on homework when the sound bites of our culture undercut parental authority in myriad ways? Some days it feels as though we are swimming upstream, cutting against the current of all that is valued in our market-driven society. In late-twentieth-century America, parenting has become a countercultural activity of the first order.

There is much that is new and nourishing in our work together. Strange as it may seem, the identity of being a parent—unlike those based on race, gender, or class—is relatively undeveloped in American society, and enormous potential lies in identifying people first and foremost as mothers and fathers. Conservatives and liberals, rich and poor, blacks and whites, men and women, easily splinter over policy issues, whether the problem at hand is welfare reform or new rules for divorce. But when these same people are forced to confront these issues as parents, they can often find common ground. By utilizing the lens of parenthood, we are able to shed new light on old problems and bring an entirely fresh perspective to the shrill and tired debate over the American family.

Thus, this book provides comfort and hope on both the intimate and the societal front. It contains affirmation of and support for individual parents. And there is not a father or a mother among us who is not thirsty for such relief. Even more important, it puts forward a programmatic agenda capable of underpinning our collective future. If we can create the conditions that allow parents to do a good job by their children, we will contribute mightily to the health and wealth of this great country.

The two of us met in the summer of 1992 when Senator Bill Bradley and William Bennett invited us to join the Domestic Strategy Group, an advisory panel convened at the Aspen Institute in Colorado during the lead-up to the 1992 presidential election. The mandate of the panel was to explore the causes of our social malaise—the fracturing of families, the hollowing-out of community. The group didn't get very far. Despite the best efforts of David Gergen, who moderated, liberals and conservatives clashed on ideological grounds and disagreed on most items of substance. Some months later, the panel broke up in disarray. But the two of us continued to talk—and talk and talk. Whatever its failings, the Aspen project seeded a partnership that grew enormously in scope and depth. Intense discussions over Monday lunch at Princeton, and later Harvard, evolved into joint paper-writing, shared political activism, and eventually this book.

We begin by asking a central question: why are hundreds of thousands of American children dangling and dangerous and millions more failing to thrive? It is a fact that too many children are being born without a skin—with none of the protective armor that in the past was provided by parents and communities. We demonstrate that at the heart of our children's plight is a truly frightening erosion of the parental role—of the ability of moms and dads to come through for their children. This is happening not because parents are less devoted than they used to be. They do not love their children less. The truth is, the whole world is pitted against them. One of the best-kept secrets of the last thirty years is that big business, government, and the wider culture have waged a silent war against parents, undermining the work that they do. Some of the hostility has been inadvertent, and some of it has been deliberate. But whatever forces are responsible for the war against parents, one thing is for sure: parents have been left twisting in the wind by a society intent on other agendas.

As a nation we have a hard time acknowledging the significance of what is going on. Until recently, the failure of our government to support parenting was masked by the existence of a deep—and largely invisible—reservoir of unpaid female labor. For generations, wives and mothers raised our children and tended our communities, creating the web of care that the rest of society depended on—and took entirely for granted. But relying on free and invisible female labor as the fountainhead of our social and human capital no longer works. In the 1990s, women have new agendas and other responsibilities, and society has been left with a dangerous void—a vacuum in which children are diminished and destroyed.

Precisely because parenting has been so very invisible, we have great difficulty grasping its enormous importance. Simply put, the parent-child bond is the most powerful of all human attachments. All of us who are mothers and fathers comprehend this on an intuitive level. How can any of us forget the bewildering rush of gut-wrenching, life-bending emotion we felt when we first held a newborn son or daughter? But despite the power of this shared experience, we generally do not understand the larger significance of the parent-child bond. We do not realize that when this elemental connection weakens and frays, devastating consequences ripple through the nation, for the sacrificial, other-directed work that parents do is the wellspring of compassion, competence, and commitment in society. In fundamental and far-reaching ways parents affect the strength of our communities, the capacity of our economy, and the vitality of our democracy. We demean and devalue these precious parental energies at our peril. Which brings us to the main thrust of this book: *what can this society do to revalue and revitalize the art and practice of parenting and thus replenish our children and renew our nation?*

As we tackled this huge challenge and searched for the alchemy that might produce a new kind of parent power, we triggered a series of policy initiatives to help us in our quest. In October 1995 we created and chaired the Task Force on Parent Empowerment. The idea behind this endeavor was to pull together a group of eminent scholars, policymakers, business leaders, and parent activists from both white and black America to help us create the intellectual foundations for a parents' movement. For two years this task force deliberated, sifting through the relevant research, listening to testimony from parents around the country, analyzing the power of various policy instruments, and trying to figure out how and why parents have become one of the most disadvantaged groups in our nation. In October 1997 we completed our labors and presented our main result, a blueprint for parent empowerment entitled "A Parents' Bill of Rights." This document comprises a pragmatic, programmatic agenda that delivers on two fronts: it tells us how to relieve the intense economic pressures on parents and solve the parental time famine, and it shows us how to rewrite our cultural script so as to lend new status to the parental role.

In a parallel exercise, we obtained foundation funding to underwrite the first ever nationwide poll of parents' political priorities, an exercise that we undertook in the fall of 1996, just before the presidential election. Despite all the political posturing on family values, up until this survey there were virtually no hard data on what kinds of support parents want and need, from government and from the community at large. With all the hand-wringing in Washington over family disintegration, it is astonishing that no one has seen fit to ask the views of those most deeply affected— moms and dads. This survey allowed us to listen to the voices of parents and tease out their most desperate needs, desires, and yearnings. What these parents had to say was invaluable, and we used it to draw up our blueprint for action. Our Parents' Bill of Rights thus incorporates this additional element of authenticity and legitimacy.

Last but not least, in 1994 and again in 1996 we reached out to a special set of youngsters, the schoolchildren of New York City, and asked them for images of their moms and dads. What does it feel like to grow up in the belittled and besieged families of the 1990s? With paint and poetry, these children created images of stunning clarity. Some of their work is lyrical and inspiring; much more is quite brutal. As a tribute to these remarkable youngsters, we use examples of this powerful art to illustrate the jacket of this book. Through the exquisite honesty of these paintings and poems, we learn anew of the power of parents to make or break a child's life.

One final note: this book is built on more than its fair share of passion and commitment. Throughout our labors we have been touched by the singular joys and responsibilities of a project that goes to the core of our beings. We feel the healing power of the work we have done together in the recesses of our souls. Over the past year we have been made particularly aware of these profound connections by the birth of a grandson, Kalen, into the West family and of a daughter, Emma, into the Hewlett-Weinert family. As we were caught up in the miracle of birth, we were once again inspired—and humbled—by the astonishing power of a small child to evoke our most sublime and selfless feelings. Parenthood does indeed present astonishing opportunities—for individuals and for nations.

In September 1997 we held an event in New York to celebrate and give thanks for new life. Both families participated. For this special occasion we were inspired to exchange some words, which included poetry and dialogue. These words are for Emma:

> I glory in her wide gummy grin which lights up the whole
> world,
> and her infectious giggle.
> When she lets loose that bubbling crescendo of pure joy,
> I stop whatever I am doing and allow it to wash over me.
> Such unstinting, unedited delight cleanses the soul.
>
> I revel in the steady stare of her forget-me-not eyes,
> knowing that despite the intense scrutiny, this is not a judg-
> ment thing.
> No need to suck in the belly or touch up the makeup;
> babies don't know that wrinkles and bulges are bad.
> Emma is merely drinking me in, learning my lines, my sounds,
> my smells,
> learning to love and be loved.
>
> I adore her sated, trusting body, when, on the verge of sleep,
> she snuggles deep in my breast,
> her pudgy fingers spread out like a fan or a gill.
> Dreaming of nourishment, her mouth makes small, sucking
> motions,
> and for a moment she looks like a diminutive, celestial fish.
> It is this total abandonment, this extraordinary trust, that
> I remember from my other babies.

Emma has not yet learned to measure or modulate,
to dole out her joy in manageable dollops.
She does not realize that she needs to hold something in
    reserve.
She does not understand that she can be hurt.

These days such vulnerability can tear my heart out.
I now know just how many babies are rebuffed and rejected
    by a harsh and unforgiving world.

I am deeply grateful for this bonus child,
for Emma brings with her special joys and special responsi-
    bilities.
In midlife I am much more in touch with that which is
    miraculous and glorious in a new life.
But I am also more in touch with the awesome risks—hers and
    mine.
Some are straightforward enough;
Emma can choke on a pea or drown in three inches of
    bathwater.
Others are much more complicated.

I now have another hostage to fortune,
one more life that is more precious than my own. And I now
    know what that means.

It means a loss of freedom. It means dealing with an undertow
    of care and anxiety that permeates every hour of every day.
For I know full well that if I fail to keep my children safe,
    I will not find life worth living.

One thing is clear, the loss of freedom is a small price to pay
    for this,
most sublime of earthly connections.
Being a parent, cherishing a child, brings out the better angels
    of human nature,
drawing upon our most selfless instincts.
For myself it has brought a measure of wisdom, and a great
    deal of happiness.

As recent beneficiaries of liberation movements (feminist and
black), we find it particularly hard to face the bare, bald truth:

children deserve prime time and attention and need to sit in the center of life. This is bound to curtail some of our hard-won freedoms. So be it. At least for the sweet, short years of childhood, everything else in a parent's life should be negotiable.

Of course, our negotiations and accommodations would be a lot less painful if we could count on the support of the wider community, which simply is not there. We all know the grinding toll of doing battle every day with the snipes and sneers of our culture. Modern America expects every parent to be both a hero and a saint. But who among us has a private supply of altruistic energy that can be dipped into on a daily basis for a couple of decades? Not you, not we.

We deal with so many layers of betrayal that it cuts deep into the space we have for watching a newborn child dream; we thus lose out on the magic unleashed by an unfolding life. The selfless passion most of us mothers and fathers conjure up for our children is the nearest we come to transcending earthbound limits. We cannot afford to waste this precious energy. Our best hope for this book is that it gives new support and sanctity to the work that parents do and ensures that all the Emmas and Kalens of this world flower and flourish.

PART I

Struggling Parents Then and Now

ONE

························

The Partnership

ONE OF THE GREATEST surprises of our partnership has been the discovery of profound commonalities in our experience of parenthood, as children and as adults. On the surface of things our lives began very differently—for what could be more different than black blue-collar America and white working-class Wales? But at a deeper level of reality there were extraordinary similarities in how we were raised and the values we took from our parents. Even more unexpected—and certainly more fraught—is what we share in our adult struggles to be a good father and a good mother. We have both discovered that adequate resources and a desperate desire to do a good job by our kids are no guarantee of success in this parent-hurting society. Like millions of other mothers and fathers—black, white, and every shade in between—we have unwittingly been caught up in this war against parents, and our tales from the front lines share a load of gratuitous isolation and struggle.

Let's start with some of the obvious contrasts.

Sylvia Ann Hewlett The landscape of my childhood was littered with reminders of a troubled past. In the 1950s, the South Wales mining valleys looked like a film set for the industrial revolution. I remember going on walks with my grandfather and trying to take in the significance of the shuttered collieries, abandoned slag heaps, and row upon row of ramshackle terraced houses straggling up the hillsides. Even the omnipresent silly sheep were dirty and dilapidated, their woolen coats clogged with the same coal dust that infiltrated my skin and clothes. When I was a teenager there was a new round of closures—many of the remaining mines and steel mills shut down, and unemployment hovered around the 20 percent mark. The young people I knew, particularly those with spunk and energy, left in droves. ❧

Cornel West Six thousand miles away, the backdrop was very different. In the 1950s, California was entering its golden era. Postwar prosperity was in full bloom. Economic growth was moving along at an impressive clip, pulling in workers from out of state who were lured by good jobs and a great climate. I remember Sacramento in the 1950s and 1960s as a place where pretty much everyone was upbeat about the future. Even for black families with modest means in segregated neighborhoods, it was a land of pleasant single-family homes, of barbecues and baseball diamonds. All of us kids had dads, most with jobs—that, we took for granted. ❧

Despite these startling differences, we soon learned that we came to our writing partnership from oddly similar backgrounds. First and foremost, our fundamental roots lie not in California or in Wales but in two specific sets of parents who placed children center-stage in their lives and gave these children the gift of unconditional love, in generous and imaginative measure. Second, we were both raised in impressively strong extended families that were nourished by a rich web of social support emanating from the wider community. We see this as critical. After all, our life histories are not those of lone individuals pulling themselves up by their own bootstraps, or of people who just lucked out, who happened to inherit a set of stellar parents who found the inner resources to do an exceptional job. Vernon and Jean Hewlett and Clifton and Irene West were highly effective parents, but they were able to draw strength from a popular culture that nourished and supported them and a political culture that enabled and empowered them.

Finally, our childhoods were conditioned by our outsider status as a black male and a working-class female. In strangely similar ways we both spent an important chunk of our early lives fighting a legacy of discrimination centered on race, class, and gender. Again, these were not private or lonely battles. In the United States and

Britain, civil rights legislation, affirmative action, and class- and gender-sensitive educational policies all played a role in vastly improving the odds in our favor. However, despite this rich array of supports, one thing is crystal clear: none of these external factors would have done any good without the central ingredient—the unstinting, sustained love provided by our parents.

Cornel West Mom and Dad definitely gave me the armor to survive and thrive in a racist society. They gave me a deep spirituality and morality that sustained me as a black male in America. When those white brothers acted devilish, I had all kinds of inner resources to fall back on. This not only helped me with my teenage struggles but, down the road, enabled me to reach out to others. Looking back on it, I tell you, the love I got from Mom and Dad was supernatural. Lord have mercy! This is what has supported my spirit and soothed my soul. ❧

Sylvia Ann Hewlett My parents, for their part, gave me all kinds of armor—competence and confidence, yes, but also a kind of in-your-face audacity that enabled me to cross class and gender lines in what was still an extremely traditional society. When I arrived at Cambridge University at age eighteen and discovered that I belonged to the wrong sex, spoke with the wrong accent, and came from the wrong side of the tracks, I needed all the parent-inspired armor-plating I could get my hands on. ❧

The Biographical Backdrop

Cornel West I was born in Tulsa, Oklahoma, in 1953. My family then spent three years in Topeka, Kansas, before moving on to Sacramento, California. I consider my real growing-up place to be Glen Elder, a black, working-class community on the outskirts of Sacramento. During my childhood, my father worked in the supplies department at McClellan Air Force Base. When I was five, my mother went back to school to finish her college degree, eventually becoming a schoolteacher and a principal. I was the second of four children and have an older brother, Clifton III, and two younger sisters, Cynthia and Cheryl.

Glen Elder was built just after the war, and its modest homes were mostly bought by hardworking black folk, many of whom were returning veterans. When I was a kid growing up, it was a blue-collar community where most grownups—men and women—had steady, decent jobs as bus drivers, waiters, construction workers, barbers, salesclerks. No family had much money, but every kid on my block had two parents and a back yard. It may sound ironic, but despite the fact that Glen Elder at that point was segregated—the banks and the real estate agents worked out a deal that restricted blacks to three subdivisions on the outskirts of Sacramento—it was a wonderful place to grow up in. Neighborhood ties were close and supportive. Most evenings someone would come knocking on the door asking for a cup of sugar or a pint of milk, either because they had run out or to tide them over until payday. We kids learned to figure out who the needy ones were, and would do our best to help out: "Here's the milk for your baby, Mrs. Burton, but do my mama a favor and take this rice we have left over."

The ingredients were not complicated—a plenitude of jobs, involved mothers, fathers on the case, vigilant neighbors—but the end result was that the streets of Glen Elder were free of crime. From age five or six, my brother, my sisters, and I were allowed to play anyplace in the neighborhood. My mama just gave us a time when we were expected home. Until darkness fell, we were given almost complete freedom. Today, if you go back, you'll see these same streets infested with guns and drugs. You would never believe we had that kind of childhood. ❦

Sylvia Ann Hewlett I was the second of six daughters and was born in Pyle, a small working-class community on the southern edge of the South Wales coalfield. During my childhood my father held various teaching jobs, eventually becoming principal of a technical school. My mother also trained as a teacher, but she gave up teaching when her first child was born. As the family expanded, we moved to nearby communities—Cwmbran, Croesyceiliog, New Inn—seeking larger, affordable accommodation and better schools for us girls.

Partly because we moved so many times, I do not remember close neighborhood ties. Instead, I feel that as a child I derived enormous support from a close-knit extended family. As a young girl I particularly idolized my paternal grandfather, Anthony Hewlett, a tin-plate worker who left school at age twelve and spent most of his life engaged in backbreaking physical labor, a fact that did not stop him from engaging in various kinds of political activity. For many years he was the leader of the South Wales branch of the Steel Workers Confederation. A self-taught, learned man, he won all kinds of essay competitions and in his thirties was awarded a scholarship at Cambridge University. However, despite all of his intellectual gifts, this working-class bloke was never able to earn a degree—in the end he was not able to matriculate in Greek and Latin—and ended up back in Wales dipping metal in molten tin and supporting a family on three pounds a week. From my grandfather I learned to understand the power of collective bargaining and class struggle. But I also absorbed the lesson that credentials are enormously important, especially for people born on the wrong side of the class divide. The advice of my grandfather was to "go get those fancy degrees and beat the upper classes at their own game."

My father, following family tradition, led impassioned discussions over the evening meal. Was any cause worth risking one's life for? Personally, he thought not. Should the Welsh language be made a compulsory subject in school? It seemed a little daft to him. And how about reincarnation? What did we all think of Buddhist ideas on this subject? A committed pacifist and religious maverick, he liked to get his teeth into ideas like these over high tea.

In the late 1950s my father became involved in the Campaign for Nuclear Disarmament and did his best to persuade his family to share this enthusiasm. I can still remember the scene at one local CND rally—my father and a row of small daughters in plastic macs and Wellington boots listening to Bertrand Russell expound on the perfidy of the superpowers. Needless to say, the whole event was way above the heads of us kids.

Despite a rich vein of debate and political passion, life was pretty threadbare in our household. The family had no refrigerator, telephone, television, or car until I was in my mid-teens, and we girls were very much thrown back on our own resources. Whether it was dealing with dank winters in unheated bedrooms by cuddling up three to a bed, or helping one another with homework or violin practice, we developed intense bonds. Camaraderie was also fostered by an enormous amount of shared household labor—fetching coal for the kitchen fire, doing the family wash with the aid of a boiler and scrubbing board, figuring out what to do when the sheets froze on the clothesline. ❧

The Economic Struggle

Sylvia Ann Hewlett Eking out small amounts of money, pinching and scraping, was a way of life in my childhood. My quite dreadful parachute blouses are permanently etched in my memory. At the grammar school we older girls attended, students were required to wear crisp white blouses teamed up with bottle-green pleated skirts and jackets, all of which added up to a tidy sum in the local stores, and this was especially true if you needed to buy six of everything! So my mother hit upon the ingenious idea of investing in large quantities of surplus parachute material. Since it was left over from World War II, it cost next to nothing. The only problem was, it was quite hideous, being dirty beige in color and resembling a thick, textured plastic. My mother struggled to fashion this slippery, sliding stuff into blouses for her girls, but her valiant efforts were not up to the task at hand. The collars puckered and curled, and the seams jutted out at odd angles. The result was a garment guaranteed to make any teenager look remarkably unattractive. To add insult to injury, this fabric, made to withstand the Normandy invasion, literally never wore out. I was still sweating it out inside my parachute blouses when I left school at eighteen. ❧

Government Support

Cornel West On the important economic front, Uncle Sam was pretty good to the West family in the 1950s and 1960s. You know, Mom would not even have met Dad had it not been for the GI Bill! He was only able to study at Fisk, where Mom was a student, because he was a veteran and the tuition charges were paid for by the government. A few years later, when they were a young married couple with kids, the GI Bill kicked in once more. By guaranteeing a low-cost mortgage, the Veterans Administration made all the difference. My mother remembers the numbers so clearly because it seemed like a miracle to her. She and my dad were able to buy our three-bedroom home in Glen Elder because they were able to put down just $500 and take out a 3 percent mortgage. At that time they had practically no savings. In the 1950s and 1960s family finances were stretched real thin—I mean, no one with four young children has much money. Without government help, home ownership for our family would have been out of the question. ❧

Sylvia Ann Hewlett For my family, the government-provided family allowance of fourteen shillings a week was a godsend in the 1950s. It underwrote a chunk of the weekly grocery bill and helped with gift-giving at birthdays and Christmas. It also gave my mum a precious degree of financial independence. Only mothers could sign for the family allowance, so this sum of money was truly hers. Picking it up at the post office on Fridays was one of the high points of her week. All of us, especially the babies, also benefited from the new National Health Service—created by the first Labour government of postwar Britain—which provided family health care free of charge. Obstetrical care, hospital stays for childbirth, at-home midwife services, well-baby doctor's visits, vaccinations, and dental care were now there for the asking. My mother was especially grateful for the milk, orange juice, and cod liver oil that nursing mothers and small children received free of charge. When we were babies, Britain was still dealing with wartime rationing—it lasted until the early 1950s—and you just couldn't get these basic supplies for love or money. Back then, my parents saw the government as truly committed to helping parents raise healthy children. ❧

A Family-Friendly Popular Culture

While government policy in the 1950s bolstered parents in their struggle to do a good job by their children, whether they lived in South Wales or California, the popular culture of this era kept a respectful distance. It intruded relatively little on private family space, and when it did impinge, it was mildly or enthusiastically supportive of family values.

Sylvia Ann Hewlett I remember my childhood as much less invaded by the media than is true for my kids. For example, my parents did not buy a television until I was fourteen years old, and then they imposed strict rules. We older children were allowed to watch one show during the week and three at the weekend, while the younger children were allowed to watch "children's hour." To this day I remember the excitement of turning on our flickering black-and-white TV set at 7 P.M. Thursday evening to watch *Dixon of Dock Green*. By today's standards *Dixon* was a singularly tame show featuring a kindly policeman in a blue helmet doing good in the neighborhood, but to me and my sisters this was heady, suspense-filled drama. ❧

Cornel West I remember the Mouseketeers, a Disney show featuring children in Mickey Mouse ears getting into all kinds of exciting scrapes. On weekdays we kids watched this show together; it came on at 5 P.M., just after dinner. When the show was over, the television set was turned firmly off so that we kids could concentrate on our homework and on reading. Sunday evening the family got together to watch *The Ed Sullivan Show*. And as far as television watching was concerned, that was pretty much it. ❧

It wasn't only a question of network television in the 1950s being low-key and respectful; home life almost entirely lacked the high-decibel bombardment from the media we have gotten so used to today. There was simply no equivalent of MTV, trash talk shows, slasher movies, Calvin Klein underwear ads, or local TV news. Our parents tended to buy one of the more sedate newspapers on Sunday, but we were not pounded by a daily Technicolor fare of drive-by shootings in Detroit and massacres in Rwanda, nor were we tempted to buy gangster rap or rent *Natural Born Killers* at the local video store. As kids we delighted in buying the occasional forty-five, but James Brown, Curtis Mayfield, and various Motown artists (in the West household) and Mozart and the Swingle Singers (in the Hewlett household) were about as daring as we got.

Parental Involvement and Education

By and large, our families had time rather than money, and as a result they were much less likely to offload a child-related problem on an expert—whether a therapist, a tutor, or a coach—than families are today.

Sylvia Ann Hewlett I have vivid memories of the hundreds of hours my mother put in preparing me for the eleven-plus examination. This was not an easy task, given the fact that she had five other small children and was running a home that lacked such modern conveniences as a washing machine and a refrigerator. However, my mother understood that the stakes were huge. If I was not among the lucky 15 percent that made it through the eleven-plus examination to grammar school, I would be relegated to the local secondary modern school and a third-rate education. The problems facing her were twofold: at age ten I was an indifferent student, somewhere in the middle of my class, and we couldn't begin to afford a private tutor. So she set to work with daily spelling tests and arithmetic exercises, telling anyone who was interested that I was just a late bloomer. I don't know where she found the time or the firmness of purpose. For twelve months I squirmed and I squiggled, doing my level best to drive my poor mother up the wall as we sat at the kitchen table for an interminable sixty minutes a day. But her doggedness prevailed, and I managed to get over the eleven-plus hurdle and earn a coveted grammar school place. Even at the time, with my rather limited ten-year-old vision of what was important, I remember being immensely grateful. ❧

The Luxury of Time

But it wasn't just the occasional examination emergency; we both recall, with considerable awe, the impressive amount of time our respective parents—particularly our mothers—devoted to the care and supervision of us children. Some of this time was surely "quality time," but more than the intensity of interaction, we remember the sheer, unstinting quantity of it all. Our parents were simply available and on call, day in, day out, year after year.

Sylvia Ann Hewlett My mother's trek to and from primary school stands out in my memory with particular clarity. When I was about nine, the family moved to a house that was sited alongside a heavily trafficked main road. The primary school we children attended was some distance away—about two thirds of a mile—and the route to school involved crossing several busy and somewhat dangerous intersections. These were the days before crossing guards, school buses, or school lunches, and my family did not own a car. So four times a day, my mum walked us to and from school: at 8:45 A.M. and 12:15 P.M., and again at 1:30 P.M. and 3:15 P.M. Eight times a day she made this trip on foot, pushing the youngest child in a stroller. Looking back, I am staggered at the magnitude of the time commitment and the relentless rhythm. How did my mum find time to clean, shop, and cook, let alone do anything for herself? And all that walking can't have been much fun, as the local climate didn't exactly make things pleasant or easy. Sheets of cold, driving Welsh rain often accompanied these treks to and from school. Several times a week, we all arrived home with wet socks and chattering teeth. And yet my mother was often cheerful and good-humored. At 12:15 and 3:15 she always seemed so pleased to see us. We used to run up to her, eager to share a drawing or a piece of inconsequential school news. When I was eleven I left this primary school and moved on to grammar school, but four younger sisters remained in the pipeline. My mum was to make this trek for an additional twelve years. ❧

Cornel West What I recall most clearly is the extraordinary amount of time my parents—particularly my mother, but also my dad—devoted to my various "discipline" problems. I was a devilish child, at least some of the time, and got into some serious trouble. I had tremendous energy but didn't know how to channel it. At age eight I was the head of the local gang, if you could call it that. More like a group of kids that hung out together, and I was their leader. We could be real mean. We had an operation where we'd take little kids' money. We'd line them up and they would give us their lunch money—thirty-five cents. We'd then go buy candy at

Sam's store and hand it out to the kids. It was just inexcusable. It wasn't ugly physically, but it was mean and wrong.

Luckily, we didn't have weapons to speak of. Every once in a while someone would pull out a switchblade, but mainly it was fists, and Mom was somehow always around looking out for us—I think she had eyes in the back of her head! Whenever my mother caught me fighting, she would step right in to make sure it was fair and square. First she would ask us if we really wanted to fight. Of course we would say yes. Then she'd say, "Okay, but you're going to have a fair fight, so put on your gloves." Mama would stand right there, hands on hips, watching us go at it with gloves, and we'd fight fair until we collapsed. If for some reason she wasn't there, which was rare, we'd do some bad stuff—bash heads against walls, that kind of thing.

My mom did the day-to-day supervision, but my dad was in charge of the heavy-duty discipline. When I got into real trouble, which seemed to happen a lot, he got the belt out and whipped me. I'll never forget in third grade I beat up my teacher. She was pregnant and it was a terrible thing to do, but I just lost control. You see, she tried to make me salute the flag. I refused—being newly in touch with the hypocrisy of this racist society, I mean, who are you kidding, even in third grade I realized that America was not "one nation under God, indivisible, with liberty and justice for all." This sister didn't know what to do with my intransigence, so she slapped me. My rage and impotence just boiled over and I laid into her with my fists. I guess I didn't really hurt her—the baby was fine—but God, was this a big thing. West punched out the teacher. I got suspended for a month or so.

I was sent home early that day. I remember it so clearly. As I walked in the door of my house, the phone rang. It was my dad. "Corn," he says, "have your pants down to your knees and my belt next to you when I get home. I'm leaving early. In fact, I'm leaving now." My heart sank to my boots. I knew that he would give me the beating of a lifetime. He did, and he was justified.

My dad was so upset by this incident that after the beating he just went into his bedroom and shut the door. He stayed there for a long time, quiet and sad. I cried like a baby, but there was nothing I could do to ease my father's pain. I knocked on the door and tried to apologize. But he felt as bad as I did. In all kinds of ways, my father's disappointment in me was much harder to bear than the beating. ❧

Anger and the Legacy of Race

Cornel West Looking back, I now understand that at least part of the aggression and rage I felt as a child was tied up with the special burdens of being born black in a racist society. By and large, folks in my family did not see themselves as victims, but nonetheless, family history was infused with a heavy load of discrimination and oppression.

Mom used to tell us kids of her girlhood in Crowley, Louisiana. She told how in downtown Crowley blacks were not allowed to drink from the water fountains, sit downstairs in the movie theater, or try on hats or dresses in the local clothing stores. Negroes, as they were called then, were simply not thought to have civilized habits when it came to personal hygiene. They were allowed to buy any clothing item they wanted, but they needed to know their exact size and were expected to pay in cash. Returns were not allowed.

When I was a kid these stories made my blood boil, but they did not make me as fighting mad as another family story that stands out sharp and painful in my memory. It revolves around my maternal grandmother, who died when she was just thirty years old. It sounds unbelievable, but she died because she had a tooth pulled. In those days they put a string around your tooth and attached it to a door. Then they slammed the door and your tooth—hopefully—came out. Well in my grandmama's case, part of the decayed tooth stayed in her gum, and it became infected. Unfortunately, there was only one black doctor in town, and he was on vacation. So they wrapped up her head and waited. One afternoon she got so bad they rushed her to the white hospital in town, to find that the hospital wouldn't allow her in. Some hotshot white doctor stood in the doorway declaring, "Over my dead body will we have black people in this hospital." So she died on the steps of the hospital. My granddaddy was with her, and he went berserk. But some of the other black folks—deacons from the church—jumped on Granddaddy to prevent him from hurting this guy. You see, he could have been lynched—Granddaddy, I mean. In the end, they ran him out of town with his kids. My mom was just three months old. And so my mother never knew her mama.

Mom was always careful to put these stories in perspective for us children. Yes, her family of origin was poor and discriminated against, but it was also true that within the cocoon of her family, her church, and her segregated community, she was a cherished and celebrated child. She often pointed out that she was better off than many poor black children today, who often have no refuge in terms of home and family. Back in Crowley, money was undoubtedly in short supply—the family budget was tight enough to preclude indoor plumbing and children's toys—and yet she did not know she was poor until she was a grown woman. She recalls her childhood home as being a center of community life. In summertime neighbors gathered on the porch with its swing and rockers for conversation—slow, comfortable conversation about births, deaths, Sunday's sermon, and the cotton crop. Winter evenings were spent indoors. After the children had done their homework, they would spread out a jigsaw puzzle and the whole family would work on it together. She remembers the rocklike presence of her father. The first black to own a service station in Crowley, a deacon of the local Baptist church, and a powerhouse in the black community, he often filled in as a surrogate dad. One story Mom told was of a neighbor whose husband had passed and who was struggling to raise two high-spirited boys on her own. This lady used to come visiting on Fridays, saying to my grandfather, "Mr. Bias, please come by tomorrow night, I want you to give my boys a spanking, I need help in keeping them in line." And he would do just that.

Mom's fond memories of her girlhood in Louisiana and Texas went some way toward preparing me for my own encounters with racism. A bitter taste came in the early 1970s, when I had a run-in with the Cambridge police. During my second year at Harvard, a young woman who lived in my dorm was raped. The police immediately rounded up four black students, including me, and subjected us all to hours of interrogation. Immense pressure was put on the victim to identify one of us—it didn't much matter which—as her assailant. She refused, saying that she did not recognize any of us. To this day, I am profoundly grateful. I owe a lot to this white sister. The expectations were intense. Had she cracked, one of us would have been locked away for half a lifetime. ❧

The Importance of Fathers

Cornel West One thing I am clear in my mind about is that Dad put extraordinary energy into fostering and facilitating a childhood involvement in sports, which proved to be tremendously valuable to me. My passionate commitment to baseball from age eight to age fifteen focused my energies and gave me something to be proud of and belong to during those dangerous adolescent years. Through baseball I learned to understand and appreciate the value of loyalty, determination, integrity, and camaraderie. It also deepened and strengthened my relationship with Dad.

My father was one of the founders of the Glen Elder Little League. Can you imagine it today, one small community fielding fourteen teams, all coached by black fathers between the ages of twenty-one and thirty? The dads actually built the diamond for our games. They got together and spent weekends and evenings leveling the ground, laying the sod, and building the bleachers. In my childhood, baseball was one of those incredible communal activities where the men and boys came together. It was an excuse to stand around and shoot the breeze, to holler and cheer, to swap scores and averages, to coach the kids, and to bask in their accomplishments. The strange thing is, we really were a talented lot. Eight of the kids on my team ended up playing professional baseball. One of my closest friends was Roland Office, and he went on to play for the Atlanta Braves. When I was thirteen, my hero was Willie Mays and my aspiration was to be a major-league baseball player—I've clearly been a failure in that regard. I sometimes seriously think that all this intellectual stuff is all on the side—baseball is what life is all about.

Sports were so central to my life as a kid that I get enraged when they cut back on athletic programs. Seems like those are the first things to go when budgets are slashed, because they're seen as a frill. But sports are essential if you are interested in socializing young males. I'm living proof! ❧

Sylvia Ann Hewlett For his part, my father was passionately committed to our musical education. An amateur pianist and Mozart enthusiast, he would spend hours listening to the BBC

Third Programme, sharing various pieces of arcane knowledge with us children. As little girls we could guess the composer and key of a piece after having heard just a few bars of music. Despite the tight family budget, all six of us were given private music lessons and required to practice every day. This regime yielded impressive results. By the time I was twelve, there was a family string trio, and eventually we older sisters became members of the Welsh Youth Orchestra.

But looking back on my musical education, I have powerful cross-cutting feelings. The pressure to practice and perform was heavy-handed and relentless. My parents tended to give me sheet music for Christmas, when I really craved normal teenage stuff like bell-bottom jeans and Cliff Richards recordings. But I loved playing in the youth orchestra. Contributing to the splendor of Mahler's Fifth is an extraordinary experience for a fifteen-year-old. It also gave me a circle of friends from all over Wales who shared my cultural interests.

My father was a charismatic, unconventional man, and once he had adjusted to the fact that there was to be no son—I will never forget the look on his face when told that his forty-five-year-old wife had just given birth to a sixth girl—he set about guiding and shaping the aspirations of his daughters. "Marriage is no solution to your lives," we were told with broken-record repetition from our earliest years. And in the Welsh mining valleys, this was clearly true. With the industrial base in steep decline, decently paid jobs were increasingly scarce, and my dad simply didn't want his girls to marry a miner or work in Woolworth's. He had feminist instincts before it was fashionable. And so he set to work and told us and showed us in every way he could that we had to get ourselves an education and find a better life.

When I was thirteen, my father took me to visit Cambridge University, to show me its astounding beauty and to tell me that if I worked hard enough and set my sights high enough, I could gain admission and transform my life. It is only in retrospect that I realize the audacity of this gesture. Why did my father believe that I could make it into one of the most elite universities in the world? A child who had never before been out of Wales, who spoke English with a thick working-class accent, who had never eaten in a restaurant or stayed in a hotel, and who attended a school that in eighty years had never sent a student to Cambridge? Besides which, didn't the memory of his own father's Cambridge experience give him pause? In the 1930s Anthony Hewlett had been allowed to taste the delights of an elite education, but the fruits of his labors had been snatched from him by a rigid and hostile establishment. But wherever my father's confidence and courage came from, it rubbed off on me. Encased in those dreadful parachute blouses, which had the decidedly mixed blessing of discouraging boyfriends, I learned determination and ambition and got down to the hard, grinding work of preparing for the entrance examinations. Four years later I did squeak into Cambridge University, and true to my father's promise, this experience did expand and enrich my life.

However thrilling this tale of a lone individual defeating the odds, I now feel that this is only part of the story. In my childhood, hard work and parental support were aided and abetted by imaginative government policies. In the 1960s the Labour party, led by Harold Wilson, was back in power in Britain, and a great deal of official attention was being given to the challenge of breaking down entrenched class barriers. Oxford and Cambridge universities, which over the course of many centuries had helped create many of these same barriers, were under new scrutiny and beginning to feel real pressure to diversify. By the mid-1960s, when I was applying to university, most of the Cambridge colleges were bending over backward to find acceptable candidates from state schools. The result: I was probably given some small edge in the cutthroat competition for places, precisely because of my class origins. ❦

Cornel West My story is similarly complicated. In the early 1970s, civil rights legislation combined with affirmative action to dramatically change the range of choices faced by academically gifted black students. My mom always told me, "Cornel, you would never have gotten into Harvard had it not been for the civil rights struggle, which produced government support. Affirmative action opened the door. You sure got the talent, the grades, and the board scores—never think you didn't earn your Harvard place— but in the old days such an elite institution would not have made you welcome." And I really lucked out with regard to timing. The

Ivy League was only just opening up for blacks. Harvard admitted a handful of African-American students in 1969, but in 1970, my year, they took in nearly a hundred. ❧

Hindsight

We both find looking back on our childhoods a sobering experience. We are struck by the sharp contrast between the child-centeredness of our parents' lives and our own adult struggles to balance family with a whole slew of competing demands. In all kinds of ways the priorities of our mothers and fathers were stunningly straightforward, undiluted by high-flying careers or marital breakdown. As children we had absolute confidence in the fact that we were the guts of our parents' lives. Looking back at what they did to raise us, we are amazed. Even when they went after us—perhaps especially when they went after us—there was so much love and attention coming our way. That's the bottom line. What we were given by our parents was just phenomenal. It's virtually unimaginable today to put together the kind of devotion and attention our parents gave to us.

Sylvia Ann Hewlett The most difficult challenges in my life have been wrapped up in my ongoing effort to balance work and family, and I am painfully aware of how the rigors of a high-profile career clash and collide with the struggle to bear and raise children. For me, an important crunch came in September of 1979, when I discovered that I was pregnant with twins—the same month that my tenure review started at Barnard College. It was a problematic pregnancy from the beginning, with a variety of worrisome symptoms, and I gave serious thought to taking time off from work to grow my babies. I consulted my dean and was told that since the college had no maternity or parental leave policy, I wasn't entitled to a leave of absence; if I took time off, I would lose my job. Twelve years of hard, grinding work had gone into this career of mine, and I was only eighteen months away from tenure. Given a cutthroat academic job market, could I really give up the possibility of lifetime job security? I agonized, but finally decided to stick with my job and stamp down my worries.

Two months later, on November 17, at 6:30 in the evening, I was sitting in my office in a state of utter exhaustion after a ten-hour workday, trying to summon up enough energy to go home, when liquid began to trickle down my legs. As the trickle turned into a stream, I realized in horror that my water had broken and that it was much too early to go into labor—I was only twenty-three weeks pregnant.

Later on that night, in the emergency room at Lenox Hill Hospital, the attending physician was pessimistic about the babies' chances. He predicted that over the course of the next few days I would go into labor and my babies would be born. Given their estimated size, they would have no chance of survival. This grim prognosis turned out to be only too accurate. On the morning of the third day, one of the babies died in utero and my obstetrician induced labor. It was a dreadful fourteen-hour experience. I screwed up my eyes and plugged my ears so that I could not see or hear my dead and dying babies being born, but I felt them through my agony, warm and wet against my thighs.

Afterward, for quite a long time, life was truly hard to bear. I mourned my children with an intensity that frightened me. In addition to my terrible grief, I was ridden with guilt. If only I had given up work, if only I had had the guts to risk my career. I felt I had failed to protect my babies and therefore had no pity for myself.

Just over a year later my husband and I had a healthy second child, and gradually the dreadful sense of failure ebbed away. But losing those babies left an indelible mark. The dark winter of 1979–1980 permanently changed my priorities and my perspective. It put me profoundly in touch with the deep tradeoffs between self-fulfillment and child well-being. The fact is, the needs of children often run full tilt into adult agendas. It also put me in touch with the far-reaching significance of social supports. The right to parental leave would have made an enormous difference to the life chances of those twins, as would a set of colleagues who understood the value of parenthood. But at Barnard College in the late 1970s, having a child was definitely seen as a countercultural activity. For the newly liberated women on the faculty, childbirth was decidedly unchic, and the less said about it the better. Indeed, my subsequent attempts to organize a committee to press for child-related benefits were beaten back; such initiatives smacked of special privilege in an era when professional women were focusing on "cloning the male competitive model." At the time I wondered how other women dealt with hostile work environments, for if I, a highly educated person with at least some market power, was having a hard time, surely millions of American women were pushed under when they attempted both to hang on to a job and to raise a child. Even today, in the wake of the 1993 Family and Medical Leave Act, 30 percent of working women have no right to time off for pregnancy or childbirth.[1] They are in precisely the same position I was in in 1979: they have to choose either their child or their job. ❧

Cornel West The greatest challenges in my life center on the logistical hurdles and limited rights I have experienced as a noncustodial father. From the time of the breakdown of my marriage to Cliff's mother in 1979 to my marriage to Elleni in 1990, I was forced to deal with a difficult but nonetheless standard set of problems. My ex-wife was awarded custody of two-year-old Cliff and then decided to move to Atlanta. I had no recourse, legal or otherwise. And yet in my struggle to build a close relationship with my son, I now had to cope with an almost impossible set of barriers. Hundreds of miles separated me from Cliff, and I had limited visitation rights—a few specified weekends during the year plus three months in the summer. Besides which, what would I do with my son during our precious time together? My bachelor cribs in New York, New Haven, and Princeton did not provide a supportive context for a four-year-old or a nine-year-old—there were no kids on the block, no basketball hoop in the back yard. But I wrestled with these problems and over time developed a strategy that worked, albeit imperfectly.

I hit upon this great solution for the summers. I would take Cliff back to Sacramento, back to the loving, child-centered home that had been so good to me and my siblings a generation ago. It required a lot of stretching and bending of the rules, but I organized life so that I really could take two and a half months out of the year. It meant postponing book deadlines and taming an almost impossible travel schedule, but it was well worth it. Those summers in Sacramento stand out like jewels in my memory. My parents' home turned out to be a profoundly healing place in which

Cliff and I could reach out to one another. It provided the deeply needed (and yet so hard to contrive) rhythms and routines of normal family life. Three meals a day; regular bedtimes; clean clothes; a bevy of cousins—Kahnie, Phillip and Phyllis, Cornel and Erika— just around the corner, on tap for casual play; bicycles and baseball gear in the garage all ready to be put to use whenever a grownup was available. And hovering in the background, loving, eagle-eyed grandparents. I did manage to squeeze in a few hours of reading and writing each day, but mostly I tried to help weave this tapestry of normality. The evening meal was particularly important, as all three generations gathered for a cookout in the back yard. Conversation and laughter flowed, advice was sought and help was freely offered, jokes and stories were traded, and the children, spellbound, hung on the edges, absorbing the spirit and meaning of family life.

The rest of the year was a struggle. I maintained regular telephone contact with Cliff, calling him several times a week just to hear his voice and shoot the breeze. But in the rushed, tantalizing visits around Thanksgiving, Christmas, and Easter, it was always hard not to lapse into the role of being a "good-time dad," showering gifts on him in an attempt to make up for real time or a deeper agenda.

It's sobering to realize how thoroughly the decks are stacked against dads' being effective parents in the wake of divorce. How do those brothers manage who need to be on the job fifty-one weeks a year and don't have the financial ability to hop on a plane and spend a weekend visiting a child? And the fact of the matter is, they mostly don't. The data tell us that five years after divorce, more than 40 percent of dads are no longer seeing their children. Many are discouraged and defeated by the next-to-impossible circumstances triggered by divorce. When you come right down to it, most of the legislation out there is disrespectful of the father-child bond. It's as though dads don't matter. ❦

Sylvia Ann Hewlett I have also been touched by the painful fallout of divorce and remarriage. My experiences involve my stepdaughter, Shira. I know the anguish of standing by helplessly as a seven-year-old or a thirteen-year-old deals with the heartache of yet another confused, complicated Christmas of shuttling between households and facing two four-course meals. On many important family occasions I have struggled to figure out which would be the lesser evil, attending Shira's bat mitzvah/graduation/exhibition opening and by my very presence making it a little harder for her parents to deal well with this special event, or not attending and letting Shira down. At different times I have made different decisions. For example, I chose not to attend Shira's high school graduation but to attend her college graduation. I am still not sure which was the better decision. Clarity is an elusive goal in the muddy world of blended families. ❧

Cornel West And success is hard to come by. Try as I might—and I have struggled enormously to come through for Cliff—all kinds of other factors have gotten in the way. In the end, I don't have as much attention available for my loved ones as Mom and Dad had. I mean I *definitely* haven't been the father or husband my father was. ❧

Sylvia Ann Hewlett It's just so hard to perform on all fronts. The other day I was thinking of the hundreds of times I have cut short a speech in an effort to get home before my children's bedtime, dashing through airline terminals in a desperate attempt to make that earlier plane. And how I invariably end up doing two things badly. I fail to fulfill the last leg of a professional commitment, and, drained and exhausted when I finally see my children, I also fail to rustle up the energy and empathy to help with a homework assignment or conjure up an imaginative bedtime story. It is on these occasions that I envy my mother. Her focus on her children seemed so simple and clear-cut, the rhythms of her life so peaceful and pared back. ❧

Cornel West I am often tempted to be nostalgic about my childhood, a time when it seemed to be a whole lot easier to be a good parent. But the fact is, we cannot recapture the 1950s and 1960s. And even if we could roll the clock back, we would not want to. The blatant racism and sexism of that period would be intolerable. I remember how my mother was treated when she returned to finish college in the early 1960s. As one of the first black students to graduate from Sacramento State College, she had a difficult time. In those days you still had this ugly, open racism. Some folks would make fun of her, saying that blacks were dumb and she would never pass her examinations. Others would spit when she walked by. We children were young, and I guess my dad kept most of it from us. If I'd known, I would have gotten out there and kicked a few behinds. As it was, Dad had to go and run interference a couple of times. Looking back, I get so full of rage . . . that I wasn't there to protect my mom when those white brothers and sisters were acting devilish. ❧

Sylvia Ann Hewlett The expectations of the 1950s pretty much obliterated my mum. Looking back, I am both impressed and horrified by the extent to which we children took over my mother's life. From age twenty-six, when she had her first child, until age fifty, when her sixth child entered school, my mother barely had time to go to the bathroom, let alone do anything more substantial for herself. Those treks to and from primary school send shudders up and down my spine. Talk about free and invisible female labor! And yet these years made up the prime of her life, the years her daughters spent earning advanced degrees, traveling the world, writing books, teaching college. I can still get stirred up and angry on my mother's behalf. To add insult to injury, at least some of this sacrificial labor was unnecessary. A few elemental social supports, starting with crossing guards and school lunches, would have given my mother a measure of freedom. But I also recognize, deep in my heart, that the tradeoffs involved for us children were real: the security and success of my mother's six daughters were undoubtedly grounded in the fact that she gave them her uncluttered attention. She was not intent on other agendas. ❧

In the end we learn some fundamental lessons from this retrospective on our lives. We now understand the enormous centrality of parents—both mothers and fathers—in raising competent, compassionate human beings. The steadfast, sustained love of our parents gave us the wherewithal both to develop our skills and to "grow our souls." But we also deeply appreciate how very much harder it is for parents to come up with this steadfast, sustained energy in the modern age.

This brings us to what is perhaps our most important insight: as a society, we often fail to recognize the importance of the external environment in shaping the ability of moms and dads to come through for their children. In the 1950s and 1960s, both of our families were nourished by a society that was, in intensely practical ways, supportive of the art and practice of parenting. As we shall see in subsequent chapters of this book, the 1990s present a sharp contrast. Corporations and government increasingly tilt against families, maximizing the economic and time pressures on parents, while the media do their level best to denigrate and displace moms and dads.

Thus, the key to the future is the creation of a new political and cultural environment that supports the work of parents. In doing this we can learn important lessons from the lives of Clifton and Irene West and Vernon and Jean Hewlett, but we cannot clone them. The main thrust of any new initiative should be to affirm and enhance the heroic energies of moms and dads in the light of the great breakthroughs of the last thirty years. The gains of the civil rights and feminist struggles cannot be lost. Blacks, women, and other disadvantaged groups now expect and deserve a fair measure of equal opportunity and self-realization. But if we can build on these progressive movements and have them condition a polity and a culture that give new value to the work that parents do, we will accomplish a great deal. We will contribute mightily to reweaving our web of care—a societal project of great significance. But we will also contribute to private lives. Today's adults, both men and women, will be able to deal much more wisely with the age-old and ongoing tradeoffs between freedom and responsibility, self and other, which haunt the daily life of any thoughtful parent. Business, government, and the media, properly molded, cannot solve all dimensions of these existential problems, but they can get us partway there.

TWO

....

Parents and National Survival

WE PARENTS are so used to being trampled on, sneered at, or just plain ignored that we often fail to understand how embattled we are. But occasionally some especially flagrant example of parent-bashing grabs our attention and we catch our breath. For a fleeting moment we glimpse ourselves from the outside in, and see and hear the contempt and carelessness American society routinely throws our way.

Sylvia Ann Hewlett A few months after my book *When the Bough Breaks* came out in paperback, I was invited to discuss issues of parental overload and child neglect on the Larry King radio show. In the early 1990s this was one of those hugely popular call-in radio shows that reached vast numbers of people across the country. It aired between 10 P.M. and 2 A.M., and all kinds of people called in to talk to Larry: lonely truck drivers spinning along interstate highways, trying to stay awake; security guards and insomniacs killing the dead hours in the middle of the night. Most of the call-ins on this particular show were eminently forgettable, but one seared my consciousness in ways I will never forget.

Gary called in to talk to Larry King and me. He was twenty-seven years old and lived in Phoenix, Arizona. Gary wanted to talk about what was going on in his family. He and his wife had just put their three-week-old baby daughter in a kennel.

"A kennel!" we cried in unison, shocked and disbelieving. "You put your baby in a kennel?"

"Hold on," Gary said, becoming defensive. "Let me explain."

Gary and his wife, Brenda, both worked full-time. He was a maintenance person at a local office complex; she worked as a checkout clerk at a convenience store. Together they earned $23,000 a year, a sum of money that "didn't go a whole distance in Phoenix." After taxes their joint take-home pay was just over $400 a week, half of which went to pay the rent. When their daughter, Jenny, was born, they found themselves dealing with some heavy-duty problems. To begin with, neither of their jobs carried medical insurance, and consequently Jenny's birth triggered some huge bills: $3,930, to be precise. As Gary put it, "Jenny will be three years old before we have paid off the obstetrician." Another problem was that neither of them was entitled to parenting leave. They worked for small employers and did not qualify for job-protected leave under the terms of the Family and Medical Leave Act, which excludes businesses with fewer than fifty employees. Brenda couldn't simply quit her job, as Gary's paycheck did not even cover rent and utilities.

They coped with the actual birth by fudging and lying through their teeth. Brenda called in sick for ten days and then used up a week of accumulated vacation. When Jenny was two and a half weeks old, they hit the day-care market in Phoenix and found that the only thing they could afford was informal family day care, which in their neighborhood boiled down to a private home where two elderly women, unlicensed and untrained, looked after eighteen babies and toddlers. When Gary dropped Jenny off, he discovered to his horror that the other children were strapped into car seats, watching television, dirty and disconsolate. Despite a frantic search, Gary and Brenda had up till then failed to find something better. Their budget was $40 a week, tops, and this was what $40 bought you on the private day-care market in Phoenix. In Gary's caustic words, "Dogs and cats have a better deal—at least kennels are tightly regulated in this city and are required to live up to some kind of standard of cleanliness and care."

Gary's parting shot was bitter: "We're not welfare cheats, we're just regular Americans working as hard as we know how to do the right thing for our kid. Why is it so difficult? Why is everything stacked against us? We feel such shame that we can't do better by our baby." His voice rose in raw, sharp pain as he faded off the air.

There was a short silence as Larry King and I struggled to absorb the meaning of Gary's poignant words. Larry then cleared his throat and offered some tentative sympathy. What a stressful situation. How could any family deal well with such an impossible set of circumstances? My inadequate contribution was that as tragic as Gary's story was, it was far from being exceptional. In a nation of plummeting wages and threadbare social supports, hundreds of thousands of Americans are in precisely the same situation when they embark on the serious business of raising a child. Unlike new parents in other rich nations, American moms and dads are expected to do a stellar job without the benefits of a living wage, medical coverage, decent child care, or parenting leave. ❧

Caring, nurturing, cherishing—the essential components of good parenting—have less and less support in our society. These nonmarket values and activities have been pushed to the margins by the dominant forces of American life. The stakes could not be higher as the painful struggle of individual adults such as Gary and Brenda is much more than a private tragedy. When parents are so seriously disabled that they cannot perform their central functions, the results are disastrous for our nation—and the fallout on children is quite lethal.

In the late 1990s, America's children are spinning out of control. Hundreds of thousands are hurting and killing; millions more are failing to thrive. Child poverty rates are up and SAT scores are down, teen suicide rates have doubled since the 1970s, and child homicide rates have quadrupled since the mid-1980s.[1] In the words of one blue-ribbon commission, "Never before has one generation of American children been less healthy, less cared for, or less prepared for life than their parents were at the same age."[2] There is an urgent and desperate need to pay attention to this state of affairs, for children are not some fringe group, some bit players. Children are 100 percent of our collective future, and if we continue on our present course, this great nation will most surely tear itself to shreds.

Highlighting our problems—and our national shame—is the fact that most of these terrible trends are unique to the United States. In Germany, France, and Japan, for example, child poverty rates and school dropout rates are extremely low and heading down, and child homicide is virtually unknown. A child is twenty times more likely to be killed in New York than in Paris or Bonn, and seventy times more likely to be killed in Dallas than in Tokyo.[3]

So why has America visited such treachery on its children?

At the center of our children's agony is an enormous erosion of the parenting role. Moms and dads are increasingly unable to look after their children, with the result that our entire web of care is breaking down, blighting the lives of young people. A 1997 study sponsored by the Ad Council shows that fully two thirds of Americans now see teenagers as rude, irresponsible, and wild. They place the blame squarely on the shoulders of parents. Children are out of control because parents are failing to do their job.[4]

The fact is, too many parents have tuned out. Too many children have been left home alone, to raise themselves on a thin and cruel diet of junk food, gangster rap, and trash talk shows. More and more babies are being born without a skin—with none of that protective armor that in the past was provided by loving parents and supportive communities. Increasingly, these exposed, "skinless" children are being buffeted by a ruthless market and a poisonous culture. Many of the more vulnerable have become infected or burned, their bodies and their souls stunted and seared by the onslaught of neglect and greed.

However devastating this burgeoning tide of parental neglect, simply heaping blame on overburdened moms and dads will not solve our problems. Modern-day mothers and fathers, like those before them, struggle to put children at the center of their lives. But major impediments and obstacles stand in their way, undermining their most valiant efforts. From early in the morning till late at night, America's parents are battered by all kinds of pressures, most of which are not of their making. The truth is, the whole world is stacked against them. If parents cannot give a childhood to their children, it is not their fault.

Over the course of the last thirty years, public policy and private decision-making have tilted heavily against the altruistic nonmarket activities that comprise the essence of parenting. In recent years, big business, government, and the wider culture have waged an undeclared and silent war against parents. Adults raising children have been hurt by managerial greed, pounded by tax and housing policy, diminished by psychotherapy, and invaded and degraded by the entertainment industry. A myopic government increasingly fails to protect or support parents, while an unfettered market is allowed to take up more and more private space. Our leaders talk as though they value families but act as though families were a last priority. Sooner or later, worn-out moms and dads get the message that devoting their best time to raising children is a mug's game—a lonely, thankless undertaking that cuts against the grain of all that is valued in our society. Despite the fact that the parental role and function is enormously important, we have constructed a public morality where all the kudos go to work and achievement outside the home. We live in a nation where market work, centered on competition, profits, and greed, increasingly crowds out nonmarket work, centered on sacrifice, commitment, and care. In the late 1990s, what really counts in America is how much you get paid and what you can buy.

Small wonder, then, that parenting is a dying art. Small wonder, then, that parents have less and less time for their children.[5] And time is, of course, at the heart of the enterprise. Being a "good-enough" parent requires providing a child with the gifts of love, attention, energy, and resources, generously and unstintingly over a long period of time. It involves nourishing a small body, but it also involves growing a child's soul—sharing the stories and rituals that awaken a child's spirit and nurturing the spiritual bonds that create meaning and morality in that child's life. The Greeks had a name for it: they called this cultivation of character and virtue in a young person *paideia*. But none of these practical or sacred tasks are easily accomplished by demeaned and devalued parents. In contemporary America, mothers and fathers are set up to fail.

Today's parents understand what the score is. In their guts they know they have been left high and dry by a society intent on other agendas, and they are trying quite desperately to respond. From parental rights propositions to ordinances that would hold parents legally accountable for the actions of their children, they are struggling to regain their footing, reestablish their bearings, and take back control. However, despite this new awareness, few recognize how fierce the external pressures have become. Regular moms and dads have a hard time comprehending the degree to which business, government, and our culture are bitterly antagonistic toward them.

A Hostile Media

Just think of the sound bites of our culture. In the opening episode of the popular television show *My So-Called Life,* the lead character, a depressed fifteen-year-old, says to herself, "Lately, I can't seem to even look at my mother without wanting to stab her repeatedly." In an article entitled "Father Knows Squat," the *Washington Post* points out that in the media, parents are one of the few remaining groups that are "regularly ridiculed, caricatured, and marginalized."[6] On television, parents tend to be blustering bores, miserly boobs, overprotective fools, or just plain dopey and twerpy. One show, *Party of Five,* has done away with parents entirely, killing them off in a car crash before the series began. Mothers in particular tend to be either dead or evil. On the long-running *Blossom,* Mom was AWOL in Paris for years, but in a number of new shows she's dead. On the *Gregory Hines Show, Soul Man,* and *Dawson's Creek,* she has long since passed away. On *Unhappily Ever After,* not only does she die, but in subsequent episodes she returns as a ghost to continue tormenting her family. And on *Hiller and Diller,* the father gets sole custody of his two children but is so "overwhelmed by the responsibility" that he admits his kids terrify him. Strong, effective parents are hard to find on television in the late 1990s.

Contemporary black culture tends to be more muted and cautious in its criticism of parents. Precisely because the black family is in such desperate straits and serious parent-bashing is dangerously close to the bone, the media are forced to reflect at least some positive images, particularly of mom. "Dear Mama," a 1996 hit song by the late rap artist Tupac Shakur, is a case in point. In this ode, Tupac describes his mother as a "crack fiend" and a "black queen." At the same time, the song is imbued with love and longing, when he acknowledges her extraordinary devotion to him in the face of appalling circumstances.

Government Tilts Against Parents

The political establishment can be as hostile as the media. In recent years government has pulled the rug from under adults raising children, because neither the right nor the left of our political culture values or supports the work that parents do.

Many conservatives refuse to recognize the ways in which market values destroy family values. In elemental ways, they do not get it. They fail to understand that we need to rein in free enterprise if we are going to create the conditions that support parents and nurture children. A free and unfettered labor market, for example, can seriously undermine family life by exerting enormous downward pressure on wage levels for young, child-raising adults. This is exactly what has happened over the last twenty years. Successive administrations, abandoning any notion of a social contract, have gotten out of the business of maintaining the value of the minimum wage, providing legal protections for labor unions, or placing limits on out-of-control corporate greed.[7] Every day we read in the newspapers of thousands of workers being downsized or laid off while senior managers are cushioned by golden parachutes or special deals. Recent events at Levi Strauss are a good example:

"Facing up to corporate miscalculations and sluggish sales of its blue jeans," Levi Strauss & Co. announced plans late in 1997 to lay off one third of its U.S. labor force and close eleven plants. At the same time the company confirmed that in 1996 it paid retiring president Thomas Tusher more than $125 million as part of a closely held stock buyback program.

Commenting on the size of Tusher's options award, the compensation expert Graef "Bud" Crystal said, "That's a lot of jeans, but it doesn't make these jaded eyes pop out of their sockets." He noted that other executives have received higher awards; for example, Disney's chief executive, Michael Eisner, had just received 8 million options in a package that could be worth $771 million in a decade. "What's interesting here," Crystal added, "is the disconnect between finding out that someone got that much money at the same time that you're seeing so many employees about to be laid off."

By apparel industry standards, the 6,395 workers whom Levi Strauss let go were decently treated—they will collect eight months' pay plus three weeks' pay for each year of service—but these severance packages pale in comparison with Thomas Tusher's golden deal. Tusher was paid $105.8 million in accumulated stock options and $21.5 million as a "gross tax offset bonus" to help cover the taxes on that income.[8]

The Levi Strauss story is not unusual; in the late 1990s, millions of workers are experiencing severe economic pressure, despite record-breaking profits and a huge increase in executive compensation. These trends have profoundly weakened family life. Fathers and mothers like Gary and Brenda have been forced to work longer and harder just to maintain living standards, and children have been pushed to the edge.

Sagging wages, mounting insecurity, and lengthening work weeks make up the vanguard of the war against parents. Rich folks have done breathtakingly well in recent years, while everyone else has gone on the skids. For example, Michael Eisner was paid $204.2 million in 1996. At the median wage—now $33,538, down from $35,959 in 1989—a regular person would have to work 6,182 years to make that much money.[9] It's hard to see how we can sustain a democracy with these kinds of numbers—and it is clearly hard to sustain high-quality parenting.

Conservatives who espouse family values face a herculean challenge on the economic front. Are they prepared to redistribute income and wealth in order to relieve the pressures on young families? It seems unlikely. Redistribution requires government action and interference with market mechanisms, and today's conservatives are virulently opposed to both. Those on the right simply do not understand that government must play a pivotal role if we are to develop the social supports we need to counter the family-destroying and parent-displacing properties of the market. Bolstering the earning power of child-raising adults is just one of the ways in which government must intervene if moms and dads are to be effective and wholehearted parents. Such intervention is taken for granted elsewhere. France and Germany, for example, have developed tax codes that give huge privileges to families with children. Other rich democracies seem to understand that parenting cannot be left to the tender mercies of the marketplace.

Not so very long ago, conservatives were willing to provide parents with serious help on the child-raising front by spearheading various kinds of family-friendly policies. Remember the 1950s, that golden age of the American family? Well, we often forget that the fifties family was a creature of supportive government programs, at least some of which were put in place by President Eisenhower, an unabashed conservative. That was an era when children were this nation's most important tax shelter: parents were able to claim a deduction of $6,500 (in 1996 dollars) for each dependent child.[10] It was a time when the GI Bill and the Highway Act significantly subsidized the education and housing needs of millions of American families. Newt Gingrich and Ralph Reed, however, seem singularly out of touch with the degree to which Ozzie and Harriet were bolstered by public policy and depended on the public purse.

But myopia is not limited to today's conservatives. Liberals are also destroying the parental role. Many on the left fail to understand that we need to rein in untrammeled individualism if we are to recreate the values that nurture family life. The extraordinary emphasis in left-wing circles on the rights and freedoms of the individual has seriously compromised those altruistic, other-directed energies that are the stuff of parenting. Liberal divorce laws, for example, have produced a situation in which adults can choose marriage partners two, three, or four times with no particular penalty, regardless of how many children are betrayed or abandoned. And liberal welfare policies permit fifteen- and seventeen-year-olds to bear and raise children out of wedlock—indeed, through Aid to Families with Dependent Children (AFDC), now called Temporary Assistance for Needy Families (TANF), government supports these teenagers, albeit grudgingly. The new freedom of individuals to choose single parenthood is, of course, not limited to poor teens. Madonna certainly didn't think she needed a husband in order to have a child. In the spring of 1996, newly pregnant, she announced to the world that she would not marry Carlos Leon, the father of her child-to-be. She had met Leon, a Cuban-American personal trainer, in 1994, while jogging in Central Park. They dated for a while and he briefly moved into her co-op on Central Park West, but his role in her life seems to have been mainly that of sperm donor. Rumor has it that when Madonna gave birth in the fall of 1996, Leon signed all rights to the child over to her.[11] High-profile show-biz moms such as Madonna, Rosie O'Donnell, and Diane Keaton have made single motherhood a chic thing to do—the ultimate liberated act of a strong woman.

African-American celebrities tend to be more supportive of conventional family structures than their white peers. Whitney Houston and Snoop Doggy Dogg, for example, are both deeply committed to marriage and the two-parent family and have hung in there with their respective spouses in the face of considerable scandal. Indeed, it's hard to identify a black movie star who has chosen to flaunt single parenthood. Perhaps because of the way in which out-of-wedlock births have devastated their community, black celebrities have felt the need to protect and defend the family.

Despite this qualification, the overwhelming message from progressive, liberal folks in Hollywood is *Who needs a husband to have a child?* The problem here is that there are real conflicts between adult rights to freedom of choice and a child's well-being. Madonna may not want to deal with a male partner, but most children do much better in life when they can count on the loving attention of both a mother and a father.

At the end of the day, both conservatives and liberals clobber children. Take your pick, right or left, it doesn't matter; in contemporary America both ideologies are dangerously blind when it comes to creating the conditions that allow men and women to give real priority to the difficult and glorious business of cherishing children.

Parenting: The Ultimate Nonmarket Activity

Whatever their political orientation, our leaders seem to have little understanding of how much the decks are stacked against parents in our materialistic, individualistic age. At the heart of the matter is the fact that from a purely economic standpoint, raising a child has become the ultimate nonmarket activity as various types of market logic have moved against mothers and fathers. Adults have never viewed children solely or even primarily as financial assets, but through history and across cultures, parents have often reaped at least some material reward from raising children—help with planting or harvesting, support in old age, and so on. None of these economic reasons for raising children hold true today. On the contrary, in the modern world children are hugely expensive and yield little in the way of economic return to the parent. Estimates of the costs of raising a child to age eighteen are now in the $145,000 range—and this figure does not include college or graduate school![12] Despite this significant investment, the grown-up child rarely contributes earnings—or any other kind of material support—to the parental household. In the late twentieth century, children "provide love, smiles, and emotional satisfaction, but no money or labor."[13]

Of course, large numbers of well-meaning moms and dads may still elect to invest large quantities of money and time in child-raising, but for the first time in history their loving energies are not reinforced by enlightened self-interest. Instead, they must rely entirely on large reserves of altruistic love—large enough to last for more than two decades per child. This is a tall order in a society that venerates the market. We are asking parents to ignore the logic of their pocketbooks and buck the dominant values of our age. If they routinely fall down on the job, who can blame them? Contemporary moms and dads are trapped between the escalating requirements of their children, who need more resources (in terms of both time and money) for longer periods of time than ever before, and the signals of a culture that is increasingly scornful of effort expended on others. Parents often feel as though they are expected to read from two or three scripts which diverge completely in terms of how they lead their lives. Should they take on a second job to pay for college, or should they stay home in the evening to do a little bonding and turn off the TV? Or should they do neither of the above, but rather work two jobs and spend the extra income on health-club membership? Life is short, and paying at least some attention to oneself is a good idea. Besides, a trimmer figure might make all the difference in the next round of promotions. It is easy for a bewildered parent to become paralyzed as he or she is besieged by a host of contradictory demands.

Free Female Labor

For more than a century, a variety of scholars and social commentators have paid tribute to the nonmarket work done by women in American society. In the 1880s and 1890s, the social feminist Jane Addams stressed the moral heft of women's traditional roles. Indeed, much of her political activism was directed toward securing for women the right to stay at home and care for their children rather than being forced into the labor market. She saw "the home as the original center of civilization."[14]

Much more recently, the psychologist Carol Gilligan has made a distinction between the voices of men and women. In her highly acclaimed 1982 book, *In a Different Voice,* she describes how men gravitate toward the instrumental and the impersonal and emphasize abstract principles, while women lean toward intimacy and caring and give priority to human relationships. Gilligan points out that the female "care" voice is not inferior to the male "instrumental" voice, as it is often treated in psychological theory; it is simply different—different and enormously important. Over the decades this voice of care has played a critical role in producing a healthy equilibrium between individual and community in American society. Because it balances self with other and tempers market values with nonmarket values, it has gone some distance toward redeeming the urgent greed that is the spirit of capitalism.

Prior to the 1960s, when more families were organized along traditional lines than is true today, women provided this voice of care, which knitted together family and community. At least in the middle classes, a clear division of labor between the sexes allowed women to devote huge amounts of time to nourishing and nurturing: they read bedtime stories, helped with homework, wrapped presents, attended parent-teacher conferences, and taught Sunday school. But in the 1970s, the myriad selfless tasks that were the stuff of raising kids and building communities went by the board as American society underwent a sea change. Traditional patterns were broken by a liberation movement that often encouraged women to clone the male competitive model in the marketplace, and by a new set of economic pressures that increasingly required both parents to be in the paid labor force to sustain any semblance of middle-class life.

Before getting too nostalgic about traditional roles, however, we should remember that the sacrificial load carried by at-home women was often hard to bear. Many spent their entire lives laboring to serve the needs of others. Gilligan tells us that the main change wrought by feminism was that it "enabled women to consider it moral to care not only for others but also for themselves." She quotes Elizabeth Cady Stanton telling a reporter in 1848 "to put it down in capital letters: SELF-DEVELOPMENT IS A HIGHER DUTY THAN SELF-SACRIFICE."[15] Despite her appreciation of the importance of women's traditional roles, Jane Addams was also convinced that women must undergo a struggle for identity and recognition. She thought that the great challenge facing women was to hold in fruitful tension the "I" of the self, the "us" and "ours" of the family, and the "we" of citizens of the wider civic world.[16] Nora struggled with this challenge in Ibsen's *A Doll's House* (1879), and women have been struggling with it ever since.

The insights of Addams and Gilligan reflect the lives of middle-class white women and have little to do with the lives of poor women, particularly poor black women. Since the beginning of this nation, women of color have toiled both in the workplace—often in a white woman's kitchen—and in their own homes. In a very real sense, their contribution to family and community has been even more heroic than that of middle-class women. In sustained and steadfast ways, they have looked after the children of affluent white women in addition to their own, and they have received very little in the way of recompense or recognition. Black women thus have done double duty and been doubly invisible.

This brief historical excursion helps explain why the shortcomings of our nation on the parent-support front were until recently cloaked by the existence of a deep and largely invisible reservoir of free female labor. For generations women spent huge chunks of their lives making the nonmarket investments in family and community that underpin our nation. By nurturing children and by nourishing a web of care that included neighborhood and township, women created the competence and character upon which our democracy and our economy depended. Thus, the invisible labor of women comprised nothing less than the bedrock of America's prosperity and power. In addition, as women grew and tended our stock of human and social capital, they masked the contradictions inherent in our political culture. Conservatives had the luxury of cultivating a blind faith in markets because women (unacknowledged and unappreciated though they were) provided the all-important nonmarket work. And liberals had the luxury of cultivating a taste for self-fulfillment—at least white men did—because women reached out to others.

As we move into the twenty-first century, it is clear that relying on free and invisible female labor as the wellspring of our social and human capital no longer works. Modern women are intent on a fair measure of self-realization, and besides, the economic facts of family life preclude a return to traditional structures. Falling male wages and sky-high rates of single parenthood make it hard to spin out a scenario in which large numbers of women (or men) have the option of staying home on a full-time basis.

It is ironic to note that the nurturing, caring roles that are so underappreciated by contemporary culture are very much factored in by the market. Career interruptions triggered by childbirth and the special demands of the early childhood years cost women dearly in terms of earning power. A study by the Rand Corporation shows that a two- to four-year break in employment lowers lifetime income by 13 percent, while a five-year break lowers it by 19 percent.[17] Of course, if we were to expand our programs of family support—paid parenting leave, job sharing, and the like—more women would be able to stay on their career ladders during the childbearing years.

Fathers Under Siege

The inability of our nation to give value to or even to recognize the work of parents has penalized men and women in different ways. If the work done by mothers has been rendered invisible—or used to exact a price in the labor market—fathers have come under special attack by programs and policies oblivious to the importance of the father-child bond. Over the last thirty years, divorce reform and the enormous expansion of our welfare system have conspired to make it extremely difficult for a large proportion of American men— somewhere between a third and a half—either to live with or to stay in effective touch with their children. Aid to Families with Dependent Children is a case in point. In retrospect, it seems clear that AFDC, the nationwide program that for three decades provided the lion's share of income support for poor families, was set up so as to deliberately exclude fathers. The rules held that if an "able-bodied man" resided in a household, a woman with dependent children was unable to claim benefits for herself and her children.[18] This caused men to be literally pushed out of the nest. Not only did these AFDC regulations create a huge disincentive to marry; they made it extremely difficult for poor men to become fathers to their children. These government-sponsored rules help explain why out-of-wedlock births in the black community leapt from 21 percent in 1960 to 69.8 percent in 1996.[19]

In recent years men have experienced a tremendous loss of power in the workplace and in the family, which is a large part of the reason why millions of men are turning to Promise Keepers and the Nation of Islam. Demoralized, displaced men are seeking solace in brotherhood and turning inward to their gods. Jesus or Allah might just come through for them in a way that is increasingly problematic for employers or government.

The antifather bias in our public policies has found its clearest expression in the demonization of deadbeat dads. Public outrage on this subject was triggered by a 1989 Census Bureau report entitled "Child Support and Alimony," which described how more than a quarter of all noncustodial fathers were absent from their children's lives and paid nothing in the way of child support.[20] Shocking and shameful as these findings are, some factors were overlooked. To begin with, almost 40 percent of the "absent fathers" described in this report had neither custody nor visitation rights and therefore no ability to connect with their children. It seems odd to call them by the pejorative term "absent" when they have no right to be present. In addition, a little-known study by the Department of Health and Human Services shows that noncustodial mothers have a far worse record of child-support compliance than noncustodial fathers: almost half of all noncustodial mothers pay nothing toward the support of their children.[21] It seems that once a parent—male or female—has lost touch with a child, that parent is unlikely to contribute financial support. It is probably unrealistic to think we can keep in place all the obligations of traditional parenthood without its main reward: loving contact with a child.[22] Yet, rather than create policies that help noncustodial parents connect with their children, all we seem capable of doing is cracking down some more on deadbeat dads—thin stuff in a country that leads the world in fatherlessness.

One thing we do know: the huge increase in fatherlessness goes some distance toward explaining why so many youngsters are out of control. There is now a weight of evidence connecting fatherlessness to child poverty, juvenile crime, and teen suicide.

The Parent-Child Bond

This brings us to the heart of the matter: if the center of this nation is to hold, we have to learn to give new and self-conscious value to the art and practice of parenting. It can no longer be left to invisible female labor or the tender mercies of the market. Make no mistake about it: the work of moms and dads is of utmost importance to our nation. At a fundamental level of analysis, the parent-child bond is the strongest and most primeval of all human attachments. When it weakens and frays, devastating consequences ripple through our nation, because this elemental bond is the ultimate source of connectedness in society.

H. F. Harlow, the animal psychologist, demonstrated in a famous series of studies of infant monkeys the extraordinary importance of parental love. Taking a group of newborn monkeys from their parents, he placed them with artificial surrogates—a wire mesh "mommy" and a terry-cloth "mommy." Despite the fact that the infant monkeys were supplied with all the ingredients for physiological development—nourishment, water, proper temperature, and protection against disease—they failed to flourish. In Harlow's study, the deprived infants became zombies, developing odd, autistic behavior of the kind one sees in severely retarded persons. To Harlow, they did not seem fully alive. And while the baby monkeys enormously preferred the terry-cloth mommy to the wire mesh mommy, avoiding the cold wire mesh and clinging fiercely to the warm, cuddly terry cloth, even the terry-cloth mommy was a long way from being enough.

These artificial surrogates failed to provide loving, tender, responsive care, and thus the baby monkeys grew up not knowing the give-and-take of talk and touch, of feeding and fondling, of learning and playing. The infants survived and eventually grew into adults, but strange, abnormal adults who could not relate to their own kind or reproduce.[23] The implication of Harlow's research for humans is clear: the mere fact of physical survival does not guarantee a person. The full development of a human being requires something much deeper and more complicated than food and water; it requires sustained and sustaining love. According to the psychiatrist Willard Gaylin, "It is necessary to care for a child with love, in order to initiate a similar capacity in the child."[24]

Who will provide this transforming love? The obvious candidates are parents, because it is mothers and fathers, above other adults, who tend to fall crazily in love with their children. As the child psychologist Urie Bronfenbrenner has shown, children thrive on huge amounts of "irrational, emotional attachment," most often the gift of a mother or a father but in exceptional cases provided by a devoted grandparent or some other caregiver.[25] This is the magical force that provides the basis for self-love and self-esteem. And once a child has learned to love himself or herself, that child is able to care deeply about others. Thus parental love not only contributes powerfully to the development of a fully human being, it also nourishes and sustains the larger society. The connections are straightforward enough: caring about the well-being of others is the foundation of compassion, conscience, and citizenship. When a child is deprived of parental love, that youngster is liable to grow up in an infantilized state—very much like Harlow's zombies—never developing a love of self, never developing the ability to reach out to others. This is a recipe for violence, against oneself and against others, for anger and aggression remain raw and exposed, untempered by a commitment to anyone or anything. It is also a recipe for civic collapse. How do you persuade a young person who is profoundly careless of his own or of others' well-being to join a Boys and Girls Club or to vote in our democracy?

Cornel West I remember meeting one of these disconnected, tortured youngsters at a talk I gave at a community center in Newark, New Jersey. After the event, a young man sixteen or seventeen years old came up to me and said, "Professor West, I hear you're a pretty smart brother, you write this deep stuff, it must take a lotta talent and a lotta work to do something like that. Well, I've got talent too. I'm the smartest guy in my class. But the rub is, I can't find any motivation. I don't see why I should try to do what you do. More and more I feel I belong on the streets, hustling, dealing, and hurting like everyone else. That's the way to survive where I live."

He then asked a question. "Brother, what made you want to keep doing all that hard work, what made you believe in some kind of different future?" So I talked about my dad encouraging and disciplining me, my mom reading poetry to me, my older brother helping me with my homework, and my younger sisters cheering me on. The young man listened closely and then, in obvious pain, said, "Here's the score—I'm in this world by myself. My mother's strung out and tuned out. I have brothers, but I don't know them, and as for my father, where he is nobody knows. I sure have never seen him."

I remember feeling totally helpless. I had no recipe to heal these open wounds. The only thing I could think of doing was to bow before the enormity of his misery, kiss the young brother's hand, and mumble some words of empathy. "My God, I can't imagine—it's beyond my experience. You've got things you can teach me—you've been somewhere I've never been. I've read a ton of books on alienation, but I cannot grasp what you are living . . . I cannot understand what it must be like to have never been loved." I then simply told him to stay strong and don't forget to pray. ❧

This bleak and bitter encounter in Newark reflects the agony of a child who was born without a skin, without the tender love of an attentive parent. For this young man, the parent-child bond—the relationship that transmits self-love and the capacity to love others—had never developed, and the consequences were quite deadly.

A World Upside Down

This young man is not alone. In modern America, across race, gender, and class, millions of children are in terrible trouble. Consider the following facts:

- The homicide rate for children aged fourteen to seventeen has risen 172 percent since 1985.
- One fifth (20.5 percent) of all children are growing up in poverty—a 36 percent increase since 1970.
- The number of homeless children has tripled since the late 1980s.
- The use of illicit drugs among high school seniors is up 44 percent since 1992.
- SAT scores have slipped 27 points since the early 1970s.
- The rate of suicide among black teenagers has more than tripled since 1980.
- Obesity among children aged twelve to seventeen has doubled since 1970.[26]

Some of these statistics (poverty, homelessness) describe the pain of disadvantaged kids; others (obesity, SAT scores) describe the anguish of middle-class kids. Problems triggered by divorce, teen pregnancy, school failure, and substance abuse are no longer confined to the ghetto. They reach deep into the middle class; they belong to "us" as well as to "them." Out-of-control children aren't always other people's kids. They come in all sizes, shapes, and colors, and from affluent neighborhoods as well as down-at-heel city 'hoods. Kids who do bad things have highly educated parents as well as barely literate ones. A recent Carnegie Corporation report describes the depth and reach of our child-related problems: "Nearly half of American adolescents are at high or moderate risk of seriously damaging their life chances. The damage may be near term and vivid, or it may be delayed, like a time bomb set in youth."[27]

The enormous surge in youth violence is perhaps the most cruel—and most costly—manifestation of our inability to nurture our young. Children are now responsible for a staggering 20 million crimes a year. Between 1985 and 1994, among those aged fourteen to seventeen, arrests for murder increased by 172 percent, and for other violent crimes (rape, robbery, and aggravated assault) by 46 percent. And while violent crime among teenagers has been escalating, comparable crime rates for adults have been falling quite rapidly: between 1990 and 1994, homicide rates among adults aged twenty-five and older declined 18 percent.[28] There are now two crime trends in America, one for adults and one for children, and they are moving in opposite directions. One poorly understood fact is the hefty price tag attached to juvenile crime, as society ends up paying for a lifetime spent in and out of jail. A recent study estimates the cost to taxpayers of one violent young person at $1.5 million.[29]

In a day and age when we associate crime with young black men, it is important to stress that increases in juvenile crime apply across the board, in "all races, social classes, and lifestyles." Although young black males are four to five times more likely to be arrested for violent crime than white youths of the same age, the increase in the rate of arrests is far higher for white youths than for black: a 44 percent increase compared to a 19 percent increase between 1988 and 1993.[30]

Daphne Abdela, age fifteen, moved in a private school underworld in New York City where belonging means playing thug, getting wasted, and committing crimes. In her case, these crimes might well have included murder. In June 1997, she and her buddy Chris Vasquez, also fifteen, were arraigned in connection with the stabbing death of a forty-four-year-old real estate agent named Michael McMorrow. The killing occurred in the vicinity of the stately apartment building on Central Park West where Daphne lived. Daphne reportedly told the police that after the murder she and Chris mutilated the body, cutting off the dead man's nose and almost severing a hand in an attempt to hide his identity. Then they tried to sink McMorrow's 220-pound frame in the park's lake, gutting it first, Daphne told police, "because he was a fatty."

Daphne cannot claim to be black, brown, or disadvantaged. She is a highly privileged youngster, even by the standards of Manhattan. Before her arrest she lived in a $3 million home and was driven to school by the family chauffeur.[31]

When we look into the future, the picture becomes bleaker still. Demographic trends indicate that when it comes to juvenile crime, the worst may be yet to come. A "baby boomlet" in the late 1980s and early 1990s means that there are now 40 million children under age ten in the United States. We can therefore expect the adolescent population to swell by a quarter over the next decade. Since so many of these children are growing up below the poverty line in fragmented families, there is every reason to expect a new surge in juvenile crime.

If thousands of American youngsters are being killed or injured at the hands of their peers, thousands more are lost in their own nightmares. These are the children who self-destruct, seeing suicide as their only way out. Their numbers too are soaring. Between 1960 and 1994, the suicide rate among teens nearly tripled, making suicide the third leading cause of death for young people. Black children and very young children seem to be at risk in new and dreadful ways: the suicide rate among black males aged ten to fourteen went up a staggering 240 percent between 1980 and 1995.[32]

A particularly shameful fact is that the United States has the highest percentage of children living in poverty of any rich nation: 20.5 percent, a figure that represents a 36 percent increase since

1970 and compares with 9 percent in Canada, 4 percent in Germany, and 2 percent in Japan.[33] Children quite simply have not shared in America's prosperity in recent years. Very young children are particularly badly off: for those under six years of age, the poverty rate is 23 percent, which means that over 5 million preschoolers now live below the poverty line.[34] Bad as these figures are, they are expected to get considerably worse as the effects of welfare reform kick in. The Urban Institute predicts that an additional 1.1 million children will have slithered into poverty in 1997 alone. Black and Hispanic children are disproportionately represented in the poor population—47 percent of black children and 34 percent of Latino children are poor—but in recent years the poverty rate has grown twice as fast among whites as among blacks. Significantly, in 1996, 69 percent of poor children lived in families where at least one adult was at work—up from 61 percent in 1993.[35] In the late 1990s, getting a job does not necessarily pull a family out of poverty.

Substance abuse is also on the increase among teens. The use of illegal drugs by adolescents increased significantly between 1992 and 1995. This represents a reversal of earlier downward trends. In 1996 the government reported troubling increases in drug use in all age groups. For example, between 1992 and 1995 the use of marijuana by high school seniors increased by 63 percent, while the use of inhalants such as glues, aerosols, and solvents by eighth-graders increased 28 percent.[36]

On the educational front the news is equally grim, since underachievement and failure continue to dog the steps of American youngsters. Across the nation, combined average Scholastic Aptitude Test (SAT) scores have fallen significantly since 1972, despite a recent recentering exercise, which had the effect of raising nominal scores. Data collected by the National Assessment of Educational Progress, which has been testing national samples of students aged nine, thirteen, and seventeen each year since 1969, show "few indications of positive trends" in reading and writing.[37] American children are also at or near the bottom in most international surveys measuring educational achievement, coming in seventh out of ten countries in physics and tenth—dead last—in average mathematics proficiency.

Another disturbing fact is that only 69.7 percent of American students who enter ninth grade earn a high school diploma four years later, a figure that has slipped seven percentage points since 1970.[38] Most policymakers see this as a national disgrace in an age where other advanced nations have near universal secondary school education. In Japan, for example, 90 percent of seventeen-year-olds graduate from high school.

Not only is a large proportion of American youth growing up badly educated and ill prepared for the world of work, but a significant number are further handicapped by increasingly serious emotional problems. According to the Carnegie Corporation, today's youngsters are having trouble coping with stresses in their lives: "Many are depressed, and about a third of adolescents report they have contemplated suicide."[39] Since 1971, the number of adolescents admitted to private psychiatric hospitals has increased fifteenfold. Experts in the field explain this alarming trend by pointing to a constellation of pressures ranging from long workdays to divorce to absent fathers, which have left many parents too thinly stretched to provide consistent support for their children. The pressures on single mothers are particularly severe. Indeed, in many instances the stress is so great that parenting breaks down and becomes inconsistent and erratically punitive.

One thing seems clear enough from this brief survey: not only are American children failing to thrive; in several critical respects, their condition and life circumstances are steadily deteriorating. Overall, they lead more dangerous and more poverty-stricken lives than children did thirty, twenty, or even five years ago. They are also less likely to succeed in school and more likely to experiment with drugs, and many are depressed and seriously self-destructive. It is particularly distressing to realize that children in America are at much greater risk than children elsewhere in the advanced industrial world. Although the United States ranks second worldwide in per capita income, this country does not even make it into the top ten on any significant indicator of child welfare.

Link to Parents

Parental love and parental attention are enormously powerful in determining what happens to a child. Genetic endowment may determine eye color and a third to a half of raw intelligence, but whether a child acquires discipline and self-esteem and becomes a well-adjusted, productive person is largely a function of parental input and how well both parent and child are supported by the wider community.[40]

Unfortunately, there is much less of this precious parenting energy than there used to be. The last three decades have seen a sharp decline in the amount of time parents spend caring for their children. Stanford University economist Victor Fuchs has shown that the amount of parental time available to children fell considerably in the 1970s and 1980s; white children lost ten hours a week of parental time, while black children lost twelve hours.[41] Using a more recent data set, economist Edward Wolff demonstrated that over a thirty-year time span, parental time has declined 13 percent.[42] The time parents have available for their children has been squeezed by the rapid shift of mothers into the paid labor force, by escalating divorce rates and the subsequent abandonment of children by their fathers, and by an increase in the number of hours required on the job. The average worker is now at work 163 hours a year more than in 1969, which adds up to an extra month of work annually.[43]

The increasing inability of adults to devote significant time to children has left millions of youngsters fending for themselves, coping more or less badly with the difficult business of growing up in the nineties. True, some children continue to be raised in supportive communities by thoughtful, attentive parents, but this is not the overall drift of society. Contemporary America is populated by overworked, stressed-out parents who are increasingly unable to be there for their children. There is now a ton of literature telling parents how to parent. Walk into any bookstore and you will encounter shelf upon shelf of advice manuals detailing the skills and techniques of parenting. However, despite the claims of the experts, there is no one recipe for raising children, no magic bullet that guarantees a well-developed child. In the wise words of the Harvard psychologist Jerome Kagan, precisely how a parent feeds an infant or disciplines a teenager is less important than "the melody those actions comprise."[44] The feelings that parents bring to the role—their pleasure in parenting, their respect for the child—are extremely important. But most important is ensuring adequate time for the role. Melodies cannot work their magic unless they are given time and space. If a divorced father hasn't seen his son in six weeks or if a mother is working a sixteen-hour day, it's almost impossible to conjure up the sustained, steadfast attention that is the stuff of good parenting. Child-raising is not some mysterious process; adults have been engaged in it since the beginning of time, long before we had experts or manuals. At the heart of the matter is time, huge amounts of it, freely given. Whatever the child-raising technique, a child simply does better with loving, committed, long-term attention from both mom and dad.

A weight of evidence now demonstrates ominous links between absentee parents and an entire range of behavioral and emotional problems in children. A study that surveyed 5,000 eighth-grade students in the San Diego and Los Angeles areas found that the more hours children were left by themselves after school, the greater the risk of substance abuse was. In fact, home-alone children as a group were twice as likely to drink alcohol and take drugs as children who were supervised by a parent or another adult family member after school. The study found that this increased risk of substance abuse held true regardless of the child's sex, race, or economic status.[45]

In a similar vein, a recent survey of 90,000 teenagers—the largest and most comprehensive study ever conducted on adolescent behavior—found that youngsters are less likely to engage in suicidal behavior, become violent, or use drugs if they are closely connected to their parents.[46] This study found that the mere physical presence of a parent in the home after school, at dinner, and at bedtime significantly reduces the incidence of risky behavior among teenagers, a finding reinforced by recent research at the Harvard School of Public Health. Jody Heymann and Alison Earle show that parental evening work has extremely negative effects on the home environment and on children's cognitive and emotional development.

A 1997 report prepared for the Department of Justice demonstrates the scope of these negative effects. According to FBI data, the peak hours for violent juvenile crime are now 3 P.M. to 8 P.M.[47] This can be attributed to a huge drop-off in the number of parents available to supervise their children after school. In 1970, 57 percent of school-age children had at least one parent at home on a full-time basis; by 1995, this figure had fallen to 29 percent.[48] Experts estimate that somewhere between 5 and 7 million latchkey children go home to an empty house after school and that fully a third of all twelve-year-olds are regularly left to fend for themselves while their parents are at work.[49] These children are at significantly greater risk of truancy, school failure, substance abuse, and violent behavior than children who have a parent at home. Children, especially adolescents, crave excitement, and if they are not supervised by parents or involved in some organized activity, they are likely to become involved in something dangerous to themselves or others.

Besides insulating a child from risk and warding off potential harm, parents make a large contribution to a child's success in school. Twenty years ago, Chicago sociologist James S. Coleman demonstrated that parental involvement mattered far more in determining student achievement than any attribute of the formal education system. Across a wide range of subject areas, in literature, science, and reading, Coleman estimated that the parent was almost twice as powerful as the school in determining achievement at age fourteen.[50] The importance of parent involvement in the educational process has been further confirmed by psychologist Lawrence Steinberg, who recently completed a six-year study of 20,000 teenagers and their families in nine different communities. Steinberg argues convincingly that in the 1990s, underachievement and failure in American schools "owes more to conditions in the home than to what takes place within school walls." One out of every three parents is "seriously disengaged" from his or her adolescent's education, and this is the primary reason why so many American students perform below their potential—and below students in other rich countries.[51]

In his research, Coleman revealed that good parenting not only improves academic performance, but is also essential to the development of human capital—that combination of attributes (skills, knowledge, work habits, and motivation) that make for a competent young person. For at least a generation economists and business leaders have wrung their hands over the sorry state of America's human capital, and they have good reason to be concerned. More than a quarter of all eighteen-year-olds fail to complete high school, and many of these youngsters lack the basic skills and discipline necessary to hold down the simplest job. According to one survey, fewer than half of all American youngsters can determine the correct change after purchasing a hamburger and a Coke at McDonald's. This distressing fact tells us something about the inadequacy of our educational system, but it tells us even more about the inability of many parents to come through for their children.

In addition, a great deal of recent scholarly attention has been given to the depletion of our social capital—that store of trust, connectedness, and engagement in community life. Robert Putnam, Francis Fukyama, Jean Bethke Elshtain, and Michael Sandel, among others, have expressed great concern that "the moral fabric of community is unraveling around us. From families and neighborhoods to schools, congregations, and trade unions, the institutions that traditionally provided people with moral anchors and a sense of belonging are under siege."[52] These scholars have advanced a variety of reasons to explain why so many Americans are newly isolated, distrustful, and depoliticized, newly "bowling alone" rather than in leagues.[53] All kinds of culprits have been put forward, including television-watching and political scandal. But despite a noisy, high-profile debate, no one has gone upstream to the source of the problem—the huge erosion of the parental role. When parenting breaks down, the mechanism that transmits self-love is shattered, and this seriously compromises society's ability to pass from one generation to the next the values of compassion and commitment to others, which are the essential raw material of community-building and citizenship.

Therefore, the erosion of the parental function has immense implications in both the public and the private sphere: it jeopardizes our society as well as our souls. When parenting breaks down, it is an unmitigated disaster for the individual child. But it is much more than that, for the altruistic energy of moms and dads contributes enormously to our store of human and social capital and thus conditions the strength of our economy and the vitality of our democracy.

So how do we turn this thing around? How do we somehow give new and self-conscious value to the art and practice of parenting? It is not a simple matter, this task of creating a public morality and a political culture that will support the heroic work of mothers and fathers. The obstacles are enormous.

On the left, we rub up against a fierce attachment to untrammeled lives. Over the last thirty years we grownups have gotten used to being extraordinarily free. We have cut ourselves loose from most moral and religious constraints and acquired a new set of emotional and sexual liberties. Many of us revel in an unprecedented range of choice. In the spirit of Tom Wolfe's *Bonfire of the Vanities*, we have tasted our new freedoms and find them "quite glorious."[54]

On the right, we rub up against a blind faith in markets and a deep distrust of state intervention. In recent years conservatives have badmouthed government so thoroughly that it has become extraordinarily difficult for anyone on the right to acknowledge that government is capable of doing any good—that it can be instrumental in providing indispensable social support and in creating a public morality that supports the sacrificial energy of parents. Conservatives seem light-years away from acknowledging that contemporary parents need enormous amounts of help—not grudging help, not marginal help, but big-time heavy lifting—if they are to conjure up the altruistic energies that allow children to thrive. In the manner of the fifties, this help should be directed to strengthening rather than displacing moms and dads.

We must also remember that the nuances of this project are critical. No progressive person wants family if "family" translates into oppressive husbands and abused wives. And no progressive person wants community if "community" translates into "black jelly beans" sticking "to the bottom of the bag."[55] Texaco, after all, developed an extremely strong and vital corporate culture, but this culture was also irredeemably ugly, contaminated by systematic discrimination against people of color. However, rejecting racism, patriarchy, and homophobia need not mean retreating to a version of the liberal project in which freedom is boiled down to the ability to function as a lone individual within a heavily competitive market society. Most grownups fail to flourish in such a thin universe, and children are seriously damaged. Unless a child is protected and cherished by the selfless energies of at least one loving adult who is uniquely committed to him or her, that young person will grow up without a skin, buffeted, bleeding, and seared.

This daunting and complex set of challenges boils down to one pivotal question: can we find the political will? Can we find the key that will unlock a new and potent source of activist energy? We are, after all, talking about radical change.

We think we have found the answer. As we explain in the final section of this book, our solution involves putting mothers and fathers front and center on the national stage. By tapping into the latent strength of our democratic processes, we craft a parents' movement that will send America's 62 million parents to the polls. This will have the magical effect of tilting our entire political culture in a direction that supports and values adults raising children. By mobilizing behind a single agenda, which we call "A Parents' Bill of Rights," and by speaking with a single voice, moms and dads can transform both our public morality and our political culture to give new and massive support to the work they do. It is important to stress that parent power can be a powerful healing force in American society. The deep and desperate concerns of parents cross the usual divides of gender, race, and class and thus feed a common vision and seed a common ground in ways that are rare and precious in our centrifugal society.

As we embark on this extraordinary journey, let us appreciate the enormous weight of the task at hand. The project of giving new status and support to mothers and fathers has extraordinary potential because of the ways in which the parent-child bond is the most fundamental building block in human society. When this is hollowed out, the wellspring of care and commitment dries up, and this has a huge impact beyond the home: community life shrivels up, and so does our democracy. America's stock of social and human capital becomes dangerously depleted. If we can produce this magical parent power, we can go to the very heart of our darkness and make the center hold.

PART II

Waves of Attack

THREE

....

Managerial Greed and the Collapse of Economic Security

"'MAMA, IF I DON'T EAT so much, maybe we can figure out a way of spending less money and have you stay home with us at night.' This is what Tiffany, my ten-year-old, told me last week, and it near tore my heart out. I know how much I miss reading her stories and putting her to bed, but I had no idea she felt it so badly. You see, I don't leave my kids alone at night: sometimes my sister sleeps over, sometimes my stepson, sometimes my neighbor. But however hard I try to fill in, it's just not the same for the kids . . . I guess we all hate dealing with this second job."

Vicki Parker, a single mom, has a schedule that is punishing beyond belief. During the day, from 8:30 A.M. to 4:30 P.M., she works in a drug treatment program of the New York City Housing Authority. Her job is to be out in the field locating drug abusers and persuading them to enroll in some kind of treatment. During the night, from 11:00 P.M. to 7:30 A.M., she works as a counselor at a group home for runaway teenagers. Her task here is to make sure the kids get back to their rooms at night, to listen to their troubles, and to ward off self-destructive acts. Vicki goes from her nighttime job straight to her daytime job. When she arrives home at 5:30 P.M., she has put in a nineteen-hour day.

"It's hard to describe how bone tired I am at the end of the afternoon. Sometimes my legs are trembling with the effort of walking those last few blocks from the subway; other times I catch myself moaning aloud, I am so out of my skull with exhaustion. Most days I walk into my house knowing there's not a prayer I can be a good parent to my kids. First off, in my weary state it's all too easy to find fault. Why hasn't Tiffany stacked the dirty dishes? Why didn't Tyrone pick up the groceries? Or worse still, how come Jasmine forgot to pick up her little sister from school and left her stranded with an annoyed teacher? Seems like I am always chewing them out for something or other. They're good kids, but the resentment builds when I pile so many responsibilities on them.

"I know they need me to fix dinner and help with homework, but more often than not I just collapse on the sofa and wave them away, saying, 'Not now, give me an hour.' Of course, in an hour or so I need to leave for my second job, which is all the way down on 17th Street, an hour's subway ride away."

At the nub of Vicki's problems is her struggle to earn enough money to support her kids. Her day job pays $26,000 a year, which boils down to $148 a week in disposable income once taxes ($402 a month), rent ($624 a month), and her college loan repayment ($168 a month) are taken out. This simply is not enough to cover basic living costs—utilities, food, clothing, transportation, school supplies—for Vicki and her three children. Last winter, when Con Edison turned off her electricity and Vicki found herself too deeply in debt to borrow an additional $80, she figured the time had come to take a second job.

Vicki did not plan on having her life turn into such a treadmill. She spent five difficult years, from 1985 to 1990, going to school at night so she could earn the college degree she thought would get her a well-paid job. She got the job she was after—she had always wanted to be a social worker and help kids—but there was no way it paid enough to live on.

Vicki has also tried very hard to build a relationship with a man. She knows that her kids need a dad. Her first husband, the father of her two oldest children, was shot dead at age thirty—he was an innocent bystander in a shootout between rival gangs. More recently she has tried to construct a long-term relationship with the father of her third child, but as luck would have it, he was recently let go from a job he had held for fourteen years. According to Vicki, "He doesn't come around as much no more. I figure he's ashamed that he can't contribute as he knows he ought. But he's a beautiful person. When Tiffany wants something bad, he puts away a dollar a day towards it. He can manage that."

The day we interviewed Vicki, she was worried sick: Jasmine, fourteen, had not been home for three days. Vicki knew that she had gotten into some bad company recently. She was "hanging" with a twenty-one-year-old man who kept her out until all hours. Vicki is desperately worried that Jasmine will get pregnant. "She's just started high school and she's a real strong student, I can't stand the thought that she might be about to throw her chances away. But I guess my not being there at night has just made it too easy for her to act out."

Vicki had one last bitter comment. "I know what happens to neglected kids. I work with them nineteen hours a day. In fact, I am forced to work with them so long and so hard that I end up doing all kinds of bad stuff to my own kids."[1]

Plummeting wages and lengthening work weeks, joblessness and mounting insecurity—these are the hallmarks of our age. For large numbers of workers, wages have fallen relentlessly for the past twenty-five years while time spent on the job has risen significantly. Like Vicki Parker, most Americans today are working longer hours for less pay; like hamsters in a wheel, they are running harder and harder just to stay in the same place. Since adults raising children make up the group most seriously affected, these trends have grim implications for family life. Parents are newly squeezed and stretched; children are increasingly home alone.

If steadily deteriorating economic conditions haven't made parenting hard enough, they are juxtaposed with surging corporate profits and huge increases in managerial compensation, which adds to the load of frustration. When Michael Eisner can take home $204.2 million, as he did in 1996, why on earth can't Vicki Parker make ends meet?[2] Why does it now take two—or three—jobs to keep a family above the poverty line? On Labor Day 1995, Labor Secretary Robert Reich gave a speech entitled "Frayed-Collar Workers in Gold-Plated Times," in which he pointed to the increasingly obvious fact that although profits were at a twenty-five-year-high, the majority of Americans were taking home smaller paychecks than they had three or five years before. This can be a bitter pill to swallow. Workers find it hard to tighten their belts and shortchange their families when they can smell a gravy train that feeds an elite class of managers a rich diet of salary raises, bonuses, stock options, and other perks.[3] Christmas 1996 brought the point home. Shoppers in the Big Apple discovered that Hermès had a waiting list for its $4,000 Kelly bags, Patek Philippe had back orders for a $44,500 watch, and Neiman Marcus was sold out of $75,000 Jaguar cars. For ordinary Americans, Christmas buying was much less brisk. The holiday season saw sales for luxury goods grow by 21 percent while overall sales remained flat.[4]

This new and extraordinary gulf between the haves and have-nots in American society is the result of the huge and growing discrepancy between how we treat senior managers and how we treat everyone else. Recent developments at IBM are illustrative. At the end of 1995, after a draconian restructuring exercise during which more than 60,000 workers lost their jobs, IBM handed out $5.8 million in bonuses to its top five executives. Chairman and CEO Louis V. Gerstner, already slated to receive a compensation package worth $12.4 million, was given a $2.6 million bonus. For Gerstner's staff, however, the year-end news was quite different. His executive secretaries were told to expect salary cuts of 36 percent.[5] This kind of gross inequity creates an undertow of bewilderment and bitterness among employees struggling to pay the mortgage or underwrite day care and braces.

In the late 1990s, the private sector seems much less constrained by any notion of justice or equity, much more convinced than ever before that greed is simply good. The way in which this corporate vision differs from the past is underscored by events at the Bank of America.[6] In February 1993, the bank proudly announced the highest profit for any banking institution in U.S. history: $1.5 billion. It then proceeded to lay off 28,930 workers. Its CEO, Richard Rosenberg, who had taken more than $18 million in compensation over the previous five years, followed this move with the news that 8,000 of the bank's white-collar employees would be reduced to a workweek of nineteen hours—one hour shy of eligibility for benefits. This decision left a fifth of the bank's employees with severely reduced paychecks, no health care, no paid vacation time, and no pensions. The objective: an additional savings of $760 million, designed to impress Wall Street and boost share values and executive compensation even further.

Claire Giannini, the granddaughter of the founder of the Bank of America, was so appalled by these actions that she gave a series of press interviews deploring the fact that executives no longer cared whether the lower ranks kept their jobs. She recounted how her grandfather, in the depths of the Great Depression, had ordered executives to take a 20 percent rollback in salary to keep the bank solvent and maintain a full complement of jobs. This action contrasts sharply with the brutal layoffs in 1993—the bank's most profitable year ever.

Though Claire Giannini attempted to blow the whistle, that is more than can be said for our national leaders. Politicians have mostly tried to pretend that none of this is happening. Take President Clinton's claim in his 1998 State of the Union address that these are good times, that incomes are rising across the board. This simply is not true. Childless families—particularly older ones— have experienced real income gains in recent years, but families with children have seen their incomes fall 3.9 percent since 1989. Indeed, a 1997 report by the Children's Defense Fund shows that income for parents under thirty dropped by one third over the past two decades.[7] On the rare occasion that a politician acknowledges any wage slippage, he or she usually blames it on external factors over which the American government has no control. Fierce international competition and the availability of Koreans or Mexicans who will work for significantly lower wages than their U.S. counterparts are favorite culprits. Unfortunately, the real villains are much closer to home.

These are the facts of the matter: over the past two and a half decades, America's business and political leaders, abandoning the idea of a social contract, have moved systematically against workers. Despite an official effort to blame the wage squeeze on foreigners, declining income levels for the average American worker and frightening levels of insecurity have little to do with Korean workers or global competitive pressures; rather, they are the result of rampaging managerial greed, newly endorsed and facilitated by government. The savings resulting from a twenty-five-year-long wage squeeze have not been used to reduce the wage bill (the overall amount of money spent on wages and salaries), thus improving America's ability to compete in global markets. Instead, the money realized from all of this belt-tightening has gone to fatten the compensation packages of senior executives.[8] The ongoing and entirely real problem of fierce international competition has not been resolved, it has merely been used as a smokescreen to hide a huge redistribution of income from workers to managers. The result: the most remarkable trickle-up of income in U.S. history. Back in 1960, the average American CEO earned 41 times more than the average worker. By 1996, the average CEO earned a staggering 209 times more than the average worker.[9] Sad to say, America is now the most unequal country in the advanced democratic world, the only rich nation in which a majority of working people actually have lower incomes than they did twenty-five years ago. With working and middle-class parents newly stretched and squeezed, no wonder so many American youngsters are growing up dangling and dangerous. Children are not in some magical way freestanding or self-sufficient. Out-of-control kids in Oakland or the Bronx do not fall out of the clear blue sky; rather, their distressing circumstances are a direct consequence of the increased inability of moms and dads to earn a living wage.

Falling Wages

On the wage front, the bottom line is brutal for a great many working parents. Various analysts have crunched the numbers and discovered that for most Americans, wages are stagnant, sinking, or in free fall. Economist David Gordon looked at the period from 1973 to 1993 and found that real (inflation-adjusted) hourly take-home pay for production and nonsupervisory workers—representing more than 80 percent of all employees and the vast majority of parents—declined by more than 10 percent.[10] And this is despite the fact that per capita gross domestic product rose 33 percent during the same period. Robert Reich examined the 1980–1995 period and found that while the inflation-adjusted earnings of an adult in the top decile rose by 10.7 percent, the median adult worker's wages fell by 3.6 percent and the wages of a worker in the bottom decile fell by 9.6 percent.[11] Surveying a slightly later time period, 1979–1997, Princeton economist Alan Krueger discovered a more complicated but equally distressing picture. From 1979 to 1989, the real wage rate of workers in the bottom tenth percentile fell by an astounding 16 percent, while the real wage of median workers fell by 2 percent. Only workers in the highest brackets did well: at the ninetieth percentile, pay increased by 5 percent. Between 1989 and 1997, the trends were a little different: real wages for workers at the bottom stopped falling; real wages for workers at the top continued growing but at a more moderate pace, and real wages for the majority of workers in between—the American middle class—continued to erode quite rapidly. In fact, the median workers' wage fell 5 percent between 1989 and 1997.[12] Despite different data sets and time periods, each of these analysts describes trends that have grave implications for child welfare, since the vast majority of families with dependent children fall into the middle- and lower-income brackets, those that have suffered long-term wage decline.[13] Reflecting on these data, Senator Edward Kennedy offered the pointed comment that "the rising tide that once lifted all the boats now lifts only the yachts."[14]

This prolonged and ongoing wage squeeze is new to the American experience. According to the MIT economist Lester Thurow, "At no other time since data have been collected have American median wages consistently fallen for a two-decade period of time. Never before have a majority of American workers suffered real wage reductions while the real per capita GDP was advancing."[15]

The Good Old Days

Most Americans who were children in the 1950s and 1960s grew up with an optimistic and generous take on the future. The economy was moving along at an impressive clip, doubling every ten years, and most people participated in the expanding affluence. Every sector of society—rich, middle-class, and poor—experienced at least a doubling of real income during the three decades after World War II, with the bottom fifth of the population advancing faster than the top fifth.[16] Firmly embedded in the consciousness of this prosperous period was the notion that each generation would be more successful than the previous one. The cumulative, egalitarian progress of this era became the stuff of the American Dream.

These happy results were a long way from being inevitable. As we shall see in the next chapter, the government of this era created a tax code that privileged families with children. It also sponsored programs such as the GI Bill, which did a splendid job of making sure that young people had the resources to get married, buy a house, start a family, and acquire an education. And government support of working people and their families was buttressed by a strong labor movement, which was determined that as American workers became more productive, they would share in the bounty they produced. In the mid-1950s, unions represented 35 percent of all American workers. Not only did they have a powerful voice in setting wages and benefits in sectors such as auto and steel, but they set the pace for the entire economy. As a result, as workers came through with an almost 90 percent increase in productivity between 1947 and 1973, almost in lock step their real wages increased by 99 percent.[17]

The Tide Turns

The early 1970s, however, brought difficult economic times and less generous attitudes. Corporate profits began to drop precipitously, largely because of repeated oil shocks, increased global competition, and productivity growth rates that lagged behind those of other countries. The business community decided to get tough. It is possible to trace this change in attitude to a series of eight meetings convened in the fall of 1974 by the Conference Board, a New York–based private-sector think tank. At these meetings, 350 CEOs reflected on their mounting problems and decided that growth was slowing down because workers had gotten out of line. In the words of one CEO, "They have little or no appreciation of the fact that their jobs, their prospects of an improved standard of living in the future, their chance of advancement are all tied to the success of the business enterprise in which they participate."[18] And so began a more mean-spirited era, when corporate leaders focused much more narrowly on their own self-interest, moving vigorously against workers and lobbying for policies that would help weaken the labor movement.

By the late 1970s, various business associations were offering union-busting services to their member companies. Leading the way, the National Association of Manufacturers created the Council on a Union-Free Environment, which gave advice on how to tame or maim union activity, and with it a new brand of consultant emerged: industrial psychologists and lawyers who specialized in beating back the demands of labor. One consulting firm was unusually direct in advertising its services: "We will show you how to screw your employees . . . how to keep them smiling on low pay, how to maneuver them into low-pay jobs they are afraid to walk away from."[19] These "new Pinkertons," as these consultants were sometimes called, developed a rich array of aggressive strategies which included firing organizers, threatening unions with decertification if they made wage demands, and telling workers that unless they fell into line, management would relocate the plant. By the 1990s there were more than 1,500 such consultants, earning $500 million a year between them, advising employers on how to defeat union organizing campaigns. With this reservoir of expert help, corporations were able to exploit every loophole in the labor laws.

In addition, by the early 1980s corporations were able to rely on substantial political support in their campaign to weaken labor. The Reagan and Bush administrations pursued policies that specifically strengthened corporate managers against the demands of their employees. For example, when Reagan broke the air traffic controllers' strike in 1981 by permanently replacing striking workers, he set an important precedent. Soon a number of large corporations, including Greyhound, Phelps Dodge, and Eastern Airlines, were routinely breaking a taboo that had existed since the passage of the National Labor Relations Act in 1935: using strikebreakers as permanent replacements for workers out on strike. This tactic discouraged strikes and further tilted the balance against labor. In 1995, there were only 32 strikes involving 1,000 workers or more, compared with 250 in 1975.[20]

In another important move, Reagan and Bush appointed conservatives to the National Labor Relations Board (NLRB) who favored employers' wishes on most major issues. In 1981, Reagan selected as the NLRB chairman John Van de Water, a UCLA law professor who had a history of helping management defeat labor in union representation elections. The data on NLRB decisions over a ten-year period show a pattern of growing antagonism to labor. Back in 1975–1976, for instance, 84 percent of unfair labor practice complaints against corporations were sustained in whole or substantial part by the NLRB. A decade later, that number had dropped to 52 percent.[21]

Thus, backed by an army of consultants and emboldened by

friendly administrations, corporate America has spent the past two decades systematically weakening the labor movement, which has made it much easier for companies to cut wages and jobs. By 1995, only 13 percent of private-sector workers in the United States belonged to a union—down from 35 percent in 1960—and givebacks in wages and benefits had become a standard feature of contract negotiations. This type of concession was unheard of in the 1950s and 1960s. In recent years, wage growth among unionized workers has actually fallen below the pace of wage growth among non-union employees. Surveying the scene for a 1995 cover story, *Business Week* concluded that "U.S. companies now dominate the labor market to an unprecedented degree."[22]

The Great U-Turn

As government and the private sector moved against workers, wages began to sag. Beginning in 1973, wages for male production workers took what economists Barry Bluestone and Bennett Harrison have called "the great U-turn," and they have continued on a downward curve ever since.[23] The wage squeeze first affected blue-collar workers, but these reductions gradually fanned out across the workforce, so that by the 1990s wages for men were falling in all occupational categories except management. Wages of white men have fallen slightly faster than those of black men, and young men have suffered disproportionately. Overall, since 1973 wages are down 25 percent for men aged twenty-five to thirty-four.[24] Since 1993 male wages have fallen almost three percentage points, a particularly disturbing trend which demonstrates that wage levels are newly unaffected by the business cycle. During the 1993–1996 economic expansion, wage rates continued to decline despite high growth rates, nearly full employment, and record profits. Productivity gains, for example, no longer seem to translate into wage gains: in 1994 and 1995, productivity rose by 3 percent per year while wages fell by more than a percentage point each year.[25] The implications of these figures for family life are dire: *32 percent of all men between twenty-five and thirty-four when working full-time now earn less than the amount necessary to keep a family of four above the poverty line.*

Cuts in fringe benefits have compounded the belt-tightening associated with the wage squeeze. Employer-provided health benefits are declining—between 1979 and 1994, the percentage of the workforce with health insurance fell from 69 to 57—and copayments, deductibles, and premiums are rising.[26] Defined-benefit pension plans are giving way to 401(k)s without employer contributions, or to no pensions at all. And the widening wage gap is mirrored in a widening benefits gap. Top executives and their families are receiving ever more generous health benefits, and their pension benefits are soaring in the form of compensation deferred until retirement. Although they have no greater job security than lower-echelon workers, when top executives lose their jobs, it is not uncommon for them to receive golden parachutes studded with diamonds.

The wage squeeze appears not to have had such a dramatic impact on women's salaries. While male workers in the bottom 80 percent of the income distribution experienced an unprecedented decline in real hourly earnings between 1973 and 1994, women workers in this same income category enjoyed a modest level of real wage growth—2.8 percent.[27] The gender gap has gotten smaller, but primarily because male wages have fallen, not because female earnings have greatly improved. However, even these small gains in female earning power are fading fast. Median wages for women started to fall in 1989 and are now slipping for every group except college-educated women. Such a decrease makes it more difficult for women to contribute significantly to family income or deal with the heavy demands of single parenthood.

But what about those on the lowest rungs of the economic ladder? Sadly, more than 12 million Americans work at jobs that fail to bring them over the poverty threshold. Part of the problem is a declining minimum wage, which despite the recent upward adjustment buys just two thirds of what the minimum wage bought in the mid-1960s. The minimum wage was frozen from 1981 through 1989, and again from 1991 through September 1996. Indeed, the last time the minimum wage enabled a family of three to live above the poverty line was in 1980.[28] Freezing the minimum wage for long periods of time has contributed to the growth in the number of the working poor. Not only does the minimum wage determine earnings for the 4 million Americans who receive it, it also holds down earnings for employees in industries that pay workers just a little more. Workers clustered around the minimum wage often lack benefits as well as a living wage—health care and pensions but also paid sick leave, paid vacation leave, and job flexibility. All of which severely impact children. As Jody Heymann and Alison Earle point out, the problems of low-wage working parents are compounded by "working conditions that make it difficult or impossible for them to care for their children well while working."[29] In the late 1990s, a decently paid job with benefits has become a rare and much sought after commodity.

Gayle Blanding pulled on her best dress, the navy one with the gold buttons, painted her lips cranberry, and repeated her mantra: "I have great confidence, I have great skills." But thirty-eight-year-old Blanding still trembled as she rode the A train from Harlem to midtown Manhattan. "Don't worry, Mommy," whispered her daughter, who accompanied her part of the way.

The lure that drew Ms. Blanding from her home before dawn yesterday was a tiny classified advertisement in the evening paper and the possibility of a steady job with medical benefits. The Roosevelt Hotel is scheduled to reopen next month, and two days ago the hotel management ran a classified advertisement announcing seven hundred new jobs. The hotel needed housekeepers, maintenance workers, desk clerks, security guards, and a host of others. The pay ranged from $6 to $15 an hour, and the jobs carried benefits. By early yesterday morning 4,000 people were lined up in a twisting, turning human chain that extended for several city blocks. The hotel staff was taken unawares. "I've never seen anything quite like it," said Ted Knighton, of Interstate Hotels, the hotel's management company. Police officers had to set up barricades to control the surging crowd, which snaked around 46th Street and down Vanderbilt Avenue. Many job applicants arrived as early as 3 A.M. and waited for up to eight hours in the slow-moving line just to fill out a job application. But they said it was worth it.

"I got a three-month-old daughter to support, so I'll do anything for a real job," said Martiza Rivera, twenty-three, who lost her job as a supermarket cashier six months ago and arrived at the hotel at 7 A.M. "I just want her to have the things I've never had. A bank account. A college education. It's hard waiting out here for so long. But when I get tired, I just think of her smiling at me."[30]

Downsizing

In 1994, a nationwide poll indicated that nearly 40 percent of American workers worried that they might be fully or partially laid off or have their wages reduced. This pessimism is well placed. According to this same poll, one quarter of all workers had actually been laid off, had their hours reduced, or taken pay cuts during the previous two years.

The fact is, the contemporary labor market is characterized by a high level of employment insecurity. In an effort to boost profits and impress Wall Street, hundreds of corporations have rushed to downsize, merging operations, purging employees, buying this company, selling off that division. The result is that a large proportion of working Americans have lost their jobs, at least temporarily. The New York Times, in a major series on downsizing, estimated that more than 43 million jobs were wiped out in the U.S. labor market from 1979 through 1995—most of them decently paid jobs with benefits.[31] These mass firings continued during the economic recovery of the mid-1990s. Announced firings soared to 500,000 in 1994 and 600,000 in 1995 and involved some of America's most prestigious corporations. AT&T fired 40,000 workers over a twelve-month period; General Motors, 75,000; IBM, 60,000; and Sears, Roebuck, 50,000.[32]

In some instances, downsizing hasn't reduced the number of production workers; production has simply been shifted to outside suppliers. When this happens, downsizing becomes "a highly effective technique for reducing wages without having to cope with an unhappy workforce that had just had their wages reduced."[33] In essence, high-wage workers are fired at major firms and lower-wage replacement workers are added to the payrolls of smaller supplier firms.

Political leaders often remind us that the economy generated 23 million more new jobs than were lost between 1979 and 1995, but for the victims of downsizing this is cold comfort. A significant minority of downsized workers fail to find new jobs, while a majority end up in lower-paying positions with inferior benefits. Labor Department data show that 12 percent of downsized workers are pushed out of the labor force entirely, 17 percent remain unemployed two years later, and of the 71 percent who find new employment only 37 percent find new jobs that pay as well as or better than their old ones. A study of 2,000 workers let go by RJR Nabisco revealed that 72 percent found new jobs, but at average salaries that were 47 percent of what their old jobs had paid.[34]

For Craig Feldner and his family, it has been a rough few years. In 1993, the architectural firm Craig worked for began to restructure. A handful of people were let go, and those who remained began working longer and harder. The name of the game was to prove you were indispensable. Craig found himself mired in a daily grind, leaving home at 6:30 A.M. and getting home at 8:30 P.M. stressed and anxious, with a briefcase full of paperwork. In retrospect, he feels that his children got the brunt of his preoccupation and irritability. His younger daughter, Lauren, now seventeen, recently accused him of bailing out on her. She told him that for two years he had simply "shut down and tuned out."

In August 1995 the other shoe dropped. One Friday late in the month he was simply fired—told to clear out his desk and leave that very day. He was given five weeks' severance pay. Craig couldn't believe what was happening to him. How could twenty-three loyal years at the company count for so little? A mild-mannered, low-key guy, he still talks bitterly about the way he was treated. To add insult to injury, the month Craig was fired the company reported that business was up 10 percent above projections. Craig knew full well that he had personally secured some of this new business.

So at age fifty he hit the job market again, painfully combing the classifieds, making cold calls, sending out hundreds of résumés. Given his age, Craig thinks he was lucky; six months later he landed another job at a smaller firm. But his new job pays 10 percent less than his old job did and the fringe benefits—medical coverage, pension, vacation—are much less generous. These cutbacks hit at a bad time. His older daughter recently enrolled at a private college, and Craig has taken out a loan to pay the tuition charges. He now pays $700 a month to service this new debt. The carrying charges on his house and the tuition loan impose a heavy financial burden, currently soaking up 60 percent of his take-home pay. Even with his wife back at work full-time, the future looks scary. It's hard to know how they are going to find the money to send a second child to college.

But finances are the least of Craig's problems. What worries him most is the ways Lauren is acting out. "We kind of lost her three, four years ago," he says wistfully. "I guess she just felt abandoned with me coping with my job situation and her mother back at work . . . she got into some real bad company. She used to be such a good student, but recently her grades have fallen out of sight and at weekends she stays out until all hours. To tell the truth, we don't know how to reach her anymore. She has these tattoos and pierces all over her body and often seems kind of spacy. We're worried sick." Craig has a stricken expression as his voice trails off.[35]

Lengthening Work Weeks

While wages and job security are on the wane, the number of hours spent at work is on the rise. These trends are obviously related. In the late 1990s, it takes more hours of work—or an additional job—to provide the level of financial security that one forty-hour-a-week job delivered a generation ago. In 1996, 7.5 million adult Americans held two or more jobs, a figure that has grown 64.6 percent since 1980.[36] In February 1995, *Money* magazine ran an article on one of these new four-job families.

Most days, Cincinnati science writer and biology teacher Chris Curran, thirty-seven, starts cooking dinner at seven—in the morning. With a full-time day job, a part-time night job, and three daughters, aged seven, eleven, and thirteen, she has given up sleep and made friends with her Crock-Pot. Her husband, Andy, thirty-nine, a language and grammar teacher by day and a radio disk jockey on weekend nights, is also on overdrive. "Some days," says Chris with a sigh, "I just dream of sleeping until noon."

The Currans' four jobs began as a stopgap measure but soon evolved into a routine. Eleven years ago, when Chris was pregnant with their second child, Monica, Andy lost his $14,000 job as a research director at a radio station. They switched over to Chris's health insurance plan, but that policy didn't cover her pregnancy. To make up lost income and cover medical expenses, Chris put in about five hours of overtime a week at the television station where she then worked as a reporter and producer. "I never want to have that experience again," she says. Now, referring to the four jobs, she adds, "If we lose one, we won't lose our minds."[37]

As we have noted, Harvard economist Juliet Schor estimates that compared with twenty years ago, the average employed American is now on the job an additional 163 hours a year, or the equivalent of an extra month.[38] Men are working nearly 100 more hours a year, or two and a half extra weeks. Women—many new to the paid labor force—are working approximately 300 additional hours, which translates into seven and a half extra weeks a year. This rise in work time affects the great majority of working Americans: hours have risen for assembly-line workers, hospital orderlies, and Wall Street lawyers.

Harriet Patton is surprisingly matter-of-fact when describing her schedule at her last law firm. "I used to go in around 8 P.M. on Sunday and work right through the night until 7:30 on Monday evening. Tuesday through Friday were just regular days, 9:30 A.M. to 7:30 P.M. These hours might seem long, but they are increasingly normal at prestigious law firms. Expectations have shot up over the last decade, and a young associate is now expected to bill a minimum of two thousand hours a year. Where I worked, this seemed to boil down to sixty-plus hours a week. Working all through the night on Sunday was my way of coping. It enabled me both to rack up my billable hours and to salvage the weekends for my family. My children were little—the youngest was just two years old—and I was determined not to cut into precious weekend time. But it was totally exhausting. Come midday on Monday, I would have killed for sleep. In the end I just couldn't keep it up."

So three years ago Harriet threw in the towel and took a part-time job. But part-time in the world of New York law firms might not be anyone else's idea of part-time. Her new job requires her to work from 10:30 A.M. to 6:30 P.M. five days a week—a mere forty hours. Harriet is particularly grateful that her new schedule allows her the luxury of breakfast with her children. "My five-year-old is a regular 'babbling brook' in the morning. It is such a privilege to be there to hear this bright, sparkling child unleash a stream of consciousness at eight o'clock in the morning." While appreciative of her new arrangement, Harriet is aware of the price that is being exacted. She is permanently off the partnership track and can expect a lifetime earning stream roughly half of what it would have been otherwise.

These financial repercussions are of consequence to her family, since Harriet is the sole breadwinner. For the last five years—ever since their third child was born—her husband has been home with the kids.[39]

Schor argues that the incentive structures of market capitalism tend to produce what she calls "long-hour jobs." In her view, the short work week typical of the middle years of this century was profoundly aberrant. It came about as a result of a "monumental struggle" staged by trade unions and social reformers rather than through some natural evolutionary process. This struggle gave us, among other benefits, the weekend. Sometime in the sixties and early seventies the movement to limit work weeks collapsed, and the relentless pressures toward long hours reasserted themselves.

Schor makes the point that in recent years, the lengthening of the work week has been off the public agenda. In a real sense it has become a "nonchoice" or "hidden tradeoff." This is in sharp contrast with the historical situation. In the nineteenth century, for example, limiting the work week was one of the nation's most pressing social and political issues. Employers and workers fought bitterly over the length of the working day, and political leaders endlessly debated and legislated minimum and maximum hours. Today these debates are long forgotten, despite the fact that for contemporary families, the stakes are extremely high.

An extra 163 hours of work a year can be devastating in a world in which a majority of both moms and dads are in the paid labor force. Half the population now say they have too little time for their families, and the problem is particularly acute for working mothers. A Boston study found that employed mothers spend eighty-five hours a week at work if essential household tasks are included.[40] As a direct consequence of lengthening work weeks, the amount of time parents spend with their children has dropped significantly. Hallmark now markets greeting cards for overburdened parents who find it difficult to actually see their children. "Hope something brings you a smile today," chirps one card, meant to be left under the cornflakes in the morning. "Even though I can't be with you right now . . . consider yourself hugged," says another, designed to peek out from under the bedcovers at night. The message contained in yet another card—"I know I'm in trouble when my computer has more memory than I do . . . Now what was your name?"—may not be very comforting to a small child left home alone.

The emerging parental time famine is having an extremely negative effect on children. A central problem is that children are increasingly left home alone to fend for themselves while their parents are at work. Nationwide, estimates of children in self-care range up to 7 million, and at least 500,000 of these are preschoolers.[41] As we have seen, research in the field has uncovered ominous links between absentee parents and a whole range of emotional and behavioral problems among children. For example, a study that surveyed 5,000 eighth-grade students in southern California found that the more often children were home alone after school, the greater the risk of substance abuse.[42] And a recent survey of 90,000 teenagers confirmed that the mere presence of a parent in the home after school, at dinner, and at bedtime significantly reduces the incidence of risky behavior among adolescents.[43]

New economic pressures on parents mean that there is less time and energy for parenting than ever before, yet the irony is, given the challenges of modern society, children require more intensive and longer periods of nurturing. If children are to become economically viable in an increasingly skill-intensive era, they must be well educated, and if children are to become socially viable in an increasingly complex culture, they must have strong, stable attachments to adults. In other words, the need for parental investment and involvement in children has reached new heights just when moms and dads are increasingly unable to be there for them.

The Face of Work in Other Countries

The wage squeeze seems to be largely an American problem. Despite the fact that we often blame falling wages on global competitive pressures, other rich countries, which are part of the same international trading system, have managed to maintain steadily rising wages. For example, workers in Japan and Germany have fared much better than U.S. workers, with real wage growth at 2.2 percent and 3.1 percent per year, respectively, in the years from

1973 to 1993. Indeed, real wage growth in eleven other advanced industrial countries was much more rapid than in the United States over this same time. Despite the advent of a "global hiring hall," the kind of wage crunch experienced by American workers is far from inevitable.[44] To be fair, several European countries have experienced much higher unemployment rates than the United States in recent years, and some economists see this as the price Europe has paid for higher wages. However, even if one believes that there is a tradeoff between employment and wages, from the vantage point of child well-being, the European system is far superior to the American one. European parents are either well paid or they are unemployed, with an impressive package of benefits—but either way they have more time for their kids than their underpaid, overworked American counterparts. Children in fact are doing much better in Europe than in America, with child poverty rates well under 10 percent and secondary school graduation rates well over 90 percent.

Lengthening work weeks also seem to be a peculiarly American phenomenon. In the United States, work weeks are long and getting longer, while in Europe they are short and getting shorter. In the European Union, a powerful trade union movement has kept the issue of shorter hours at the top of the agenda throughout the postwar period. Even in bad economic times, unions have resisted the inevitable pressure for longer hours, arguing that a shorter work week actually combats unemployment by spreading the work around, and employers seem to be listening. In the early 1990s, the large German union IG Metall, for instance, won a thirty-five-hour work week for its members, a gain that spread through the German labor force.[45] In a similar vein, the recent economic downturn in France has prompted Prime Minister Lionel Jospin to propose a law that would cut the French work week from thirty-nine to thirty-five hours. He is also proposing state financial aid of $1,500 per employee to any company that will reduce the work week of employees by 10 percent while increasing its staff by least 6 percent.[46] U.S. manufacturing employees currently work 320 more hours a year than their counterparts in Germany and France. What's more, French and German employees have five to six weeks of paid vacation a year, while American workers had an average of sixteen days off in 1994, down from twenty days in 1981.[47]

Joblessness

If mainstream workers are being squeezed, stretched, and generally overworked, poorly educated workers, especially black men, are failing to find any kind of foothold in the labor market. In the words of the Harvard sociologist William Julius Wilson, "For the first time in the 20th century most adult men in many inner city ghetto neighborhoods are not working in a typical week."[48] Analysis by the Center for the Study of Social Policy shows just how far this process has gone. In 1993, nearly half of all adult black males (43 percent) were without jobs. They were unemployed, had stopped looking for work, were in prison, or simply had no fixed address and could not be found by the census.[49]

The extraordinarily bleak situation of black men has been obscured by the fact that the official unemployment figure constitutes only the tip of the iceberg. While 8.8 percent of black males aged eighteen to sixty-five are officially unemployed—that is, out of work and actively seeking a job—another 20.6 percent are outside the labor force because they are discouraged workers who have given up looking for a job. A further 4.4 percent are in penal institutions, and 9.3 percent cannot be found by the census. The net result: in 1993, just under half of working-age black men were in the mainstream workforce, compared to over three quarters of working-age white men.[50]

Not only are millions of black men not working at all, but those who are working often earn very low wages. In 1990, for example, 22 percent of black men aged eighteen to sixty-five who worked full-time for the entire year earned less than $12,195—that year's poverty threshold for a family of four. The proportion of black men who earn extremely low wages has increased dramatically since the early 1970s, when only 13 percent of black male full-time workers earned wages that put them below the poverty threshold.[51]

Why is decently paid work disappearing for so many black men? The answers lie in a set of factors ranging from a shrinking manufacturing base and the suburbanization of employment to underinvestment in inner-city school systems and a "war on drugs" that disproportionately targets—and incarcerates—young black men. Some of these factors are structural; others are politically inspired.

All have contributed to undermining the economic circumstances of black males.

The extremely large number of black men either without jobs or with exceedingly low earning power has contributed to the devastation of family life in inner-city communities. Out-of-work, poverty-stricken men tend not to marry or support their children. The data show that the rate of joblessness among black men and the rate of female-headed households follow identical trends. Between 1960 and 1992, a period during which joblessness doubled for black men, the number of black female-headed households also doubled, reaching 46 percent of all families by 1992.[52] It seems that the declining economic power of black males has gone hand in hand with a declining male presence in the home.

The economic plight of black men and the conditions and policies that trigger that plight have been almost entirely ignored in the long-drawn-out debate over welfare policy. Yet the destruction of male earning power helps explain why so many women and children are dependent on government in the first place. The fact that an astounding 47 percent of black children are now growing up in poverty is due in large part to black men opting out of family commitments. This in turn results from the interaction of three factors: the structure of AFDC, which over a thirty-year time span deliberately excluded men; structural shifts that have phased out many blue-collar jobs; and crime control policies that target young black males.[53]

Against this stark backdrop, the current wave of welfare reform seems seriously off-base. Precisely because it concentrates on the needs and obligations of single mothers, it largely ignores the economic plight of disadvantaged men and its implications for women and children. To the extent that men enter the welfare loop at all, they are discussed almost exclusively as sources for child support payments. But this is not the gut issue. With so many minority men either outside the labor market or earning poverty-level wages, the issue is not enforcing child support but creating the opportunities that allow black men to earn a decent living and reconnect to family life, as Michael Garcia has struggled to do.

For the last two and a half years, twenty-five-year-old Michael Garcia has worked—off the books—as a garage attendant in midtown

Manhattan. He works the night shift, from 11:00 P.M. to 7:00 A.M., and earns $5.50 an hour. Despite the fact that he works seven days a week and all holidays, including Christmas and New Year's Day, his take-home pay averages just under $260 a week. More than half of his wages go toward rent. Michael's share of expenses for a small apartment in the North Bronx, where he lives with his girlfriend and her son, comes to $540 a month. He barely has enough left over to cover subway fare and food. He does without a telephone and is generally a month or two late on his utility bill.

Eighteen months ago, Michael enrolled at Long Island University, intending to get himself the credentials to upgrade his job prospects. A resourceful and determined young man with a respectable high school record, he was able to piece together a package of grants and loans that covered his tuition expenses. Despite this minor triumph, his new schedule was relentless. After leaving work in the morning, he would get on the subway for the forty-five-minute ride to school, sometimes falling asleep and missing his stop. He would then drag himself through six hours of classes. At the end of the afternoon he would take the subway home (a complicated trip that involved three trains and took almost two hours), where he would grab something to eat and sleep for four hours. He would then get on the subway again and return to work.

By the fall of 1996, when we interviewed him, Michael had accumulated seventy-six college credits in media arts and communication, but he was discouraged and bone tired. A couple of months before, he had felt it was time to try to get what he called a real job, one that would allow him to make some kind of commitment to his girlfriend and her son. He was thinking of marrying his girlfriend and adopting her eight-year-old, who is fatherless. One hundred and fifty job applications and twenty-seven job interviews later, he had come up with precisely nothing. It's not that he was asking for the moon. When asked what kind of job he wanted, Michael talked wistfully about some kind of desk job—he does, after all, have all these newfangled computer skills. His wage goal? Maybe $10 an hour.

So why can't this highly directed, hardworking black person get to first base in the job market? Because Michael Garcia has a criminal record. When he was eighteen, he and three older friends mugged a guy in Brooklyn and made off with a gold chain and $37 in cash. Michael was sentenced to two and a half years in prison, which he served at Rikers Island and at Coxsackie jail in upstate New York. This was a heavy sentence, given the nature of the crime and the fact that it was a first offense. In Michael's eyes, the severity of his sentence had a lot to do with the color of his skin and his family's inability to afford a fancy lawyer. Bad things happened to Michael in jail—he was raped and his face was slashed—but he is mostly upset about the damage done to the rest of his life. He despairs of ever landing a job that uses his skills, pays decently, and opens up some kind of future. Any prospective employer can conjure up his criminal record at a stroke of a key; he has seen them do it dozens of times. College credits, computer skills, work experience—none of these things seem to make any difference.[54]

Michael's predicament is distressingly commonplace. A criminal record makes it extremely difficult to get a job, and most men, like Michael, continue to see obtaining a "real" job as a prerequisite for marriage and fatherhood. Although Michael says he loves his girlfriend and her son, he is not about to make a formal, long-term commitment to them before he has that job in hand, a prospect that is fast receding given the reaction of prospective employers to his criminal record. Our labor market remains singularly unforgiving of young felons, no matter how motivated or qualified they are to make their lives anew.[55] When next we blame black joblessness on the decline of our manufacturing base or a shortfall in education, we should remember that our criminal justice system is a powerful contributing factor. Experts in the field agree that our decade-old war against drugs has disproportionately targeted small-time drug dealers, who are mostly young black males, and let off the hook drug users (mostly white folks) and the big bosses (again, mostly white folks). The result: fully a third of black males in the eighteen-to-twenty-four-year age bracket are either behind bars or on parole.[56]

Duped and Betrayed

On the rare occasions that politicians mention this litany of economic woes—falling wages, lengthening work weeks, heightened insecurity, joblessness—they tend to focus on the following explanations. First, these unfortunate trends are a result of forces beyond their control. Global competition has forced down wages, because there simply is no way American employers can pay textile workers $12 an hour when the going rate in South Korea is $2 an hour, or pay physicists $75,000 a year when the going rate in Russia is $12,000. Second, growth rates and wage levels have been dragged down by big government and an extremely onerous welfare burden. In the not too distant past, the story goes, irresponsible liberals increased our tax burden and spent the resulting revenues on "them." In the category of "them," politicians tend to group together black welfare moms and brown immigrants.

By and large, Americans believe this combination of half-truths and self-serving lies. In a recent Harris poll commissioned by *Business Week,* when asked why incomes for working Americans have fallen over the course of the last fifteen years, 73 percent of respondents blamed increased government spending, while 52 percent blamed increased global competition.[57]

Despite a powerful consensus, these popular explanations are highly misleading. The welfare burden, for example, is way off base as a meaningful explanatory factor. AFDC/TANF has not significantly exacerbated the deficit, dampened growth, pumped up our taxes, or put downward pressure on wages. The sums involved are simply too paltry. By blaming welfare mothers and immigrants for our economic woes, we merely add to the mean-spirited mood of the day and create convenient scapegoats for opportunistic politicians.

At first blush, increased global competition would seem to provide at least part of the explanation. Yes, there is a new, fiercely competitive global economy, and this has the potential of producing downward pressure on wages. However, despite this logical connection, it turns out that the central cause of falling income levels and heightened insecurity is the overweening greed of American managers, not Korean textile workers or Russian scientists.

In fact, all of the cruel belt-tightening, all of the new stress and fear, have had absolutely no impact on America's competitive position in the world. Smaller paychecks for 80 percent of workers have surely shaved an enormous amount off the wage bill, but this huge savings has merely been transferred to the pockets of managers. From the important vantage point of competitive strength, the entire debilitating exercise has been irrelevant.

Just look at the numbers. Over the last twenty-five years, the wage bill has remained virtually stagnant, moving from 56.6 percent of national income in 1973 to 58.6 percent in 1993. But this seemingly stable situation masks a seismic distributional shift from workers to managers. In 1973, 40 percent of total national income went to production workers while the rest of the wage bill—16.2 percent—was paid out to supervisors and managers. By 1994, the share of total national income going to production workers had fallen six percentage points, while the share going to supervisors and managers had increased from 16.2 percent to 24.1 percent.[58]

It is hard to exaggerate the size and scope of this shift. Managerial compensation as a percentage of national income increased by almost eight percentage points between 1973 and 1993. This amounts to seven times the amount of money involved in the defense buildup of the 1980s!

Managerial Bloat

The size and cost of the American managerial class have grown enormously in recent years. By 1994, 17.3 million employees worked in managerial and supervisory jobs at various levels of the corporate hierarchy. This veritable army of bosses was paid $1.3 trillion in total compensation, if we include salaries, benefits, stock options, and other perks.[59] As a nation we wring our hands and beat our breasts about big government, but the cost of most government programs pales in comparison to the sums involved in managerial bloat. For example, the $1.3 trillion paid to managers in 1994 was *four times* the bill for social security and *fifty times* the bill for AFDC. When Ralph Reed, Newt Gingrich, and Rush Limbaugh next fulminate about the cost of government, they should be reminded of the enormous amount of money tied up in managerial compensation. Even within business circles, compensation packages for top management are increasingly seen as out of line. Respondents to a recent *Industry Week* survey called the soaring levels of executive pay "disgraceful," "infuriating," and "sickening."

But what about downsizing? If we have had a problem with managerial bloat, isn't it receding? Surely downsizing is creating a world where corporations are increasingly lean and mean? The fact of the matter is, although many managers and supervisors have been fired, even more have been hired. Laid-off managers are quickly rehired, and large numbers of new recruits have been brought into the managerial ranks. For all the concern about downsized executives, there were many more managers in the mid-1990s than there were in the mid-1980s, before downsizing began. For example, between 1989 and 1994, employment for managers and supervisors rose by 1.4 million, increasing the number of managers in total nonfarm employment by 5 percent. This little-known trend is finally being recognized in the business press. In the fall of 1995, the *Wall Street Journal* admitted that reports of management cutbacks "have proved much exaggerated." Even corporate giants who have reported dramatic levels of managerial layoffs "have more managers per 100 employees today than they did in 1993."[60]

Which brings us to an important question: is this enormously expensive army of managers remotely necessary? Various analysts have put forward the view that keeping a company profitable in today's harsh business climate is extremely difficult, and it is therefore appropriate for the market to reward CEOs who have the ability and skill to generate high rates of return. The problem with this theory is that the data fail to show a connection between executive pay and profitability. Management consultant Alan Downs has demonstrated that there is no relationship at all between compensation of CEOs and return on investment. Instead, he finds a powerful correlation between CEO compensation and the number of employees laid off. According to Downs, chief executive officers who fire the largest number of workers are those who are paid most generously.[61]

This is how layoffs translate into huge rewards. Mass firings have become a highly profitable strategic ploy in the executive suite because of the way in which they play on Wall Street. Investors increasingly interpret the news of a layoff as a sign of a corporate turnaround. In the words of one analyst, "The payroll is a large, ongoing liability to the balance sheet, and investors are titillated by anything that reduces it."[62] Given these expectations, a common shareholder tactic is to pressure management to lay off workers to generate a spike in earnings and higher dividend payments. If a CEO is willing to sign on to this strategy and lead the charge, he or she can expect to share in the windfall.

Another reason put forward for maintaining huge compensation packages is that we need to pay CEOs 209 times what the average worker earns to remain competitive in global labor markets—to prevent top managerial talent from being lured away by German or British corporations. The problem with this theory is that the United States has more and better-paid managers than any other country, and there is little incentive for senior executives to seek employment elsewhere. According to data from the International Labor Organization, managers make up 13 percent of total non-farm employment in the United States, compared with an average of 4.4 percent in the rest of the advanced industrial world.[63] What's more, American managers are paid a good deal more than their colleagues overseas; top-level managers here earn, on average, almost twice as much as their counterparts in Germany, Japan, and Britain.

In the end, neither of these theories wash. It all seems to boil down to pure, unadulterated greed. Corporate elites, increasingly unfettered by government, seem newly able to reward themselves with an extraordinary panoply of goodies, the sumptuous dimensions of which we have not seen since the days of the robber barons. It's hard to comprehend, but over a twenty-year span, the wildly successful accumulation of wealth by corporate elites has combined with a wage crunch to make the United States the most unequal country in the advanced industrial world. The top one percent of the American population now controls 39 percent of national wealth, compared to 26 percent in France, 16 percent in Sweden, and 18 percent in Great Britain.[64] So much for our cherished egalitarian traditions! One thing we can be sure of: this unprecedented trickle-up of wealth has been driven by private-sector greed, but it could not have happened without the collusion of government.

Campaigns and Collusion

Nineteen ninety-six was the year when all semblance of restraint in campaign financing went by the board. Candidates for president and for Congress raised and spent an estimated $2 billion on their campaigns, almost double what had ever been spent before on an election.[65] According to the Center for Responsive Politics (CRP), by far the largest source of money for all candidates was corporate America. During the 1996 election cycle, business contributed $242 million, while organized labor contributed a mere $35 million.[66] "Money is not coming from ordinary Americans," said Ellen Miller, the executive director of CRP. "We have a political system paid for by Wall Street and Tobacco Road."[67] Even Marty Sobo, the chairman of the House Budget Committee, matter-of-factly explained that the serious money today is given by the large corporations: "That's where the campaign money comes from now—in the 1980s we gave up on the little guys."[68]

The momentum behind this recent surge in corporate financing of election campaigns has come from tremendous growth in so-called soft-dollar contributions—money given to national political parties which is then distributed to individual candidates. The soft-dollar conduit is increasingly used as a loophole to allow donors to avoid federal campaign finance restrictions. Direct contributions to candidates are capped at $1,000 for individuals and $5,000 for businesses, but contributions to political parties are unlimited.

So who are the major donors? In 1996, the biggest donor of soft money was the financial services industry, which includes Wall Street and the insurance and real estate industries. This sector gave $59.8 million, 64 percent of which went to the Republican party. The largest single corporate donor was Philip Morris, which gave $2.7 million, 78 percent of it to the GOP, followed by AT&T, which gave $2.2 million, 60 percent of which went to the GOP. The Association of Trial Lawyers gave $2.1 million, 80 percent of which went to the Democratic party. Other big soft-dollar donors were Joseph E. Seagram and MCI, both of which favored the Democratic party, and Atlantic Richfield, which favored the Republican party. Hedging their bets, most big donors gave to both parties.[69]

Political fundraising always has been a game of selling access. The dangerous characteristics of the 1990s are that the sums involved in running for national office have become astronomical and that corporate America is supplying a larger and larger proportion of the huge amounts involved. Obviously, when elected officials of every hue and stripe are heavily indebted to and dependent on business, corruption taints the political process. In the words of

Ellen Miller, "When candidates for political office solicit and receive big bucks for their political campaigns, big favors are incurred. Both parties know it. Both parties do it."[70]

In some instances, corporate attempts to influence policy are very specifically targeted. Philip Morris, for example, is after a looser regulatory environment for cigarette smoking and is betting on some Republican help, while the Association of Trial Lawyers is heading off efforts to restrict lawsuits against business and is counting on some Democratic help. But even more damaging than these kinds of pressure are the ways in which enormous corporate contributions create a brutal probusiness, promarket environment that constrains the actions of politicians across a broad array of issues. In this brave new world progressives are defanged, labor is emasculated, and sixty-year-old rights to welfare benefits are thrown out the window. In the late 1990s it takes a singularly courageous—or foolhardy—politician to mess with the private sector. This explains why Congress failed to make any progress on campaign finance reform in 1997 despite the scandals. It also helps explain why political leaders will not even talk about reducing the obscene levels of executive compensation. An unholy alliance between corporate America and government policymakers has tilted the balance of power against working Americans and created a situation in which the fruits of growth are increasingly monopolized by senior executives and other members of the elite.

The Cover-Up

Luckily for elite groups—and surely not coincidentally—this squeezing of workers in order to fatten the compensation packages of managers remains "one of the best-kept secrets of the U.S. economy."[71] Aside from Gordon's book and a smattering of obscure articles, this is an entirely untold story. It is also enormously distressing. The deliberate creation of a yawning chasm between managers and everyone else is profoundly destructive of family life in America. As we have seen, the vast majority of parents are being forced to work much harder for less money, and children are being pushed to the edge, or in some cases pushed under. In the late 1990s, there are hundreds of thousands of Vicki Parkers and Craig

Feldners—well-intentioned parents working as hard as they know how to raise their kids but hopelessly undermined by the labor market.

Most of these serious ramifications are lost on our leaders. Business commentators, policy wonks, and the media have tended to celebrate stagnant or deteriorating wage levels. A recent report on wage trends welcomed the fact that real wages are growing at zero percent and American workers are "obtaining less in pay and benefit increases from employers these days." Indeed, the press becomes extremely nervous if wages show any sign of heading up. In September 1996, the *New York Times* told its readers that "the half-percent increase in wages since August is deeply disturbing" because it might well put pressure on prices. Oddly enough, there is little evidence to support the notion that wage increases would trigger inflation. Economist Alan Krueger points out that the cost of fringe benefits is actually decreasing for many employers and that this should allow wages to grow without creating pressure on prices. In his view, "there is some room for wages to grow without igniting inflation."[72]

Our cavalier disregard for the real-life consequences of a twenty-five-year-long wage crunch has undoubtedly been helped along by the masking power of race and gender. In contemporary America, black pain and female labor tend to be heavily discounted, often to the point of invisibility. The folks who have suffered most from the wage squeeze and joblessness, those "faces at the bottom of the well," are overwhelmingly black and brown, and it seems to be all too easy to ignore the increasingly desperate plight of this group of Americans.[73] As the wage squeeze tightens, however, and more and more middle-class workers are directly affected by declining wages and heightened insecurity, it becomes harder to avoid these grim realities.

Another piece of camouflage has been provided by the extraordinary work effort of women. In recent years huge numbers of wives and mothers have entered the paid labor force to bolster family living standards; the percentage of mothers at work who have children in the six-to-seventeen-year age group rose from 55 percent in 1975 to 77 percent in 1996.[74] In many respects, these women are the unsung heroines of our age, routinely working two jobs fifty weeks a year, in the manner of no other women in the rich world. They have bailed out their loved ones, maintaining family income levels in the face of a huge decline in male wages. However, this particular safety valve is about to clog up. In the future, wives are unlikely to offset their husbands' falling real earnings to nearly the same extent. Most wives are already working full-time and have little spare capacity. Besides, female wage rates have begun to fall, and this diminishes the appeal of additional paid work. Both of these factors make it probable that from here on in, falling male earnings will translate into falling family income as the buffer of increased work effort by women becomes weaker. This means that in the future, neither race nor gender can be relied on to mask the size and scope of the wage crunch.

A Window of Opportunity

As mothers and fathers are increasingly squeezed and stretched by various types of economic pressure, they are almost entirely unaware of just how thoroughly they have been duped and betrayed. If they knew that the wage crunch was neither necessary nor inevitable, that they were working longer hours for less pay and shortchanging their children merely to enrich an executive class, working men and women might well become militant in new and serious ways, providing a window of opportunity for concerted political action.

This leads us to the good news: hidden in these depressing changes is some powerful potential. Precisely because sagging wages and frightening new levels of economic security are homegrown problems—artifacts of out-of-control managerial greed—*we can do something about them.* We clearly cannot control wage levels in Korea, Mexico, or Russia, but if working parents were to find some new political clout, we might be able to turn our policies around and reintroduce notions of fairness and equity in the labor market. We might even reinvent the social contract and recapture the American Dream! This is the silver lining in an otherwise grim economic reality that profoundly debilitates American parents and their children.

FOUR

....

Government Tilts Against Parents

OUR GOVERNMENT has become bitterly hostile to parents. Compounding the economic pressures produced by sagging wages and mounting insecurity, mothers and fathers are newly undermined by a political culture that fails to give support or value to the work they do. Starting in the late 1960s, successive administrations, both Republican and Democrat, have pulled the rug from under adults raising children, progressively dismantling programs and policies that underpin family life. Indeed, in some instances government has intervened with the deliberate intention of disabling and displacing moms and dads. Given these new political realities, devoting time to family and children has become an increasingly difficult and thankless task.

Today the lack of support for mothers and fathers in American society borders on the absurd. Take one small example: our government now does a better job underwriting the breeding of horses than the raising of children. If you own a horse, you can deduct from your tax bill the cost of food, stabling, training, vet and stud services, transportation to and from horse shows, attendance at horse shows, insurance, and a host of other expenses. Compare this to raising children. Can a parent deduct from his or her tax bill the cost of a child's food, housing, medical care, or preschool education? Of course not. We are light-years away from such a scenario.

The contrast between these two situations is ludicrous. Obviously the health of our nation is much more centrally tied up with the fate of children than with the fate of horses. A few years back, Wilhelmina du Pont Ross, a member of one of the wealthiest families in the world, hired her husband to run their stables and wrote off his salary on their joint tax return—a perfectly legal maneuver. Would that a husband could hire his wife to look after their children and write off her salary on their tax return.

The original idea behind government subsidies for horse breeding was that horses, like cattle, were critical to the working of a farm. Since the vast majority of farms in the United States are now mechanized, this logic no longer applies. However, the breeding of horses has kept a privileged place in our tax code through the lobbying efforts of the American Horse Council, whose well-heeled members "can barely tell a horse from a donkey, but recognize a nice tax shelter" when they see one. According to the *Wall Street Journal*, "Some of the people breeding horses . . . are up front about their motivation, as can be seen from the names given racehorses in recent years: My Deduction, Tax Dodge, Tax Gimmick, My Writeoff, Another Shelter, and Justa Shelter."[1]

How did this happen? How did a nation so desperately concerned about the collapse of family values develop a tax code that ranks horses above children? The answer to this troubling question lies deep within our political culture.

The Abdication of Government

In recent years the American government has largely gotten out of the business of supporting moms and dads. Parents have become the victims of a set of ideological contradictions and antagonisms that have frozen political will and dramatically undermined the social supports that used to reinforce parental energies.

Particularly since 1980, conservatives have maintained that markets should be free and unfettered, that the economy does best—is most efficient—when there is as little interference by government as possible. In the social sphere, by way of contrast, conservatives have argued for controls and constraints. Women should not be allowed to choose abortion freely, divorce should be made more difficult, and children should be required to pray in school. In private life, right-wingers espouse traditional family values rather than free-market choice.

Granted, elements of social conservatism do provide important protections for parents and children. Tightening the rules around divorce, for instance, would seem to be a good idea if we want to preserve more "good enough" marriages and allow more children to grow up in two-parent families. However, economic conservatism can be enormously destructive of both parents and children. During the 1980s, for example, when Ronald Reagan embarked on a series of promarket initiatives, private enterprise was allowed to invade ever-widening spheres of public and private life. Television was deregulated, gambling was legalized, trade unions were beaten back, and the minimum wage was frozen, all in the name of freeing up markets. In different ways, each of these conservative policies—many of which continue to the present day—has diminished parents' ability to do a good job by their children.

For their part, liberals have developed a set of contradictions that are the mirror image of conservative beliefs. By and large, left-wingers advocate controls over the economy. Deeply appreciative of how free enterprise can pollute the environment, create hazardous working conditions, and fail to come through with medical care for poor children, liberals have fought long and hard for government intervention in economic life, to minimize the human costs of capitalism. In the social sphere, however, they are staunch supporters of freedom and choice. Whether the concern is reproductive choice, career path, or marriage partner, liberals believe that all persons—black, white, brown, male, and female—should be able to pursue their individual potential with as few external constraints as possible.

Thus, both right and left are caught up in substantial internal contradictions. More important from our point of view, both schools of thought clobber kids. Neither the conservative nor the liberal worldview is able to deal coherently or constructively with the critical challenge of supporting parents—or grandparents.

"Fresh-faced and direct, sixteen-year-old Chaz Cope would seem to be the ideal poster boy" for Youngtown, Arizona. Instead, this retirement community of sunshine and orange trees sees him as human contraband. While Youngtown allows dogs, the City Council has voted unanimously to fine Chaz's grandparents $100 a day for illegally housing a child. "All we wanted was permission for him to stay until he finished high school, only sixteen months," said Lynne Rae Naab, the boy's grandmother, explaining that Chaz moved in a year ago to escape physical abuse by his stepfather.

A few miles away, a similar expulsion order hangs over the head of another sixteen-year-old, Deserae Carrie. She lives quietly with her grandmother in the retirement community of Superstition Heights. The lawyer for the community calls her presence a "nuisance." Deserae counters that she has nowhere else to go because her mother is dying of cancer in a nursing home.

Like a great many sunbelt communities, Youngtown and Superstition Heights bar permanent residents under eighteen through age covenants written into deeds. These covenants are thoroughly legal. While the Federal Fair Housing Act bars discrimination on the grounds of race, religion, sex, or family status, it does allow discrimination against children.

At the heart of this antagonism toward children is a logic born of the marketplace. Leaders of the Youngtown community say they bar children to avoid having to provide schools, which would mean higher taxes for residents, and elected officials tend to go along with this because retirees spend tens of billions of dollars in Arizona. "This is a huge sector of our economy, and there are a lot of people with a vested interest in making sure that these age covenants are maintained," said Jason Morris, a Phoenix zoning lawyer.

Some members of the community justify the ban on children by talking about freedom of choice and individual rights. "Most of the elderly do not want to live in that type of segregated community," said housing expert George Galberlavage, "but a significant minority do, and we support their right to choose." Indeed, this right is enforced with tactics reminiscent of those of a police state. At the town offices in Youngtown, a form is available for any resident who wants to denounce a neighbor for harboring an illegal child.

Jerry Lee Naab, a former painting contractor and the grandfather of Chaz, has a few blunt words: "We are family oriented. These folks, they're me oriented."[2]

The attempted expulsion of Chaz and Deserae demonstrates the degree to which our laws and policies undercut family functioning. It is extraordinary that members of these retirement communities fail to understand that loving grandparents should be supported in their efforts to look after their grandchildren. This is the right thing to do, but it is also the rational thing to do. If Chaz and Deserae are allowed to finish high school, everyone benefits—the children themselves and the entire community. Instead, market forces and a knee-jerk regard for individual rights, at least as they apply to adults, are allowed to ride roughshod over the needs of these struggling families.

The Blindness of Conservatives

Conservatives undermine family life because they fail to see the ways in which market values destroy family values. Committed as they are to free and unfettered markets, they forget that values are the "black hole of capitalism," to use Lester Thurow's memorable phrase.[3] Indeed, market capitalism leans on some of the least attractive human traits—avarice, aggression, self-centeredness. This is because when individual men and women focus on greed, free enterprise can produce amazing results, generating the highest rates of growth and the highest standards of living in recorded history. But precisely because markets have no moral compass, they cannot address issues of social order or social investment. Free enterprise is thus singularly ill equipped to deal with the nonmarket work that parents do. Even though, as we have seen, this nonmarket work is the fountainhead of our nation's social and human capital, it can be completely ignored by free enterprise, because it lies outside the cash nexus.

To give conservatives their due, they have identified the serious consequences of family decline. They believe that strong families are vital to this nation, and they know that there are fewer of them than there used to be. Ronald Reagan, Dan Quayle, and Newt Gingrich are just three among many Republican leaders who have made political careers by stressing the importance of families and bemoaning their erosion, but none of these conservative leaders seems to appreciate the family-destroying properties of the market. On the contrary, they have done their level best to unleash free enterprise in new and more powerful ways, stacking the decks even more completely against moms and dads.

Parenting: The Ultimate Nonmarket Activity

What the right wing fails to appreciate is that from a purely market standpoint, raising children has become a financial drain of the first order. As we saw in Chapter 2, estimates of the cost of raising a child are now in the $145,000 range, and this figure does not include college tuition, which can cost $125,000, or foregone income, which can be extremely significant in the case of a professional who decides to stay home to look after a child.[4] In the late twentieth century, a child is simply a huge economic liability. There are, of course, deep psychic, emotional, and spiritual rewards wrapped up in being a parent, but moms and dads can no longer expect any economic return on their parental investments.

This brings us to a critical contemporary dilemma that confounds our political leaders, particularly those on the right. We increasingly expect parents to spend extraordinary amounts of money and energy on raising their children when it is society at large that reaps the material rewards. The costs are private; the benefits are increasingly public. If you are a good parent and come up with the heroic energy to ensure that your child succeeds in school and goes on to complete an expensive college education, you will undoubtedly contribute to America's store of human capital and help this nation compete with the Germans and Koreans, but in so doing you will deplete rather than enhance your own economic reserves. From the parent's standpoint, a child has become a pure nonmarket good. Individual mothers and fathers may still invest large quantities of time in this critical activity—critical both for the child and for the nation—but for the first time in history, their energies are not supported by enlightened self-interest; they must rely completely on a large store of altruistic love. Large enough to span more than two decades, for in our increasingly complex society, a mom or dad cannot easily offload an eighteen-year-old; nowadays children rely on parental resources well into their twenties. At age twenty-four, 42 percent of adult males are still living in the parental home![5] Coming through with this kind of long-term commitment is clearly a tall order in an age when the market dictates what is valued in life.

Right-wingers in particular are poorly prepared to do anything about this serious collision between market values and family values. Rather than mitigate the growing friction between the private costs and public benefits associated with child-rearing by socializing some of the costs of childbearing—which is, after all, the rational thing to do—conservatives have moved in the opposite direction. Since 1980, the right wing has strenuously, and often successfully, led a charge to cut back on a whole range of social supports that run the gamut from food stamps to prenatal care to housing subsidies to student loans. Because of these conservative roadblocks, American parents lack even the most elemental kinds of public support. The United States is the only rich country that fails to guarantee new mothers maternity benefits and paid, job-protected leave.[6] And it is one of the few rich countries that fail to provide housing subsidies for low-income families and free higher education for qualified low-income youngsters. More than any other wealthy nation, America expects individual parents to foot the child-raising bill from childbirth all the way through college, and more than any other wealthy nation, America is facing profound and systematic child neglect. These two phenomena are clearly related. In an age that venerates the market, relying solely on parental altruism to underwrite the costs of raising children is risky for the nation and cruel for the child. Try as they undoubtedly do, millions of contemporary parents are simply too stretched and squeezed to do a stellar job.

Left-wing ideologues can be equally careless about family well-being. While it is true that liberals have spearheaded a set of government programs that have improved the lives of poor children—WIC and Head Start, for example, have improved the health and educational circumstances of small children—it is also true that the extraordinary emphasis in liberal circles on the rights of individuals has frequently compromised the welfare of both parents and children. Untrammeled choice and uncluttered freedom get in the way of the altruistic, other-directed energy that is the stuff of parenting. The recent liberalization of our divorce laws is a case in point.

In 1970, California passed the first "no fault" divorce law, and over the next fifteen years forty other states followed suit. The new laws removed a long-existing framework of guilt and innocence and allowed for divorce whenever a husband or wife claimed irreconcilable differences. They also largely eliminated alimony and reduced waiting periods. This easing of the rules reflected a liberal resolve to treat people as unencumbered individuals free from duties and responsibilities they choose to reject." The impact has been to transform our entire conception of marriage. Instead of serving as a mechanism through which adults express their commitment to others—especially children—marriage has become a vehicle for the emotional fulfillment of adult partners.

Twenty-five years later the results are in, and they are decidedly mixed. No-fault divorce has undoubtedly opened up a new range of choice for many adults. By reducing the penalties attached to divorce, it has enhanced an individual's ability to shed family roles and responsibilities with ease and speed. But this new freedom of choice is a long way from being cost-free, as it visits considerable hardship and suffering on children. An impressive body of research now demonstrates that the children of divorce experience serious problems ranging from economic deprivation to school failure to long-term emotional distress.[7] According to Judith Wallerstein, divorce is often the "single most important cause of enduring pain in a child's life."[8]

The Antipathy of Liberals

If conservatives find it difficult to support or protect parental energies because of a blind faith in markets, liberals can be critical of the core endeavor. An important strand of liberal thinking is deeply antagonistic to the parental role and function. Scratch the surface and you will find at least some folks on the left who don't particularly like marriage or children. In their view, the enormous quantity of other-directed energy absorbed by families gets in the way of freedom of choice, and ultimately of self-realization. This is particularly true for women, which is why radical feminists tend to see motherhood as a plot to derail equal rights and lure women back to subservient, submissive roles within the family.

Rugged individualism is of course a distinctive feature of American liberalism. Individual rights sit at the center of our self-understanding as a people, from the libertarian First Amendment of the Constitution to the liberal classic *A Theory of Justice*, by Harvard's

John Rawls. This rich tradition is grounded in a deep fear of government unduly shaping the moral character of its citizens and warns against any authoritarian imposition of religious or ethical values. According to Rawls, a just society provides a neutral framework of rights within which individuals can pursue their own conception of the good. His fear is that when government seeks to shape the moral character of its citizens, it imposes on some the values of others and in so doing fails to respect the inherent capacity of free individuals to choose their own values and ends.[9]

This is a singularly appealing set of ideas. Liberalism, however, can go too far. As Michael Lerner has pointed out, "Fetishizing the freedom to choose as our highest goal in life" can easily degenerate into selfishness and materialism.[10] It can also lead to tremendous isolation, for the liberal worldview glorifies autonomy and independence and downplays connections among people. The goal becomes the maximization of choices available to an individual who has learned to stand on his or her own two feet without depending on or needing others. The problem with this "thin" liberal perspective is that people are healthier and happier in relationships and in communities than they are on their own. The fact is, we humans need one another, and the sharp decline in long-term, loving relationships in contemporary America is a significant problem. Unchecked, radical individualism has produced a society in which people are increasingly unable to sustain relationships or look after their young. This is no longer "just a particular set of choices, but a social pathology."[11] We can't have our cake and eat it: unlimited choice and uncluttered freedom get in the way of family strength and community well-being.

Nothing brings this point home more than the responsibilities of the parental role. Children do in fact hopelessly confound the liberal project of maximizing autonomy and choice. Because young children are inherently dependent and cannot survive without the energy and support of others, they cannot be conceived of as unencumbered individuals. What is more, they seriously limit the ability of responsible grownups to be unencumbered individuals for large chunks of adult life. In a nation where approximately 87 percent of all adults become parents and the "parenting emergency," to use the psychologist David Guttmann's felicitous phrase, lasts approximately twenty-five years, one thing is abundantly clear: we are not talking about marginal decisions or small-scale responsibilities.[12] Children sit right at the center of adult life and require major compromises with other life goals.

That being said, it is important to stress that we are not recommending that society resolve the contradictions inherent in the liberal project by returning to a traditional division of labor between the sexes—to a situation in which women (especially black women) pay all of the opportunity costs associated with the care and nurturing of family and community. Women are no longer able or willing to produce all of this sacrificial energy, and it is not right or just for them to attempt to do so. What we are recommending is, quite simply, that we share the responsibilities—and the joys—of parenting. Husbands and fathers, employers and government, all need to pull their weight. It is time to demonstrate collectively, in our public policies and in our private priorities, that we honor parents and treasure our children. Then and only then can we ensure that families thrive.

It seems that as far as our political culture is concerned, it's a pox on both our houses. Conservatives are blind to the ways in which unfettered markets undercut the energy and efficacy of moms and dads, while liberals are oblivious to the ways in which untrammeled individualism undermines the very essence of parenting. But if both political traditions are complicit in the destruction of our web of care, our elected leaders are a long way from acknowledging this fact, let alone wrestling with the consequences. Maybe they honestly don't see the powerful tradeoffs between market and family, between self and other. Maybe there is just too much vested interest in the status quo.

Government Support, Fifties Style

In the 1990s, an age of disillusionment with government, it is hard to comprehend that the conservative 1950s, that golden age of the American family, was largely a creation of public policy. In that decade, tax policy, education policy, and housing policy worked together in powerful ways to create a society in which families were impressively strong and children flourished. Contemporary conservatives who espouse family values but attack social spending seem unaware of the degree to which the families of the 1950s were subsidized by public programs, many of them designed or at least endorsed by President Eisenhower, an unabashed Republican. The fact of the matter is that Ozzie and Harriet as well as Clifton and Irene West depended on the public purse to an extent that would appall Bob Dole, let alone Newt Gingrich.

The fifties conjure up ambivalent feelings in many Americans. This decade and its family values were rejected and ridiculed by the rebellious youth of the 1960s, who saw the fifties as both boring and oppressive. And there were grounds for their scorn. It was an age of conformity and gray flannel suits, of cold war hysteria and McCarthy-inspired attacks on civil liberties. It was an era of segregated buses and whites-only drinking fountains, an epoch when lynchings were commonplace throughout the South. It was also a time when women were either lured or forced back into domestic roles and constituted a mere 35 percent of college graduates, down from 40 percent in the 1930s, a time when "The Theory and Preparation of a Well-Marinated Shish Kebab" replaced "Kantian Philosophy" at elite women's colleges.[13]

Yet despite all the legitimate criticism, the period from 1946 to 1963 was a glorious era for the American family. In 1946, after fifteen years of deep depression and a bloody and destructive war, there was enormous pent-up demand for comfortable family lives. And the 1950s came through for a great many people with both material abundance and family togetherness. In this decade, millions of young people were able to take for granted an abundance of well-paid, secure jobs, an affordable house in the suburbs, a late-model car, an elaborate collection of household appliances, a stable marriage, and a brood of healthy, high-achieving children. These were—and maybe still are—the ingredients of the American Dream. So how did this all come about? What fed the golden age of the American family?

Bolstering Parents Through the Tax Code

In the late 1940s and early 1950s, the federal government developed a tax code that was profoundly supportive of adults raising children. It promoted marriage through income tax schedules that halved the married wage-earner's tax liability. It offered an incentive to bear and raise children in the form of a significant tax exemption for each dependent. And it helped make housing affordable through sizable home mortgage deductions, which were channeled to young families.

In the late 1940s, Congress adopted a uniform $600 exemption per dependent person, which would be worth $6,500 in 1996 dollars.[14] The idea was to privilege families with children. As a Ways and Means Committee report explained, the intention was to impose a "lesser burden on the taxpayer with a large family and a greater burden on taxpayers with a smaller family."[15] In 1948, a tax reform bill introduced a radical promarriage measure called income splitting. Married couples were allowed to total their income and then split that sum down the middle, so that each spouse was effectively taxed only on half. Given the highly progressive income tax structure of the time, married couples experienced a dramatic improvement in their tax status compared with single people.

The 1948 bill also expanded the tax breaks accorded to owner-occupied homes: the interest on mortgages was exempted from taxation, as were capital gains from the sale of a house if a new one was purchased within a given time period. The Veterans Administration and Federal Housing Administration regulations made sure that most of these new tax-favored mortgages were given to young married couples.

Thus, as the fifties dawned, the United States could legitimately claim a powerful pro-family tax code. At this time there was a strong financial incentive for adults to marry and a significant penalty for divorce. The personal exemption underwrote a sizable portion of the costs of child-rearing, and the tax code worked with other government programs to create a generous supply of low-cost, high-quality family housing.

Buttressing Parents Through the GI Bill

If a pro-family tax code set the stage for the golden age of the American family, the GI Bill of Rights, as the Serviceman's Readjustment Act of 1944 was generally known, produced the unemployment insurance, educational opportunities, medical coverage, and housing subsidies that transformed the prospects of countless young parents.

Fueled by the fear that unemployed veterans selling apples on the streetcorner would create "chaotic and revolutionary conditions" in America, a reluctant Congress signed off on the bill in the spring of 1944.[16] It was a close call. Only a vigorous campaign by the American Legion prevented the adoption of a much meaner-spirited bill. In the words of the political theorist Theda Skocpol, "The American Legion pressured both conservatives in Congress and the somewhat elitist planners of the wartime Roosevelt Administration" to cast the net wide.[17] Founded in 1919, the legion, a cross-class voluntary association that had posts in communities throughout the nation, committed itself early on to large-scale and generous programs of support for veterans of World War II— programs that did not discriminate against blacks or women. For two years the legion waged an aggressive campaign, using radio spots narrated by wounded veterans and gaining the support of William Randolph Hearst, who controlled a major chain of newspapers. The legion persuaded Hearst to make passage of the GI Bill a personal challenge.

The GI Bill went on to become extremely popular, and in retrospect, it is hard to appreciate the fierceness of the opposition. Southern segregationists disliked the idea of equal rights for black veterans, bankers were leery of government interference in the mortgage business, and educators were afraid that GIs would "dilute" higher education. Indeed, Robert M. Hutchins, the president of the University of Chicago, went so far as to warn that an influx of GIs would turn colleges into "educational hobo jungles."[18]

Despite this rocky start, the GI Bill of Rights became one of the most admired government programs in American history. Its educational benefits enabled 2.2 million World War II veterans to attend college. It helped pay for the training of 450,000 engineers, 180,000 doctors, dentists, and nurses, 360,000 schoolteachers, 150,000 scientists, 243,000 accountants, 107,000 lawyers, and 36,000 clergy.[19] Its housing benefits helped 12 million Americans buy a house, farm, or business. In addition, it offered dependent allowances, disability pensions, and mustering-out payments; retirement pensions and emergency relief; medical care and unemployment insurance. More than any other government program before or since, the GI Bill helped a broad spectrum of Americans—blue-collar as well as white-collar workers, black as well as white workers—attain the American Dream. In the words of actor Harry Belafonte, "I didn't hardly finish first term high school. I had no desire to read, to learn. And how do you then compete for jobs if you have no training? . . . It is in this respect that I think the GI Bill became a God-send." As a result of the bill, the proportion of blacks attending college went from 1.08 percent before the war to 3.6 percent in 1950.[20]

What is more, the GI Bill more than paid for itself. The huge cost of this program (estimates are in the $14 billion range) was more than recovered in the higher taxes paid by beneficiaries as a result of enhanced education and increased productivity; for every dollar spent on educational benefits, the nation received as much as eight dollars in additional tax revenues. But the true value of the GI Bill is incalculable. How do you figure out what a Nobel Prize is worth to a nation? Ten beneficiaries of the GI Bill went on to win Nobel Prizes.[21]

In retrospect, it is quite clear that while the GI Bill targeted servicemen, it was a de facto family support policy of enormous power. Think of what the provisions of the bill meant for a young veteran in 1946 or 1952. The mustering-out pay underwrote the costs of getting married, and the educational provisions together with generous dependent allowances convinced many young men that there was no contradiction between pursuing their education and starting a family. And down the road, the education and training those men received as GI Bill beneficiaries enabled them to acquire well-paying jobs and support a family in a decidedly comfortable, middle-class style.

The housing provisions of the GI Bill proved to be as important as the educational benefits. Long years of depression and war meant that very little new housing had been built since the late 1920s, and in 1946 an extremely pressing housing shortage was the biggest bottleneck to family formation. Six million families were doubled up with relatives or friends, and another half-million were housed in temporary dwellings. In Omaha, a seven-by-seventeen-foot icebox was advertised as a potential dwelling, which gives some indication of the severity of the housing crunch. By providing long-term, low-cost mortgages—guaranteed loans for thirty years at 2 to 4 percent interest were the norm—the GI Bill transformed this desperate scene. Over the course of the decade from 1947 to 1957, 12 million families became homeowners courtesy of the U.S. government. This was not tentative or marginal support but big-time heavy lifting. Single-family housing starts rose from 114,000 in 1944 to a record 1,692,000 in 1950. Most of these units were in suburban subdivisions like Levittown, on Long Island, where the new government subsidies brought a single-family home within the reach of most returning veterans. In just five years, from 1950 to 1954, the suburban rings around American cities increased their population by 35 percent.[22]

Despite these powerfully upbeat developments, there were some notable problems with postwar suburban growth. People of color were often excluded from the new suburban communities. For example, the standard lease for the first Levittown houses included the words "This home cannot be used or occupied by any person other than members of the Caucasian race."[23] Although this provision became illegal and was dropped, ugly racism left its mark, and Levittown remains 97.37 percent white. Another problem concerned the larger family unit. Although these new suburbs promoted the nuclear family, they often weakened the extended family, as grandparents were left behind in the old urban neighborhoods. Moreover, public subsidies increasingly favored homeowners and penalized renters, which meant that low-income urban housing never got its fair share of government support. The trek to the suburbs and rededication to family life also came with some gender-specific costs, as wives and mothers became isolated from most job opportunities and the larger world.

Nonetheless, the tax code and the GI Bill, the most significant of the pro-family public policies of the 1950s, undoubtedly contributed to the prosperity and strength of this decade. During these years, the United States enjoyed both unprecedented economic expansion and a remarkable level of social coherence. The proportion of adults who married reached a historic high, and following a postwar spike in 1946, divorce rates actually fell. A baby boom roared into high gear, with fertility nearly doubling between 1944 and 1957. But it was not just a question of moms and dads producing more children. These children did much better than any previous generation of American children. Child poverty rates fell, as did juvenile delinquency and infant mortality rates, while high school graduation rates showed sharp improvement. Across a wide range of criteria, American children flourished as never before.

One final note: if the golden age of the American family was grounded in supportive government policies and a great deal of public money, it was also sustained by a strong labor movement, which made sure that the fruits of high growth and high productivity were shared by both workers and managers. Indeed, as Robert Reich has shown, the income of workers actually rose more rapidly than the income of managers in the 1946–1978 period. Given distributional trends in the modern period (1978–1997), we cannot assume that the additional education underwritten by the GI Bill would have translated into rapidly rising wages for production workers without the presence of powerful trade unions.

Tax Policy Tilts Against Parents

After the conservative fifties came the rebellious sixties, a decade in which critics on the left began to speak out against a favored treatment of marriage and children. By the late 1960s, liberals were not at all sure that they approved of either marriage or the bourgeois family. As Harvard sociologist Barrington Moore put it, the time had come "for advanced industrial societies to do away with the family and substitute other social arrangements that impose fewer unnecessary and painful restrictions on humanity." In a famous speech in 1968, Moore announced—with evident satisfaction—that the family was dying, if not already dead, and the only thing left for society was to ensure "a decent burial."[24]

Given this backdrop, it is not at all surprising that the pro-family tax code was jettisoned by the more liberal administrations of the 1960s. Direct dismantling began mildly enough, with John F. Kennedy's 1963 tax cut, which failed to raise the value of the personal exemption.[25] Indeed, Kennedy's tax bill instituted a new minimum standard deduction that paid no attention to the presence or absence of children. Richard Nixon's tax reform package of 1969 went further, limiting the gains from income splitting to 20 percent of total income. This not only reduced the marriage incentive, it actually created a marriage penalty for certain income groups, so that some two-income couples were better off single than married. At about the same time, the housing provisions of the tax code were changed so that they lost their pro-family effect. FHA and VA eligibility standards were loosened, with the result that many more loans were funneled to single-person households. In addition, the high rates of inflation typical of the 1970s accelerated the erosion of the personal exemption. The cumulative effect of these various factors on families with children was dramatic. As Eugene Steuerle has shown, between 1969 and 1983, single people and married couples without children showed no real increase in their average tax liability. In sharp contrast, married couples with two children saw their income tax rate rise an average of 43 percent, while a couple with four children faced a dramatic 223 percent increase.[26]

In the mid-1970s, new income tax pressure on families with children was exacerbated by rapidly rising social security or payroll taxes. Back in 1947, payroll taxes were minimal—a mere $30 a year per individual. Indeed, as late as 1965, the maximum annual payroll tax was still a modest $174. But then came the dramatic expansion of social security benefits, and an equally dramatic increase in social security taxes to pay for them. By the early 1980s, the payroll tax had reached $2,400 annually—$4,800 if one includes the employer's contribution. This new and heavy burden was (and is) borne disproportionately by moms and dads, since social security taxes are a regressive levy that fall most heavily on young, low-, and middle-income workers—precisely those segments of the population where most parents can be found.

Thus 1963 to 1985 was a period when tax policy turned fiercely against families with children. Self-conscious policy changes combined with inflation to produce a situation where adults raising children faced dramatically heavier taxes, both in absolute terms and in comparison with single people and childless couples. Historian Allan Carlson argues persuasively that this radical shift in the tax treatment of families was at least partially responsible for "the negative turn in family life that began in the mid-1960s."[27] The divorce rate rose 140 percent between 1960 and 1981, the marriage rate fell 30 percent, and rates of child poverty began to edge upward.

Since 1986, various tax reform packages have had an ambiguous effect on family well-being. There have been both gains and losses. On the positive side, the increase in the personal exemption from

$1,080 to $2,000 is a significant gain, as is indexing the exemption to inflation, which has put a halt to the erosion of its value. On the negative side, however, the marriage penalty has reappeared in a new and more virulent form. In 1996 the Congressional Budget Office estimated that 42 percent of married couples were penalized for being married, the average penalty amounting to $1,400. The penalty is particularly large for poor Americans (marriage reduces a couple's eligibility for the earned income credit) and for high-income couples.[28] A variety of smaller changes in the tax code also work against parents. The recent downward adjustment in eligibility for the dependent care tax credit, from age fifteen to thirteen, is just one example.

Housing Policy Weighs in Against Families

Our housing policies have also moved against families with children. In the early days of his presidency, Ronald Reagan ran into a storm of criticism when he slashed the number of new families receiving "section 8" rent vouchers to 40,000 from the previous level of 400,000. In retrospect, this looks magnanimous. Just before the November 1996 election, President Clinton cut the number of new families receiving rent subsidies to zero. Despite his progressive credentials, Clinton seems intent on breaking "new ground in the revision of the social contract."[29] As of 1996, the federal government had essentially abandoned the project of making housing affordable for low-income families.

It is not that families don't need help. Two decades of rising rents and falling wages have created a record number of people—many of them working full-time and many of them raising children— who are either homeless or close to the edge. A recent survey by the Joint Center for Housing Studies at Harvard University shows that in 1996, 6 million low-income households paid more than 50 percent of their income for rent. According to this study, the situation is rapidly getting worse. Not only does federal assistance continue to fall—1996 marked the "first time in the history of federal rental housing programs that the number of assisted units actually fell"—but the recent wave of welfare reform "seriously limits the rent paying ability of many low income households" by reducing various income transfers, such as food stamps.[30]

Twenty-nine-year-old Yvonne Spaulding lives in one room in a run-down motel called the St. Paul Tourist Cabins on the edge of St. Paul, Minnesota. Her new quarters are a little crowded, since she has four children, aged eleven, ten, seven, and five.

Not so very long ago Yvonne was living in a three-bedroom apartment, working at a job, and raising her kids. Life was a struggle, but it was more or less on track. Her life took a disastrous turn in October 1997, when her landlord lost a federal subsidy and raised her rent a cool 48 percent. "Back when it was $599 it was a reach, but there was no way I could pay $825 a month. It would have eaten up three quarters of my take-home pay," says Yvonne. "The pity was, I had finally gotten my life together. I have had all kinds of jobs—deli clerk, office cleaner, food prep work—but they were mostly minimum-wage deals. Then this last summer I landed a job in a packaging plant. It paid $7.50 an hour, the highest wage I have ever had. But when I was kicked out of the apartment in October, I had to let it go. It near broke my heart, but there was no way I could live at the shelter and go to work—I had to be right there to look after my stuff and guard my kids. You should see what goes on in these shelters—the stealing, the fights and all. Well, after a month they told us we had to go. That's the standard policy—no one can stay more than a month. I had nowhere to go, so Catholic Charities put me here. Right now I am working real hard to get a section 8 voucher. If they give me that, maybe I can find an apartment. Otherwise there's no way, with the federal subsidies gone. This housing market is going crazy."

We asked Yvonne about her kids, and her positive, can-do attitude faltered a little. "I get them bused so they are in the same school, but the older boys have been acting out recently. Leroy—he just turned eleven—has started stealing from other kids, and just last week he stole some equipment from school. I guess he's picked up on all of my stress. I mean, I've been all broken up by the fear that we wouldn't have a place to live, that we'd be out on the street." Yvonne sighed. "To tell the truth, I'm worried sick about Leroy. He's already repeated fifth grade, and I'm not sure what they will do with him if he fails out this year. In the evenings I try and help him do some schoolwork, but with us being in the same room and all, it's real difficult."[31]

As this young mother will testify, it's hard to overstate the importance of a home in the construction of family life. Stable, safe, affordable housing keeps adults at work, children in school, and community networks in place. Despite these magical properties, a secure home is increasingly beyond the reach of working Americans. Nothing could be more emblematic of the shredding of the American Dream.

It is no longer just the poor and the near poor who are squeezed. Most young families are having trouble affording housing, largely because the cost has risen much faster than wages and government no longer steps in to ease the load. A few figures put this in stark relief. The median price of a new home in 1978 was 3.2 times the median income; by 1994, the price of a house had risen to 4.2 times income. Not surprisingly, for the first time since the Great Depression the rate of home ownership is declining for families with children. In 1993, 64 percent of families with children owned a home, down from 70 percent in 1978. Significantly enough, home ownership is up for families without children.[32]

The sharp increase in the cost of housing conspires with the decline in male wages to force many mothers with young children into the workforce. A 1995 study by the Families and Work Institute shows that only 15 percent of working women with school-age children want to work full-time, although 75 percent currently do so.[33] Most believe they cannot fulfill their responsibilities to their children and work a forty-hour week. In many cases, these mothers stay at work because of high rents or large mortgage payments. Housing costs are in fact newly onerous for middle-class parents. The National Association of Realtors estimates that the typical thirty-year-old man buying a median-priced home in 1973 incurred carrying costs equal to 20 percent of his income. By 1996 this figure had risen to 32 percent.[34]

"You have to work more than one job just to keep up with where you were three, four, five years ago," said Ed Gagnon, a New York City police sergeant who moonlights at two other jobs because of mortgage payments and tax bills.

Ed has spent sixteen years on the force and now earns $65,000 a year, but that only brings in $3,000 a month in take-home pay. Of this, Ed shells out $2,100 a month in carrying charges for the modest home he bought five years ago.

"We don't have a huge mortgage by New York City standards— just $150,000—but the rate is high (8 percent) and our property taxes are crazy—they just hit $700 a month. I reckon I spend close to 70 percent of my sergeant pay on housing. With a wife and two kids, there is just no way that I can make the $900 left over stretch an entire month. So four years ago I took on a second job, working nights as a security guard at a shopping mall. Then that wasn't enough, so last year I took on this third job at the weekends—I load passengers and luggage for the Royal Caribbean Cruise Lines.

"I try real hard to see my kids in the afternoons. I just got my police shift changed to the 6 A.M. to 2 P.M. slot so I can pick up my eleven-year-old from the bus stop. Now, that's made a difference. You should see his eyes light up when he sees me waiting there. He's handicapped and goes to this special school, and he kind of relies on his dad to be his buddy. It would be great to have more time for him at the weekends."[35]

Housing Subsidies for the Rich

Although government has lost interest in providing affordable homes for middle- and low-income families, it remains extremely solicitous of the housing needs of those in upper income groups. Successive administrations have continued to offer affluent Americans generous subsidies. In 1996, for example, the federal government spent $66 billion on mortgage interest tax deductions, half of which went to households with incomes above $100,000. Thirty-three billion dollars is almost four times as much as government spends on low-income housing.

Given the way our tax code has evolved, the mortgage deduction has become highly regressive. Although 63 million U.S. families own their own homes, only 27 million—fewer than half—claim the mortgage interest deduction. This is because it doesn't make sense for low- and middle-income taxpayers to itemize their deductions. What's more, the lower your tax bracket, the less the deduction is worth to you. To give an example, if a family in the 15 percent marginal tax bracket pays $5,000 in mortgage interest a year, this tax break saves them $750. But if a family in the top tax bracket (39.6 percent) takes out the same mortgage, this tax break saves them $1,980—more than twice as much. Overall, according to the economist Peter Dreier, more than 44 percent of the tax benefits associated with mortgage interest deductions go to the top 5 percent of taxpayers, who collectively save $22 billion annually.[36] In the words of Robert McIntyre, director of Citizens for Tax Justice, "This is a stupid subsidy, because the more money you make, the more subsidy you get."

Think of it: if we capped eligibility for this deduction at $100,000—which would make a great deal of sense, given the fact that 94 percent of American children live in families with incomes under $100,000—we could save $33 billion, which would then be available to meet the housing needs of middle- and low-income families.[37] Actual policy, however, seems to be drifting in the opposite direction. In the summer of 1996, President Clinton, in a preelection bid for the support of affluent voters, all but eliminated capital gains taxes on the sale of expensive homes.

Disabling and Displacing Parents

The recent changes in tax and housing policy are good examples of ways in which government has abdicated responsibility for adults raising children. But in other areas of public policy, the government goes beyond abdication and becomes actively antagonistic toward parents. The constellation of programs concerning child welfare is a case in point. The Great Society initiatives of the sixties spawned an elaborate set of programs and services for poor children. The motivation behind these initiatives was impeccable—progressive liberal folks newly aware of the extent of poverty in "the other America" (the title of Michael Harrington's famous book on this topic) geared up to tackle the problems of school failure, malnutrition, poor health, and child abuse, which blighted so many young lives. However, an unintended consequence of this well-meaning crusade to save our children was the emergence of a new class of professionals—social workers, therapists, foster care providers, family court lawyers—who have a vested interest in taking over parental function. Bureaucracies everywhere have a remorseless drive to expand—to widen their client base. If children are the clients, parents can quite easily become the adversaries—the people who threaten to take business away. Christopher Lasch for one believed that the "so-called helping professions" have functioned to undermine the confidence of families, unwittingly creating a vicious cycle of dependency on external sources of expertise.[38] Unfortunately, the move to take over parental function has tended to target families of color unfairly. In contexts in which parents are barely coping with the harsh realities of everyday life, it is often much easier to take the kids away than to deal with deep-seated problems of homelessness, joblessness, or substance abuse.

This brings us to the crux of the problem. Taking kids away from their parents is a risky maneuver, because what we then do with them is extremely problematic. Children are not just small-scale adults who, given the appropriate range of services, can somehow become self-sufficient and self-supporting. Children cannot live on their own and do not thrive in institutions. Whether we are talking about toddlers or teenagers, children desperately need a parent—preferably two of them—who will give them unconditional, devoted care over a long period of time. Buying such care on the open market is a difficult proposition, even when it is quite clear that a child needs to be taken away from his or her biological parents.

Michelle Torres is sixteen years old and thinks she has had "way too much" experience of the foster care system—not that there is any possibility that she will go back to her biological mom. "No one could make me do that. Besides which, my mom's in jail."

Michelle was born in Brooklyn in 1981, the fourth of six children her mother had by four different men. Michelle describes her mother as totally out of control. "She used to leave us kids alone in this wreck of an apartment. I remember the huge scary cockroaches and the broken-down chairs—if you touched one of them, you would get these huge splinters. She would go out gambling or turning tricks and not come home until the next morning."

Michelle first went into foster care at age seven. "One day Mom called child welfare and just offloaded five of us kids, but we were back two years later because the foster system got crowded. That was when the real bad stuff began to happen. My stepdad was out on parole—he wasn't living with us, just visiting a lot. One Saturday evening he raped my older sister and then came after me, but I wouldn't cooperate. I scratched and bit him real bad and then locked myself in the bathroom. I guess that made him crazy. He went in the kitchen, boiled up some oil—the kind you use for french fries—broke down the bathroom door, and just threw the boiling oil at me. Luckily, he missed my face, but he caught me on the shoulder and arm—I still have scars. He went to jail for this, and so did my mom. Turns out my stepdad was paying her for 'sexual access' to her daughters.

"I have been in foster care ever since. Over five years I have had six foster moms. The one I am with right now is pretty good. I mean, I've had experience, so I should know. Some of them hit me and locked me out of the house. But this one, she cooks supper and talks to me. But it's still, like, difficult. In my house right now money is a huge issue. My foster mom has installed a pay phone in the hallway because she doesn't want me to use the regular phone just in case I run up a bill. I'm also not allowed to use the washing machine and dryer because of using too much electricity. The machines are right there in the kitchen, but I have to walk half a mile to the laundromat, which is hard to do after homework and stuff. Besides which, it makes me feel she doesn't trust me."

We asked Michelle what she thought about foster care. Her response was thoughtful. "I guess it's necessary. I mean, if I hadn't been taken away, I would be dead by now. My stepdad was real violent—he had already killed some guy. But they should fix the system. Being bounced from home to home messes with you." Michelle paused and then added slowly, "You know, there must be some way of getting money out of the system. Some weeks I feel as though I am just rented out. Even my good foster mom admits that if they didn't pay her, I would be out in the street. That makes me feel bad."[39]

Depending on a variety of factors, including how good the pay is and how thoroughly foster care providers are screened, the caliber of the care offered by such providers varies enormously. Some are concerned and caring individuals; others are entrepreneurs who spend most of their time currying favor with social workers to obtain the small human beings who keep the government checks rolling in. And these checks are sizable—the average cost of foster care is now $17,500 per child per year.[40] But however noble the motivation or generous the pay, many foster parents have a hard time falling in love with their charges and an even harder time finding the wherewithal to sink a decade or two of energy into their well-being. Yet this is what a child needs, and this is what parents routinely come through with—biological parents and adoptive parents. They do this not because the pay is good—the pay is nonexistent—but because a child owns a large piece of the parent's soul. Unconditional love and long-term devotion are hard to find in the marketplace, no matter how much a government agency is prepared to pay. Despite this fundamental problem, overzealous agencies often go to considerable lengths to snatch a child from perfectly good parents.

One morning in May 1989, James and Denise Wade walked into their daughter's bedroom and found Alicia lying on the bed twisted with pain. They rushed her to a hospital in San Diego and discovered to their horror that their eight-year-old had been raped and sodomized.

The hospital immediately called the appropriate agency, Child Protective Services (CPS), and Alicia was interrogated. Distraught and semicoherent, the child said that a stranger had come through her bedroom window in the middle of the night, grabbed her, and carried her to a waiting car, where he had raped her. The CPS workers chose not to believe Alicia. Instead, they focused their attention on James Wade, whom they put through an aggressive, intensive interrogation. He was challenged to be a man and just admit that he had raped his daughter. Eventually a worn-down, bewildered Wade broke down, saying, "You're so sure I did it, but if I did it, I sure don't remember it." This tortured statement seemed to clinch the case for the San Diego CPS. It didn't seem to matter that a man corresponding to Alicia's description was known to stalk the Wades' neighborhood, or that in interview after interview Alicia consistently proclaimed her father's innocence. It also didn't seem to matter that Alicia, a high-performing student and all-round well-adjusted child, had never displayed any sign of a malfunctioning family life.

CPS decided that what Alicia needed was a "parentectomy"—the word used in the child abuse field to describe a complete severing of contact with her mother and father. Denise and James Wade were prevented from seeing their daughter in the hospital, and on her release she was shipped off to foster care, where she spent two years being shuttled from one secret foster home to another.

It cost the Wades their life savings, and untold pain and suffering, to exonerate James from the charge of rape and get Alicia back. James Wade had to deal with—and pay for—a battery of particularly humiliating tests. Over the course of the investigation CPS required him to shell out $260,000 for an elaborate series of therapeutic services and sex offender tests, including the penile plethysmograph test, which involved Wade listening to kiddie-porn audiotapes while his penis was attached to a mercury gauge. But the crippling expenses and gratuitous humiliation paled in comparison with the Wades' central agony: the loss of their child. From May 1989 to November 1991, Alicia was not allowed to see her father, and her mother was only allowed one visit a month.

In the fall of 1989, the San Diego prosecutor Jane Via made a determined effort to terminate the Wades' parental rights, to the point of ignoring evidence and obstructing justice. When a much-delayed DNA examination of the semen on Alicia's underwear revealed that it did not match Wade's—it genetically matched that of Albert Carder, a known sex offender who had been arrested for other child rapes—Via ordered a retest and pressed ahead for an adoption hearing. Luckily for the Wades, her petition was disallowed; but it was a close call. Several months later, a grand jury convened to investigate the details of the Wade case described Via's actions as nothing less than "a race against time to arrange for Alicia's adoption prior to the availability of the DNA results."[41]

What do we learn from this troubling case? Was the persecution of the Wade family unusual? Unfortunately, no. In a review prompted by this case, a San Diego grand jury found hundreds of similar cases in southern California. Indeed, as of February 1996, eleven lawsuits were pending against child welfare agencies around the country charged with overstepping the bounds and snatching children away from parents wrongfully accused of child maltreatment.

Behind all of this antagonism and anguish is an enormous shift in how we view moms and dads. Over the last thirty years, thousands of professionals associated with our burgeoning child welfare bureaucracy have developed what can only be described as a parent-bashing mentality. Precisely where these views come from is examined in some depth in Chapter 5, but whatever the source, a significant minority of those who work in the child welfare field are now firmly convinced that the American family is largely dysfunctional, that a majority of parents have the potential to abuse children, and that in many cases "parentectomies" are in order.

The victimization of parents by the child welfare bureaucracy goes back to the passage of the 1974 Federal Child Abuse Prevention and Treatment Act (CAPTA), often called the Mondale Act, after its sponsor, Walter Mondale. This legislation defined child maltreatment as "physical or mental injury, sexual abuse or exploitation, negligent treatment or maltreatment of a child . . . under circumstances which indicate that the child's health or welfare is harmed or threatened thereby."[42] This extremely broad definition made it easy for the child welfare authorities to extend the range of parental offenses. "Emotional abuse" could now apply to something as vague as "unreasonable verbal castigation" as well as to something as specific and harsh as locking a child in a closet for twenty-four hours, and sexual abuse now ranged from incest to "touching the genitals . . . or the clothing covering them." In one instance, child abuse charges were filed against a Colorado father for tickling his nine-year-old stepdaughter on the tummy. The definition of physical neglect became particularly flexible. In Illinois, it was defined as "the failure to provide the proper or necessary support . . . for a child's well-being," while in Mississippi it was defined as leaving a child without "proper care, custody, supervision or support." The results were predictable. Parents were labeled child abusers for not letting a child watch television after 7:30 P.M., or for giving a child money to go to McDonald's for breakfast too often.[43]

The motivation of the lawmakers who framed this legislation was above reproach: they were passionate in their desire to eradicate the scourge of child abuse, which had been hidden and lied about for centuries. In the words of the psychologist Lawrence Aber, "We denied it and denied it and when it finally broke through we couldn't stand the pain of it." As a result, "we went from doing nothing to trying to do everything." Mondale himself said that nothing he had seen in his time in the Senate was as disturbing as the 1973 hearings that uncovered "the stories and photos of children who had been whipped and beaten with razor straps, burned and mutilated by cigarettes and lighters, and scalded by boiling water." However, despite his anguish and empathy, he worried that the law that emerged from those hearings was too sweeping and would end up persecuting innocent families, which is exactly what happened. The net was flung so wide that the kind of horrendous case Mondale had in mind ended up representing no more than 3 percent of what came to be investigated under the rubric of "child abuse." Douglas Besharov, founding director of the National Center on Child Abuse and Neglect—an agency created by the Mondale Act—argues that the child protection system came to resemble a 911 emergency dispatch system "that could not distinguish between life-threatening crimes and littering."[44]

All of which has gotten in the way of helping the small percentage of children who are at great risk of being harmed by their parents. Michelle Torres is a good example. In 1991, she and her siblings, children who very much needed to be taken away from their biological parent, were returned to their mother because of serious overcrowding in the foster care system. False and trivial reports flood that system, cascading down on underpaid, undertrained caseworkers, stealing time and attention from children who really need help. Even people who work in the system openly question the wisdom of flinging the doors so wide. In the words of Eli Newberger, director of family development studies at Children's Hospital Medical Center in Boston, "Had professionals like me known then what we know now, we would never have urged on Congress . . . broadened concepts of child abuse as the basis for legislation."[45] Despite this retrospective judgment, CAPTA was enacted and opened the way for tremendous overreporting of child abuse cases. In the mid-1970s, 600,000 child abuse charges were filed, 60 percent of which were substantiated. Today, of the 3 million charges filed annually, only a third are ever substantiated, and of these only a fifth involve elements of serious endangerment.

Whether the charge is substantiated or not, the investigation process itself, as we saw in the case of the Wades, is terrifying for parents and children alike. Distraught, bewildered children are routinely examined, interrogated, or removed from the home at the beginning of the process, long before maltreatment is proven. According to Richard Wexler, it is not unusual for child welfare workers "to enter homes in the middle of the night, strip children naked, and probe their genitals for evidence of abuse."[46] And the agony of parents and children is enhanced by the public nature of these investigations, since neighbors and teachers are questioned at an early stage. Amazingly enough, the entire process seems to bypass most constitutional protections. By claiming emergency circumstances, Child Protective Service workers do not need to abide by Fourth Amendment search-and-seizure safeguards. *Miranda* warnings are not read to parents; nor are parents allowed access to information compiled on them.[47]

Particularly distressing is the class and racial bias of child welfare investigations. The fact is, low-income parents—particularly black and brown parents—are favorite victims of Child Protective Services. Families on public assistance are literally four times more likely than others to be investigated for child maltreatment and to have their children snatched away. According to Douglas Besharov, the child welfare bureaucracy is increasingly stacked against poor parents. Until twenty years ago, each AFDC family had its own caseworker, who delivered not only cash benefits but a set of social supports ranging from help in finding housing to parent education classes. When AFDC benefits were separated from family support services in the 1970s, these caseworkers disappeared, and in their place appeared Child Protective Services. Poor parents were suddenly faced with "a powerful social service bureaucracy that policed rather than helped them, and viewed the child, not the family, as its client."[48] A central issue from the beginning was that this new agency often confused symptoms of material want with parental neglect and was prepared to take drastic action, including removal of the children, based on this judgment. Children were and are taken away from their parents because the family doesn't have a functioning toilet or can't afford to fill a prescription. Children are taken away because the food stamps have run out and the refrigerator is empty. And children are taken away because the family doesn't have a place to live.

"Shakeina Merchant, her corn-rowed hair glittering with colored beads, squeezed onto the dilapidated couch between her brother and stepsister and popped her left thumb into her mouth. Her right thumb was wrapped in gauze, a vain attempt to break a soothing habit that was just too important to a nine-year-old child to give up.

"'Friday is my best day,' she said after removing the thumb from her mouth. 'That's the day my daddy comes to get me. We stay here together, and that's what I like. We cook together and do things. Mrs. Davis is okay, but I'd rather stay here all the time.'"

"Here" is a shabby one-room apartment in a rundown neighborhood of Freeport, New York. Shakeina would rather be here, with her brother and sister, her dad, his girlfriend, and her two children, than stay another day in foster care.

Wendell Merchant and his children are in one of the many impossible situations that characterize the foster care system. Merchant has custody of his children but has not been able to keep them because his small apartment was deemed unfit for his family to live in. While the Department of Social Services spends more than $1,000 a month to keep his children in foster care, it has no program to help him find appropriate housing so his family can stay together. "'They say I can have my kids if I find housing, but there's nothing they can do to help me find housing,' Merchant says. 'The way I look at it, if they gave me just half the money they're spending on foster care, I can make it.' Instead, last Sunday afternoon as usual, Shakeina, eight-year-old Wendell Junior, and three-year-old Felicia returned to Julia Davis's foster home, carrying black plastic trash bags filled with their clothes."

The Merchant children entered the Nassau County foster care system three years ago, when their mother was charged with neglect. Six months ago a family court judge awarded Wendell Merchant custody and said he could take his children out of foster care as soon as he found a place for them to live. But Merchant, who earns just $250 a week on a loading dock in Islip, has failed to find a three- or even a two-bedroom apartment he can afford.

Merchant is not giving up. As he searches for an apartment, he is trying to strengthen his relationship with his children. Tacked on the door of his tiny apartment in Freeport is a sheet of paper from his parenting class that recommends ways to practice Positive Parenting Behavior. "'I'm working on everything I can to get things together for us,' he said, looking at the three children lined up on the couch. 'But the system doesn't work for people who want to take care of their own.'"[49]

The system fails to face up to the fact that the overwhelming majority of child abuse and neglect cases are linked to poverty, and if more families were lifted above the poverty line, many cases of child abuse would simply disappear. One well-regarded study found that sexual abuse was five times more frequent among low-income families than affluent families, and that physical neglect was ten times more common. We should not be surprised. In poverty-stricken families, simply dealing with the demands of daily life involves a level of stress that the rest of us can hardly imagine. Consider the strain involved in figuring out what to do about an eviction notice when you have a newborn baby and no place to go, or the anxiety involved in coping with an asthmatic five-year-old when you can't afford the appropriate medications. Poverty undoubtedly provides "the fertile soil that incubates and nourishes a variety of social problems that might wither away in more comfortable surroundings."[50] Rather than targeting poor black and brown parents as likely child abusers, policymakers should devote many more resources to providing health care and housing so that low-income parents can do a better job of nurturing and nourishing their children.

What happens to the children whom our sometimes overzealous child welfare workers take away from parents? The great majority are placed in the protective custody of foster care—an enormously costly system that often manages to produce miserable results for both parents and children. Having a child taken away is one of the most devastating things that can happen to a mother or a father. But the prime victims are the children, for what can await them in foster care is "an endless series of hurried, capricious, short-term, and often dangerous placements."[51] The evils of the system are well documented. Investigations of foster care conditions have turned up cases of babies tethered to hospital cribs, eleven-year-olds warehoused in drug-infested group shelters, and fifteen-year-olds shipped off to correctional facilities where they are mixed with hardcore juvenile offenders. In addition, innumerable foster children are beaten, raped, or starved by individual foster parents in family "homes." The terrible truth is that youngsters removed to foster care are *ten times more likely to be maltreated while in the custody of the state than in their own homes.*"[52]

The potentially devastating effects of foster care on children are a long way from being short-term. A large number of the homeless, drug-addicted, criminally disposed adults who haunt our city streets were once clients in the foster care system. At some point in their childhood they were taken from their homes and subjected to a series of cruel or careless foster care placements that left them socially crippled—unable to deal with school, relationships, or any other aspect of real life. In fact, 40 percent of children who "graduate" from the foster care system end up on welfare or in jail.[53]

The Profit Motive

If the foster care system often works to disable parents and endanger children, it also works to enrich an entrenched and expanding bureaucracy. Each case of child abuse or neglect unlocks significant state and federal funds, not only for the child welfare agency directly concerned but for a satellite ring of substitute caregivers, therapists, and family court lawyers. Indeed, in child abuse cases the agencies are often able to cash in twice for foster care and therapy, billing both the taxpayer and the accused family. Take the Wade case. In addition to paying $260,000 for court-ordered tests and therapy, for instance, James Wade and his wife were billed for foster care, which ran to $484 a month—an unusually low figure. (Foster care for an older, more troubled child can run as high as $3,000 a month.) These charges were not strictly speaking reimbursements to San Diego Child Protective Services, which was routinely paid 95 percent of the cost of therapy and foster care by the state of California. The San Diego agency was therefore able to put the Wades' check into the county's general fund. The more kids in foster care, the greater the revenues for the county.[54]

All of this illustrates the power of the market to contaminate social policy. Right now there is a huge bureaucratic incentive to maximize the number of children in foster care and keep them there as long as possible. Conna Craig, of the Institute for Children, is convinced that long-term foster care has been the unhappy fate of hundreds of thousands of children because of the perverse financial incentives within the system. "The funding system," she says, "gives child welfare bureaucracies incentives to keep even free-to-be-adopted kids in state care."[55] In Massachusetts, for example, child welfare agencies are known to defer requests for termination of parental rights until children reach the age of seven. Why seven? Because at that age children are eligible for special needs money and the agencies can take the opportunity to request additional funding from the federal government. It is also true that older children are less attractive to adoptive parents, so if an agency can keep a child until seven, there is a good chance that that child will remain in the foster care system permanently. He or she then becomes a long-term money spinner for the bureaucracy, capturing thousands upon thousands of dollars of additional federal funds.

These ugly facts point to the dangers inherent in trying to buy parental love on the market. By and large it doesn't work. Obviously, there are cases in which a generous stipend does succeed in teasing out superior caregiving energy, but overall foster parents do a lousy job—much worse than biological parents, much worse than adoptive parents. It seems that once we allow the profit motive to replace love, once someone signs on to care for a child because of the money involved, not because he or she is prepared to fall in love with a particular child, we turn the child into a commodity and destroy the heart of the parenting enterprise. Money cannot conjure up devoted long-term care.

The failures of our foster care system also serve to pinpoint a second, profoundly troublesome issue. Why are we *so very extravagant when it comes to replacing parents and so very mean-spirited when it comes to supporting parents?* It is ironic to note that a foster parent who takes in a child receives, on average, one third more to care for this child than the actual parent would get from AFDC/TANF.[56] Indeed, federal funding for foster care is totally uncapped—in sharp contrast with AFDC/TANF funding, which under the terms of the 1996 Welfare Reform Bill is increasingly rationed. The amount of money spent on foster care reached $12 billion in 1997, more than double the amount we spent in 1990.[57] We are somehow able to brush aside these huge and escalating costs in an unseemly rush to get children out of the hands of their parents.

A final point: there is truth-telling by both liberals and conservatives with regard to the parental role, but as we have seen, their insights are often undercut by ideological blindness and bias. Conservatives do grasp the enormously important role played by moms and dads and are very aware of the parent-disabling properties of the child welfare bureaucracy—most of the critical literature on the foster care system has come from the right wing—but they see only part of the problem. Yes, they want Child Protective Services and other agencies out of the lives of parents, but they are singularly unprepared to underwrite the social supports these same parents so desperately need. A combination of income support and housing subsidies would dramatically reduce the incidence of poverty among families with children and stanch child neglect at its source.

And there are certain kinds of truths on the left. Liberals in the mold of Derrick Bell and Jonathan Kozol bear witness to the agony of dispossessed children and detail the devastating effects of poverty on family life. They prod our consciences, reminding us that whether we are talking about decent schools, rat-free housing, or basic health care, we need to take much more collective responsibility for the life circumstances of families with children. But those on the left have also failed to appreciate the unique properties of the parent-child bond and over the years have lent considerable support to the parent-displacing activities of the child welfare bureaucracy. Given their skepticism of the market, it is rather surprising that liberals have so readily bought into a fee-for-service approach to child-raising, particularly when many of the victims of Child Protective Services and the foster care system are poor people of color.

The Power of the Public Purse

Like it or not, government is an enormously powerful force in shaping family life. The ways in which public dollars are deployed serve either to support and strengthen or to undermine and hinder the parental role and function. A few billion dollars here, a few billion dollars there can clearly affect the lives of moms and dads. In no way is government a neutral force. It can influence circumstances for or against marriage, for or against an additional job, for or against resident fathers. It can expand the range of choice open to parents or narrow it down.

Of central importance to low-income parents is the question of how aggressively government intervenes to lift families out of poverty. In recent decades, the U.S. government has had a rather poor record in this regard. According to economist Edward Wolff, the relative well-being of parents in relation to childless households has been continuously eroded over the past thirty or forty years, with government policy being the powerful driving force. In 1959, 20 percent of families with children were poor, compared with 16 percent of families without children. More than three decades later, in 1993, the poverty rate among families with children stood at 19 percent, barely changed from its 1959 level, whereas the poverty rate among childless families had fallen to 5 percent, a reduction of more than two thirds. Indeed, across the board, families with children have seen their income slip relative to that of childless families. Between 1974 and 1992, for example, the median income of families with children fell by 2 percent in real terms, whereas the median income of childless families increased by 16 percent.[58]

The fact of the matter is that the U.S. government has increasingly abdicated responsibility for families raising children—tax and housing policies tilting against parents in the manner described earlier—while it has increasingly supplied extensive supports for senior citizens and other favored groups. What we have really done over the course of the last thirty years is socialize the costs of growing old and privatize child-rearing. This has produced gratuitous hardships for parents because this new thrust of policy has occurred at a time when wages are falling and family structure is crumbling.

Other rich nations have not abandoned families with children in this manner. Governments elsewhere have done a much better job of supporting low-income parents so that children do not grow up in poverty. For example, both France and Britain would have extremely high rates of child poverty—21 and 26 percent, respectively—in the absence of aggressive government action. However, tax and transfer policies dramatically reduce the child poverty rate, to 4 percent in France and 8 percent in Britain. In the United States, by way of contrast, government tax and transfer policies reduce the child poverty rate a mere 2 percent: it falls from 22 percent to 20 percent after government weighs in.[59]

Parents and children may have been left in the lurch, but it is not because the U.S. Treasury is somehow out of money. The federal budget has increased thirtyfold since the days of the GI Bill. In 1996, Uncle Sam spent $1.56 trillion.[60] It is just that rather few of these dollars find their way to parents and children. In 1996, for example, federal and state government spent $349 billion on social security but only $17 billion on AFDC.[61] According to economist and financier Pete Peterson, per capita federal benefits to the elderly now tower twelve to one over benefits to children. As we shall explore in Chapter 8, this enormous imbalance has not grown out of thin air; rather, it is a result of the growing political clout of senior citizens.

The Bottom Line

So what have all these policy shifts meant for ordinary moms and dads? We are clearly dealing with a profound change in the way government intervenes in family life. In the 1950s, the main thrust of public policy was to underpin and empower families across the board. Tens of billions of dollars were pumped into programs that gave parents the wherewithal to do a good job by their kids. Married couples raising children were particularly privileged.

From the 1960s on, we have tried another tack. Responding to liberal disillusionment with marriage and family life, government cut back on the programs that bolstered and braced adults raising children. Instead, starting with President Johnson's Great Society programs, there was a well-intentioned liberal effort to bail out poor families by offering them specially designed supports and services. Some of these efforts were helpful, but many backfired because they tended to disable and displace moms and dads rather than buttress them. AFDC had the effect of kicking fathers out of the loop, while the newly created Child Protective Services routinely removed children from poor parents on the grounds they were . . . well, poor!

After Ronald Reagan took office, the disabling of parents speeded up, as policymaking came to be controlled by rightwingers newly embarked on a love affair with the market. As we have seen, conservatives can be singularly blind to the ways in which free enterprise undermines the nonmarket work of parents, so they slashed with abandon. Since 1980 the broad drift of government policy has been to relinquish responsibility for mainstream family life and further shred the safety net for poor families. Meanwhile, all the serious money has been allowed to trickle up to the rich and the powerful, following the inherent tendency of market capitalism. Without strong countervailing pressure, which historically has emanated from either government or the labor movement, public resources in market economies routinely gravitate toward those who either own or manage the means of production. Think of the 1997 tax reform bill. Almost half the tax cuts in this $400 billion package went to those in the top 5 percent of the income scale. Families in the bottom 40 percent received nothing, although this is where the majority of children live.[62] So much for Clinton's family-friendly rhetoric.

The Construction of a Public Morality

While we acknowledge the immense power of government programs, public policy is much more than a bundle of regulations or a set of subsidies; it infuses our values and informs our worldview in ways that are tremendously powerful. Part of this power resides in its storytelling properties. According to the Harvard Law School professor Mary Ann Glendon, our laws and policies tell a story that projects "certain visions about where we come from, where we are now, and where we'd like to go."[63] As we now deeply appreciate, our laws and policies concerning family tell a story that is extraordinarily destructive of the art and practice of parenting. They tell a tale of unfettered markets in a money-driven nation that is increasingly oblivious to the nonmarket work that parents do, and of untrammeled individualism among a self-obsessed, narcissistic people increasingly unable to understand the unique and precious properties of the parent-child bond. The spirit of this story is uncaring, even contemptuous, and its thrust is to debilitate moms and dads and undermine their ability to weave the web of care that is so vitally important to our nation.

This tale is ugly, but it is enormously influential, for we are not just talking about our failure to support a bundle of programs, we are also talking about our failure to respect, honor, and celebrate parents, which in itself has enormous impact. Why should an overloaded contemporary mom (or dad) put twenty-five years of her life on the line when our laws and policies are constantly saying that these parenting energies are worthless? In sharp contrast to the glowing rhetoric of our political leaders, actual government policy is exceedingly scornful of parents.

We should take Glendon's advice when she tells us to be wary, to be exceedingly careful about the "stories we tell," the "symbols we deploy," and the "visions we project" in our laws and policies, because these powerful public signals mold our values and our priorities and condition what we do with our lives.[64] Parents aren't stupid; they understand the gap between rhetoric and reality. When our tax code ranks the breeding of horses above the raising of children, it becomes much more difficult for overburdened moms and dads to cobble together the conviction to put children at the center of their lives.

FIVE

A Poisonous Popular Culture

JERRY SPRINGER: Please meet twelve-year-old Amber. She says her mom had a plan all along to steal her twenty-four-year-old boyfriend.

AMBER: My mom—I'm very angry at my mom because she stole my boyfriend. She had it planned since the first day she met him, and she told a whole bunch of lies to get . . . to get me to break up with him. Now, she's using him. She came over to our house . . . my . . . me and my dad's house, and she told us, "Well, I just want his money. I just want his car. You know, he takes me places. He buys me things."

SPRINGER: Mom, why are you going out with him?

PAM: Because I love him.

SPRINGER: How could you love him? He slept with your twelve-year-old daughter! Somebody sleeps with your twelve-year-old, you don't love him. You either beat the crap out of him or call the cops. You don't see anything wrong in this story? What about your daughter? She's hurt.

PAM: I love Amber. She's . . . she's my daughter. Amber, I do love you, yes, but I do love Glen too. And I want . . . I want both Amber and Glen to be in my life. And if they . . . if Amber can't accept it, then she can just stay living with her father and she can stay out of my life.

SPRINGER: You're saying that to your own daughter? What's wrong with you? That's your daughter. That's your flesh and blood.

PAM: It's just the way it is. I'm not going to be miserable because her and her father want things their way.

SPRINGER: You know what? If you have to be miserable in life for your own daughter, then be miserable. That's the responsibility of bringing a child into the world. She wants her mother . . . she wants her mother to look at her and say, "Darling, I love you. And right now, whatever I can do to make your life good and special and meaningful, I will do." That's what a mother says to a child. I can't picture—and I'm not a hero—but I can't picture a parent saying anything else to a child. What parent says to a twelve-year-old child, "I don't give a crap what you think. I'm dating who I want"? You don't say that to a child.

PAM: I did.

SPRINGER: No? Let's take a break.[1]

DAYTIME TALK SHOWS have been called "group therapy for the masses at a price everyone can afford," and they are a powerful force in our culture. On an average weekday, the Oprah Winfrey show is watched by about 10 million Americans, while the twenty or so other daytime talk shows have a combined daily audience of around 50 million viewers.[2]

In a three-week period during the summer of 1997, we tuned in to these shows in an effort to understand how they treat parents. We came up with four examples: *Montel Williams,* "Young Women Who Say They Are Embarrassed by the Way Their Parents Dress"; *Geraldo,* "Parents Who Spy on Their Teens"; *Ricki Lake,* "Men Who Deny Paternity"; and *Jerry Springer,* "I Stole My Twelve-Year-Old's Boyfriend."[3] As can be seen from the above excerpt, the spirit of these programs is enough to make most parents cringe. Yes, there is an element of realism; we obviously can find parents who spy on their teens or steal their twelve-year-old's boyfriend. And yes, the talk show hosts, taking the role of in-house therapist, do attempt to take the high road. But the negativism of the message conveyed by these shows is unrelieved. Parents tend to be either irresponsible fools or in-your-face monsters.

Talk shows are just the tip of the iceberg. In the late 1990s, the mass media bombard us with negative stereotypes of moms and dads. It seems that every time we turn on TV, watch a movie, or read a magazine, we are confronted with yet another dismissive putdown of the parental role and function. Megan Rosenfeld, of the *Washington Post*, tells us that parents are one of the few remaining groups that can be trashed on primetime television with impunity. She calls it gratuitous parent-bashing; "Ask a typical viewer to describe how parents are portrayed on most shows and the answer usually is: stupid."[4] These repellant images are not limited to primetime sitcoms. In hugely popular movies such as *Home Alone* and *Honey, I Shrunk the Kids,* and in best-selling books such as *Toxic Parents* and *Spoiling Childhood,* not to mention the daily offerings of Geraldo and Montel Williams, parents are portrayed as dysfunctional and incompetent. Indeed, in a subset of cases—the award-winning movie *Shine* is a powerful recent example—parents are seen as veritable child abuse machines, the fountainhead of all that can go wrong in adult life.

Modern moms and dads need this like a hole in the head. Given the myriad ways in which economic and political forces have shifted against them, parents find it profoundly demoralizing to be further attacked by the purveyors of our culture.

Mothers and fathers are also seriously undercut by an entertainment industry that seems hellbent on destroying the values they stand for. Today the media are newly saturated with explicit sex, gratuitous violence, and aggressive materialism. Karen Sinclair, the mother of a twelve-year-old boy, describes coping with the onslaught: "Television, movies, CDs, Nintendo, the Internet, even print ads are all spewing out these destructive messages—kiddie porn, poor eating habits, you name it—that get imprinted on the brain of your child. Rudeness, crudeness, and disrespect permeate everything, and I particularly resent the message that all parents are jerks. Just to protect Danny, I spend more than an hour a day monitoring the airwaves so as to screen out some of the more negative stuff, but some days I feel I am shoveling shit against the tide."[5] Karen knows that as a part-time worker, she has room in her day for her self-imposed monitoring tasks. Most overburdened working parents do not have this luxury; they simply can't find the time to impose the rules that might protect their children from the onslaught of MTV, gangster rap, Calvin Klein underwear ads—or telephone sex, for that matter.

"Since its hit movie *The Santa Clause* came out in 1994, the Walt Disney Co. has been getting complaints from parents outraged because a character in the movie mentions an 800 number that promotes live audio sex."

A Suffolk County father is in agony over his daughter's victimization. Last December his ten-year-old daughter watched a home video of *The Santa Clause,* and the phone company subsequently billed him $247.09 for eleven calls to an adult talk line. "He was dumbfounded. Who, he wondered, could have made the calls?"

"After first denying it, his ten-year-old owned up. She had dialed the 800 number mentioned in the movie and heard a breathy recorded message promising hot talk if she called a 900 number for $2.99 to $4.99 a minute." Curious, she dialed the 900 number and was soon engrossed in a live conversation about sex. You can only imagine what salacious stuff she heard. Encouraged to keep calling, she did, ten more times in succeeding days.

"Soon after she began having problems in school." Her family attributes her plummeting grades and mounting behavioral problems to emotional upset caused by exposure to the sordid world of telephone sex. "Their pediatrician referred them to a therapist, who treated the girl for two months. The father says he would like her to continue in treatment but can't afford it."

Disney has taken the position "that the father is to blame for failing to supervise his daughter" and has refused to take any responsibility for the phone charges or therapy costs incurred by this child. In a letter to the father, the company expressed "regret at any bad feelings you may have over this and we will be happy to provide you with a refund for the cost of the videocassette of the film." This amounted to $29. The father is outraged and bitter. Since *The Santa Clause* grossed $144 million for Disney, he feels that the company should take a little more responsibility for the damage done to his daughter.[6]

A parent-hurting entertainment industry is a relatively new phenomenon. As recently as the 1950s, TV shows, movies, magazines, and popular songs paid homage to moms and dads. Unfortunately, much of this celebration was cast in a patriarchal mold, which tended to obscure the degree to which the media of the fifties boosted parents and paid tribute to their fundamental importance. Typical of this genre is "Oh, My Papa," the number-one hit of 1954. The lyrics are sweetly beguiling: "Oh my papa, to me you are so wonderful/Oh my papa, to me you are so good/No one could be so gentle and so lovable/Oh my papa, he always understood/Oh my papa, so funny, so adorable/Always the clown, so funny in his way/Oh my papa, to me you are so wonderful/Deep in my heart, I miss him so today."

Hackneyed, yes, but how very comforting these lyrics must have sounded to a regular dad, toiling away at the breadwinning role, attempting to come through for his family. Also in 1954 CBS premiered a program called *Father Knows Best*—a title that boggles the modern imagination.[7] Many of the shows screened for this series focused on what a wonderful father Jim Anderson was. In a typical episode, Jim doubts his worth in the business world and is made to realize by his adoring wife and children that being a father is the most important job he can do.

Mothers also came in for a share of the kudos. The magazines of the 1950s were full of bright and smiling housewife-mothers, for example, a 1956 article in *Look* celebrated the highly domestic woman of the era: "This wondrous creature marries younger than ever, bears more babies, and looks and acts far more feminine than the 'emancipated' girl of the 1920s or even 1930s. Steel worker's wife and Junior Leaguer alike do their own housework . . . Today, if she makes an old-fashioned choice and lovingly tends a garden and a bumper crop of children, she rates louder hosannas than ever before."[8]

Happy housewives were prominently featured in movies of this period. A favorite story line in a Doris Day or Debbie Reynolds movie went something like this: a glamorous, sexy woman gives her man a thoroughly hard time, threatening his masculinity, but in the last reel she discovers true love and undergoes a transformation into a devoted housewife. For the millions who saw *April in Paris* (1952), *Calamity Jane* (1953), *A Bundle of Joy* (1956), *The Pajama Game* (1957), and *Teacher's Pet* (1959), the message was simple: a woman might be as free and clever as a man, but her real destiny and happiness lay in being a wife and mother. Debbie Reynolds summed it all up in *The Tender Trap* (1955): "A woman isn't a woman until she has been married and had children."[9]

Popular TV shows further reinforced the centrality of traditional family life. Shows such as *I Love Lucy* (the first television program to be seen in 10 million homes), *Ozzie and Harriet* (television's longest-running sitcom), *The Donna Reed Show, The Life of*

Riley, and *Good Times* depicted a world where men were strong, dependable father-figures and women were loyal, lovable home-makers. *Good Times,* which featured a black family living in an urban housing project, was grittier and more working-class than the other primetime favorites but was equally celebratory in its depiction of family life.

The ideas and attitudes underlying these shows and movies are oppressively sexist to modern eyes. Support for parents was contained within a patriarchal context, creating a set of values that became increasingly unacceptable to progressive sensibilities. In the countercultural rebellions of the 1960s we jettisoned this context, but in so doing we often threw the baby out with the bathwater. We forgot that *Ozzie and Harriet* wasn't just about sexism and patriarchy; it was also about the importance of parents. This show gave tremendous honor and respect to the roles of mom and dad. Here on primetime television were loving, hardworking parents raising their children with wisdom and humor—solving problems, teaching values, and providing an all-important protective shield.

The fact that the entertainment industry in the 1950s was un-abashed in its praise of parents created a kind of public affirmation of the parental role that served to enhance the authority accorded to mothers and fathers. Themes such as family togetherness, respect for one's elders, commitment to one's spouse, and devotion to children reverberated like drumbeats through the culture of the day, and this undoubtedly had the effect of buttressing the energies of individual moms and dads. It also made their work easier. Even in its early days, television had enormous reach; by 1956, nearly 15 million Americans had at least one TV set, which was turned on for an average of five hours each day. The characters on primetime shows became powerful role models.[10] Thus when Betty, the teen-age daughter in *Father Knows Best,* listened respectfully to advice handed down by her father, or when Beaver, the mischievous son in *Leave It to Beaver,* leaped up and cleared the table after dinner, it became that much easier for real-life parents to ask for respectful cooperation from their own children.

Forty years later, the messages communicated by the entertain-ment industry are radically different. A celebratory media has been replaced by one intensely critical of family life, particularly of parents. The roles of mom and dad have been stripped of most kinds of respect and status, and parents' work has been debased.

The media message around parenting is at its most dismissive in contemporary movies, where parents are portrayed either as bumbling fools or as vicious perverts. In *Honey, I Shrunk the Kids* (1989), the father is a klutzy mad scientist who inadvertently reduces his own children, plus the kids next door, to the size of ants. Freed from their dependence on their feeble parents, the children become resilient and resourceful as they learn to negotiate the gigantic obstacles in the back yard. In *Home Alone* (1990), the third highest-grossing movie of all time, a pair of well-meaning but totally inept parents depart for Paris, leaving their eight-year-old son behind. The mother flies back to Chicago to rescue the stranded child, only to find that he is doing far better without his parents around than he ever did when they were monitoring his every move. In their absence he courageously defends his home from burglars and helps an old man in the neighborhood reconnect with his children and grandchildren.

More recently, in *House Arrest* (1996), middle-class suburban parents Janet and Ned Beindorf decide they are no longer in love, so on their anniversary they tell their kids, Grover and Stacy, that they're separating. The kids try to persuade them to get back together again, but when that fails, they decide to lock their parents in the basement and keep them there until they agree to put aside their differences. The kids try to keep their kidnaping a secret from the outside world while putting their parents through some impromptu group therapy. Janet and Ned attempt to escape but spend most of their time bonding and learning how to get along.

The message of these films seems to be that self-reliant and resourceful contemporary kids can teach their bumbling elders a thing or two. Film critic Beth Austin points out that modern movies are populated by "children who put their parents back on track . . . The calm, dependable, unbelievably wise and loving parents who once populated Hollywood have been replaced by a passel of unstable neurotics who need a good twelve-step program—or a good twelve-year-old—to bring them back onto solid family ground."[11]

If parents are frequently cast as ineffectual fools, they are also portrayed in a darker and more damaging light. Child abuse, child neglect, and nightmarish dysfunctional families seem to be particular Hollywood favorites. *Radio Flyer* (1992) is a prime example. This film portrays an evil man who repeatedly and viciously beats his seven-year-old stepson (and attempts to kill the family dog) while the child's mother, preoccupied with her job, fails to notice that anything is wrong. More recently, in the Oscar-winning movie *Shine* (1996), based on the life story of the pianist David Helfgott, a cruel and emotionally abusive father drives his sensitive genius of a son to a mental breakdown. This superb film will stand as one of the finest depictions of the perils faced by a child prodigy, yet it sheds a remarkably harsh light on Dad. There are no nuances here, no mention of the thousands of hours this father devoted to teaching his son. He did, after all, succeed in cultivating in the boy a passionate love of music and an extraordinary pianistic technique. Since the release of *Shine,* Helfgott's siblings have questioned the accuracy of the movie. "The film is brilliant," said David's younger brother Leslie, a violinist, "but it's not factual. It is a fictitious tale inspired by David's life. My father was not a brutal person."[12] Various medical experts have also protested the attribution of David's nervous breakdown to his father's cruelty. "Severe mental illness requires at least a biological predisposition, [but] *Shine* seems to continue a tradition of blaming parents for mental illness," said Dr. Kenneth Rosenberg.[13]

Hollywood's emphasis on incompetent or abusive parents has become so very pervasive that we have been lulled into taking this kind of parent-bashing for granted as a harmless quirk of mass entertainment. All too easily we assume that children can absorb countless images of inept or evil parents in movies, television, and popular songs while hanging on to the conviction that their own mothers and fathers are completely different. According to film critic Michael Medved, "We dangerously underestimate the impact of an omnipresent popular culture that repeatedly reassures our kids that they instinctively know better than the tired losers of the older generation."[14]

Parent-bashing in today's culture extends beyond television and movie screens to the CD player. The songs of Marilyn Manson are illustrative. The liner notes of his 1994 album *Portrait of an American Family* contain the following words: "You spoonfed us Saturday morning mouthfuls of maggots and lies disguised in your sugary breakfast cereals/ . . . we will grow to hate you."[15]

Rap music has a particularly harsh take on moms and dads, mixing gratuitous brutality with a type of unforgiving realism. In the mid-1980s, Body Count released a song called "Momma's Gotta Die Tonight" as part of an album that eventually sold 500,000. This song describes setting the mother alight with lighter fluid, hitting her with a baseball bat, cutting her body up into pieces, and stuffing them into a garbage bag. The chorus includes the lines "Ha, ha, ha/Burn momma, burn momma, burn bitch, burn, burn, burn."[16]

In a more self-critical vein, the bleak lyrics of songs by the rap group Wu-Tang Clan describe—with a measure of realism—the irresponsibility of young folk in the ghetto. In a 1997 hit called "A Better Tomorrow," which was number one on the charts in June 1997, the Clan tells the young "brothers" and "chicks" who are parents exactly what the score is: "You can't party your life away/ ... Cause your seeds grow up the same way."[17]

These, then, are the bare bones of our media story: over a forty-year period, the entertainment industry has moved from celebrating to denigrating the parental role and function; where once parents were portrayed as loving and wise, they are now portrayed as neglectful and abusive. The trajectory we describe is, of course, full of detours and sideshows that confound a simple story. The wholesome fifties had their share of rebels, James Dean being the best known, while the violent, nihilistic nineties have some strangely heroic parents; Mrs. Doubtfire and Roseanne are two that leap to mind. But overall, our media story holds up, which is why more and more parents feel demoralized and devalued. They listen to Beavis tell Butthead "Your mother is a slut" and remember a time when television, movies, and popular music routinely paid homage to moms and dads and reinforced the values they taught. Now they feel locked in a daily battle to protect their children from the negative messages spewed forth by these same sources. In the words of Kevin Bray, the father of fourteen-year-old Cheryl, "Being a good parent now means fighting all this stuff on the outside. It wasn't that way for my parents. Seems that they were working with the culture, not against it. Just last week a friend of Cheryl's attended a Marilyn Manson concert in Washington, D.C., and came back with a souvenir—a T-shirt emblazoned with the words 'Kill Your Parents.' It's hard to know what to expect next."[18]

The big question, of course, is why there has been such a sea change. Why have parents fallen from grace in such a spectacular fashion? The answer is wrapped up in the rebellions of the 1960s and the emergence of pop psychology as an enormously powerful force in our culture.

Starting in the mid-1960s, America experienced a veritable cultural revolution. A strong civil rights struggle, a new wave of feminism, an antiwar movement, and a sexual revolution all contributed to a seismic shift in societal values. Indeed, this brew was so potent that it succeeded in changing our entire cultural script. The results were mixed. While this cultural revolution rightly called into question certain evils in American life—white supremacy, male supremacy, and homophobia, to name a few—legitimate calls for a greater measure of personal freedom often degenerated into infantile, egotistical versions of individualism that ignored the needs of others. Millions of adult Americans became overinvolved with the self, pouring their best energies into a set of personal goals that ranged from career success to sexual freedom. As we have described, this narrow new focus on narcissistic individualism ran smack into the art and practice of parenting. Precisely because being a good parent involves giving time, attention, and priority to others, it seriously compromises goals that exclusively concern the self.

Which is where pop psychology comes in. In order to rationalize our much more self-indulgent behavior patterns and minimize our guilt, we have turned to Freud and, in a highly selective and misleading manner, appropriated his ideas. We increasingly use psychology—or, more accurately, a boiled-down, souped-up, highly American version of psychology—to legitimize a move away from family arrangements that submerge the self. It is as though bastardized versions of Freudian theory have been used to give us permission to be much more critical of family ties and much more skeptical of the value of parenting.

Pop Psychology and the Roots of Parent-Bashing

It is clearly not our task to come to grips with the legacy of Sigmund Freud. This huge challenge is well outside the scope of this book and the expertise of these authors. Suffice it to say that the Freudian revolution triggered a rich body of work in the fields of psychology and psychiatry that has contributed enormously to our understanding of the human psyche and enabled professionals in these fields to alleviate pain and suffering in ways that were not possible a century ago. As many of us know from direct experience, a well-trained psychologist or psychiatrist can both heal psychic wounds and tremendously enhance a person's capacity to fulfill his or her potential.

That being said, it is also true that in its more watered-down, popularized forms, psychology can be extremely damaging, particularly to the parental role and function. At the heart of the matter is the fact that in our increasingly therapeutic culture, external obligations, whether to parents, children, or community, are minimized, because they interfere with a person's capacity for self-love and self-realization. As scholars in the mold of Phillip Rieff, Robert Bellah, and Christopher Lasch point out, pop psychology tends to "promote a psychologically grounded ethic of individuality encouraging its many clients to pursue their own fulfillment, often to the exclusion of the good of family, community, or larger causes."[19]

There are some obvious problems associated with this therapeutic take on life. Pop psychology may liberate individuals by helping them get in touch with their own needs and dreams, "freed from artificial constraints and guilt-inducing demands," but it does not bode well for a downsized husband or wife who needs the empathy and support of a spouse, or for a troubled child who needs unconditional love from both mom and dad.[20] This is where duty, sacrifice, and commitment to others come in. Perhaps in some utopian child-free world, relationships should rest on the free exchange of feelings between self-actualized selves, not on enduring responsibilities or binding obligations. But in the real world of weekend carpools and life insurance payments, no marriage can last and no child can flourish unless adults live up to a plethora of other people's demands.

Pop psychology has enormous reach in our culture. One third of all Americans have been in therapy, and therapeutic insights and attitudes have spun off into the media to become a basic ingredient of self-help manuals, many of which are imbued with a virulent strain of parent-bashing. *Toxic Parents: Overcoming Their Hurtful Legacy and Reclaiming Your Life* is a good example. In this bestseller—it claimed the number-one spot on the *New York Times* list—psychologist Susan Forward charges parents with systematically poisoning the lives of their children. Parental oppression runs the gamut from incest to spanking to the expectation that an adult child turn up for Christmas.

> When Fred decided to go skiing instead of spending Christmas with his family, he was trying to be an individual, trying to free himself from his family system. Instead, all hell broke loose. His mother and his siblings treated him like the Grinch who stole Christmas, shoveling guilt by the trainload. Instead of skiing with his lover down the idyllic slopes of Aspen, Fred sat alone in his hotel room, nervously cradling his telephone, desperately seeking forgiveness for the misery his family blamed him for causing.[21]

Susan Forward is indignant on Fred's behalf. "When Fred tried to do something healthy for himself . . . his family formed a united front against him . . . They attacked with anger, blame, and recriminations."[22] And because he was so tied to the family, the guilt he felt was enough to bring him back into line. According to Forward, Fred's enmeshing, guilt-inducing parents were guaranteed to distort and diminish his ability to relate to lovers, bosses, and friends for the rest of his life—that is, unless he had the sense to seek therapy and free himself of parental demands.

Many of us find it hard to feel much empathy for Fred's predicament. As any mother or father actively engaged in trying to create a strong, loving family will tell you, enduring family ties, capable of withstanding bad times as well as good, are built on enormous amounts of altruistic effort. These efforts are not always convenient or even pleasurable. Whether it's getting up at five in the morning to drive a nine-year-old to ice hockey practice or having an incontinent elderly relative move into the spare room, moms and dads routinely produce impressive amounts of sacrificial energy, which is enormously underappreciated and unsupported in our culture. Why on earth shouldn't Fred rearrange his skiing vacation so that he is able to show up for Christmas dinner—not because this is his preferred activity, but because it would give enormous pleasure to his parents and siblings and reaffirm the importance of family ties? After all, when he was eighteen months old and eight years old, he depended very heavily on the generous energies of this same family unit, and when he is eighty he will hope to do the same. Families are grounded in reciprocity and the golden rule. With all of their warts and flaws, they draw out and rely on our most generous instincts.

Dysfunctional parents indeed leave deep and abiding scars on children that last well into adult life. All parents never have been and never will be good parents. Parenting comprises an extremely challenging set of tasks. Yet to condemn most parents—and thereby undermine their indispensable role and function—is to reinforce the dominant narcissistic individualism of contemporary America. It is also a shortcut to social chaos.

Forward describes a world in which almost everyone's parents are toxic. She wrings her hands over the thousands of patients she has seen in her eighteen years as a therapist who "have suffered a damaged sense of self-worth because a parent had regularly hit them, or criticized them, . . . or overwhelmed them with guilt, or sexually abused them, or forced too much responsibility on them, or desperately overprotected them."[23] She seems to give as much weight to the relatively rare and serious problems of incest and physical abuse as to the much more widespread, and one would think less serious, problems of excessive responsibility and over-protection. According to Forward, subtle, guilt-inducing pressure can be as destructive to children's lives as physical cruelty, which is why she thinks most of us qualify as toxic parents.

Toxic Parents is not an isolated case. In recent years, pop psychology has spawned a slew of books that contain extremely broad definitions of parental incompetence and failure. *Spoiling Childhood: How Well-Meaning Parents Are Giving Children Too Much—But Not What They Need,* by Diane Ehrensaft; *Parent Traps: Understanding and Overcoming the Pitfalls That All Parents Face,* by Donna G. Corwin; *How to Avoid Your Parents' Mistakes When You Raise Your Children,* by Claudette Wassil-Grimm; *When Parents Love Too Much,* by Laurie Ashner and Mitch Meyerson; and *The Emotional Incest Syndrome: What to Do When a Parent's Love Rules Your Life,* by Dr. Patricia Love have all been big sellers in recent years. According to Wassil-Grimm, more often than not children are seriously damaged by their parents. Workaholism, volunteerism, overscheduling, overeating, gambling, compulsive shopping, and compulsive jogging are just a few of the addictive behaviors that parents indulge in, and by so doing create and perpetuate dysfunctional families. Wassil-Grimm is of the opinion that "80 to 95 percent of today's families fall short of truly healthy functioning."[24]

It is clearly difficult for a parent to do anything right, as there are crimes associated with loving too much as well as too little. Meyerson and Ashner tell stories—in horrified, disapproving tones—of parents who help their adult children find jobs or give them the down payment to purchase a first home. These parents convince themselves and their children that they are loving and generous when in reality they are power-hungry and self-serving.

The discovery of toxic parenting in the late 1980s gave birth to a new movement that focused on healing the wounded inner child—wounded, naturally enough, by neglectful and abusive parents. Through his nationally televised PBS series, his best-selling books, and his workshops, psychologist John Bradshaw has led a crusade that seeks to reclaim and nurture the inner child. His mission is to help people resolve the grief caused by the myriad kinds of abandonment and neglect that are the inevitable consequence of family dysfunction and toxic parenting. Like Forward, Bradshaw casts his net wide; in his view, 96 percent of families are dysfunctional.[25]

Unfortunately for existing family units, championing your inner child seems to involve jettisoning your parents and siblings and getting yourself a new family of choice. To use Bradshaw's words, "[A] new family is necessary in order to give your inner child protection while he is forming new boundaries . . . If your family of origin is not in recovery, it is almost impossible to get support from them . . . So I advise you to keep a safe distance and work on finding a new, nonshaming, supportive family. This could be a support group of friends . . . or it could be any one of the myriad of 12 Step programs now available all over the country."[26]

The psychobabble of our age is thus replete with hostility toward parents. They are damned for doing too little and damned for doing too much. And God forbid that they be given any credit for anything that goes well in children's lives. Needless to say, this is tremendously demoralizing for individual moms and dads.

It is crucial to stress that while pop psychology, with its deep vein of parent-bashing, is important to our analysis, it is but a small part of a much larger Freudian heritage. Psychoanalytical theory, for example, has given us a much kinder perspective on children. Prior to Freud, the prevailing wisdom was that children came into this world replete with original sin and the role of parents was to break them like horses, using such techniques as "frightening them, beating them and lying to them."[27] All of this now changed. As Freudian theory spread from Europe to America, it taught us that children were not inherently bad, nor were they blank slates on which society could write its commands. Rather, children were seething with complex emotions and needs. And as we grew to understand that all the great passions of adult life—love, lust, sexual curiosity, jealousy, fear of death—flowed through childhood, we learned to go gently with our children, to listen to their fears and respect their feelings.[28] We also learned to appreciate the enormous significance of early childhood. This is when character is shaped, sexuality molded, and the mind stimulated or dulled. All of these ideas are good. From the vantage point of a two-year-old or a twelve-year-old, when families abandoned the brutal child-raising practices of earlier times and moved toward a more sensitive approach, it was a giant step forward. What is not good is that along with this new regard for children came exaggerated, impossible-to-live-up-to expectations for moms and dads, which paved the way for contemporary parent-bashing.

In both his theoretical and his clinical work, Freud made some key assumptions that have strongly shaped the way we see parents. Among the more important are that the essential elements of personality are formed by age five; that families are privileged sites for self-formation; and that much of what becomes pathological behavior is rooted in family trauma. In his theoretical constructs, Freud tended to downplay the larger world of politics, economics, and culture. It simply did not seem credible to him that political or economic structures could fundamentally mold the personality or affect the mental health of an individual man or woman.

It is easy to see how Freud's emphasis on trauma within the family paved the way for later popularizers of his work to lay much of the blame for adult pathology and dysfunction on parental failure. The work of Alice Miller is a particularly important example of how easily parent-bashing flows out of Freudian constructs. In the early 1980s, Miller, a Swiss-born psychoanalyst, wrote several extremely influential books.[29] In *For Your Own Good: Hidden*

Cruelty in Child-Rearing and the Roots of Violence, she expresses her outrage at the systematic cross-generational damage wrought by parents: "The former practice of physically maiming, exploiting, and abusing children seems to have been gradually replaced in modern times by a form of mental cruelty that is masked by the honorific term *child-rearing.*"[30] It is hard for a parent to derive any comfort or guidance from Miller's work, because her arguments are directed not against a specific child-rearing practice but against all child-rearing practices. According to Miller, the dire consequences of parenting have little to do with a particular set of values about how children should be raised and nothing to do with whether a parent is strict or permissive. Rather, parenting is an elemental, gut-wrenching power struggle that nearly always ends with the parent bruising and battering the child.

In Miller's view, a great deal of the hatred and violence in society can be traced to the sadism perpetuated every day in every home by power-hungry parents. "All advice that pertains to raising children," she writes, "betrays more or less clearly the numerous, variously clothed needs of the adult. Fulfillment of these needs not only discourages the child's development but actually prevents it."[31] In a great many cases the damage visited on the child is so significant that it amounts to "soul murder." According to Miller, such childhood "traumata" are an inevitable part of family life and flow from the fact that parents are unconscious slaves to the dark secrets of their own childhoods, when they themselves were trampled on by power-hungry parents. Parental oppression thus cycles through the generations.

In her books, Miller tackles the question of how to reverse this cycle of parental abuse and recommends that psychoanalysis and therapy more generally be used to help individuals get in touch with their narcissistic rage against the parents who mistreated them. According to her, this has the potential of liberating the next generation. Freed from their childhood resentments, new parents are thus able to disengage from the need to use and abuse their own children.

Miller presents no clinical evidence to support her theories. She does however, point to various historical examples. In her view, Sylvia Plath, Franz Kafka, and Adolf Hitler were all victims of soul murder. In *For Your Own Good,* she contends that Hitler's obses-

sive and murderous anti-Semitism was a direct result of the perse-
cutions visited on him by an autocratic father who tyrannized his
son with brutal beatings and cold contempt. If the father wanted
young Adolf to come to him, he would whistle through two fingers,
as though calling a dog. Miller makes the case that in his crimes
against humanity, Hitler was merely reenacting the crimes perpetuated against him by his father, "mistreating the helpless child he
once was in the same way his father had mistreated him."[32] Even in
his attempt to exterminate the Jews, she argues, Hitler was simply
replaying childhood battle scenes on the stage of international politics. Miller has nothing to say about other powerful factors that
undoubtedly contributed to the evil that was Hitler: Germany's
long history of anti-Semitism, the manner in which Germany was
humiliated and punished by the Treaty of Versailles, and hyper-
inflation during the Weimar Republic. As a self-styled disciple of
Freud, Miller airbrushes away such geopolitical details. In her
view, World War II and the Holocaust were simply the products of
abusive parenting. History and society drop out of the equation.

Miller's work has been enormously influential in the United
States. Her description of unreconstructed parenting—parenting
without the benefit of therapy—as an inherently pathological act
has proved to have great appeal in the more sensational reaches of
pop psychology. Over the course of the past decade, boiled-down
versions of Miller's work have made their way into the American
mass culture via that slew of bestsellers mentioned earlier, including Forward's *Toxic Parents* and Bradshaw's *Homecoming*. These
books in turn have given birth to a veritable cottage industry of
multimedia workshops in which regular Americans are encouraged
to beat up on mom and dad and blame all of their life problems on
abusive parenting. Wendy Kaminer, for one, has trouble with a
worldview that sees virtually all of us as "weak, diseased, and
helpless—so fragile that a harsh word from a parent is a serious
form of abuse."[33]

There is, of course, more than a grain of truth in Miller's theories; they clearly would not resonate so powerfully unless they
touched real feelings. Parents are tremendously important in the
lives of their children, and autocratic, power-hungry fathers—or
mothers—can be immensely destructive. However, these insights
can distort reality unless they are put into proper perspective.

The fact is, parents are not lone operators; they function within a societal context that profoundly affects what they are able to do, and Freud's tendency to disregard the economic and cultural dynamics of the wider society has left a problematic legacy. First of all, the larger world, including government policy and labor markets, seriously conditions mental health and the possibility of good parenting. We ignore this fact at our peril. If a father has just been downsized and has lost both his job and his health coverage, he may well find it difficult to be a good parent. This state of affairs has much more to do with a newly brutal labor market than with a neglected inner child. But our Freudian sensibilities tend to encourage introspection and self-absorption rather than political or social action. By explaining adult pathology purely in terms of family dysfunction, we are kept from questioning the broader society and thus abdicate a larger project—that of making our government and our culture more accountable. Pop psychology lulls us into thinking that as long as our intimate relationships are in order, life will be fine. This is clearly not true for most parents. If a mom or dad is homeless, or is working two jobs, or has a child in substandard day care, he or she needs superhuman attributes to be a stellar parent.

Thus, as a result of our therapeutic sensibilities, parents are confused about the nature of their predicament and what stands in the way of their doing well by their children. They tend to focus on internal problems, such as family tensions and individual shortcomings. They are much less clear about what the external obstacles might be, such as a tax code that discriminates against families with children or a labor market that puts immense downward pressures on wages. One thing is for sure: it is extremely difficult for parents to overcome a set of problems they do not see, and when mothers and fathers fail to identify external pressures and tensions, the tendency is to blame each other, which often weakens the family from inside.[34]

Using the image of the Trojan horse, psychologist Mary Pipher talks about how therapists sometimes help along this process of implosion from within.

Long ago, the Greeks pounded on the walls of Troy, a city-state with which they were at war. The walls around the city held, and the Greeks' blockade wasn't working. Enough food entered the city to stave off starvation. Finally the Greeks built an enormous horse and filled it with soldiers and left it as a gift to the Trojans. Then they hid in the hills and waited to see what happened. The Trojans awoke one morning to find the Greeks gone and the gigantic horse outside their gates. They pulled it into their city and had a day-long party. That night, when all the Trojans passed out, the Greeks emerged from the belly of the horse. They opened the gates to the city for the other soldiers and took over the town from within. *We therapists have sometimes been like the Trojan horse. Under the guise of friendship and gift-giving, we have sometimes invaded families and done great harm.*[35]

Faced with unidentified outside pressures and very little in the way of external support or affirmation, parents have become increasingly discouraged and unsure of themselves. In her 1997 book, *The Time Bind,* Arlie Hochschild tells us that for many American adults, work rather than home has become "the haven in the heartless world," the place where people feel most appreciated and most relaxed. According to Hochschild, most workers now feel more confident they can "get the job done" at work than at home. One study found that only 59 percent of workers feel their "performance" in the family is "good or unusually good," while 86 percent rank their performance on the job this way.[36] Hochschild's analysis has a ring of truth for many of us, not because the workplace is so very user-friendly—one third of all workers are now contingent, throw-away employees, and conditions are actually deteriorating for many people—but because being a parent has become so very problematic. In a world where a hit song by the group Megadeth tells the world that "parents are dickheads," it is hard to conjure up the commitment to be a good parent. It is difficult to allocate serious amounts of energy and effort to an activity that is so very demeaned and disparaged in our culture.

The Onslaught of the Mass Media

So far we have been talking about the media's frontal assault on parents. This is a little-known story. Generally speaking, we fail to appreciate the degree to which parents are directly blamed by the popular culture. As we have seen, these head-on attacks are immensely damaging, crippling confidence and adding to the parental load at a time when parents are already in deep trouble.

But parents are not only dealing with a frontal attack, they are also coping with an entertainment industry that floods their homes and their communities with a family-destroying mix of explicit sex, random violence, and crass materialism. Though this is a well-known story, few understand just how brutal and multifaceted the onslaught has become. In the spring of 1996, our Task Force on Parent Empowerment consulted with parents around the country and constructed a portrait that details how a typical family experiences the mass media.

Ray and Andrea Johnson have two children, twelve-year-old Derek and eight-year-old Deirdre. Time and money are tight, but with both parents working full-time jobs, they feel they are providing for their family reasonably well. Like over two thirds of American households, they own two TV sets, one in the living room (hooked up to a video game console) and the second, a portable, that they move from room to room. (To keep the kids from squabbling over who gets the portable, they are thinking of getting another set, which would put them in company with the one third of U.S. households that own three or more.) The Johnsons are also one of the nation's 75 million households with a VCR and one of the 56.4 million subscribers to cable TV. (They have heard the hype about how cable TV may soon have a five-hundred-channel capability and find it bewildering: they already get some fifty channels and don't know what's on half of them—though maybe Derek does.)

While the TV, VCR, and video games are the Johnsons' primary sources of entertainment, they also like music of various kinds. The family owns a compact disk player as well as several AM/FM radios and cassette players, with additional units in each of the family cars.

Over the past several years, however, Ray and Andrea have begun checking the music with caution. Rap music, particularly gangster rap, blindsided them with the unrelieved brutality and sadism of its themes and the extreme vulgarity of its language. Time and again they find themselves asking each other, "How can they sell that stuff to kids? How can they put it on the air when it would be unprintable in most magazines and newspapers?" So far, they haven't found any answers that make sense.

Most recently, as a Christmas present for the whole family, the Johnsons, like about a quarter of U.S. households, acquired a home computer and, like 8.5 million others, signed up for an on-line computer service. Though neither Ray nor Andrea had ever used a computer, both were seeing the handwriting on the wall and recognized that without computer skills, their children would soon be left behind in school and they themselves in work advancement. Now, however, they are paying more attention to news stories about pornography, scams, and other kinds of crime on the Internet and are feeling inadequate to provide protection, since both kids know how to use the PC better than they do and have more time to spend on it.

The Johnsons live four blocks from a shopping mall, one that Derek and Deirdre pass on their way home from school. The mall offers a videocassette rental franchise (plastered with graphic advertising posters and blaring with movie promo tapes on big-screen TVs); a video arcade (strangely dark and echoing with electronic gunfire); a store selling video games, records, tapes, and CDs (vibrating with booming bass notes and draped with still more advertising displays); a multiscreen movie theater; a toys and games shop (seemingly stocked with every TV/movie/cartoon/music promotional tie-in product on the market); and two department stores (with a warren of designer boutiques blasting raunchy music videos and pushing pricey, label-on-the-outside, gotta-have clothes for the juniors market).

Lately it seems to Ray and Andrea that everywhere they turn, they and their kids are being bombarded with seamy, violent media messages and media-driven promotions and cross-promotions. TV cartoon characters push junk food and action figures, then show up in violent movies and/or video games. Rappers parlay their street-thug personas into music videos and movie roles that promote their cassettes and CDs, which in turn are packaged to promote their movies and music videos. Movie stars hit the TV talk-show circuit to plug their latest blood-drenched films and dish up the tawdry but titillating details of what would otherwise be their private lives. Athletes turn TV appearances into ads for the products they endorse, downplaying their latest assault or drug charges to win more endorsement contracts. Then all of these media-made "personalities" turn up again as featured faces on everything from hamburger wrappers (a $2.09 Big Mac) to high-end apparel ($130 sneakers) and household furnishings (a $3,400 Mickey Mouse armchair).

Ray and Andrea try hard to keep track of all this—the TV shows, tapes, CDs, movies, video games, clothing, and just *stuff* their kids see, buy, rent, listen to, wear, or want. But there are more sources and choices than there are hours, or even minutes, in the day. It seems that most of these things, or the promotions for them, enter their home and their lives through the TV, and they think the kids watch too much TV. (To tell the truth, they think the whole family watches too much.) They've set rules. Derek and Deirdre know that they may not stop at the mall without prior permission, that they may watch no more than one hour of TV after school, that they are not to watch certain channels and programs. But Ray and Andrea rarely get home before 6 P.M., and school is out by 3. They trust the kids, but they know they *are* kids. They worry.[37]

The Abdication of Government

An out-of-control entertainment industry has something to do with the exponential growth of technology—every year, it seems, we add something new to the rich array of media options—but much more to do with the increasing reluctance of government to intervene on behalf of parents and children. The Internet is a good example. It is both an ever-expanding reservoir of knowledge and "a garbage heap of pornography, of lewd exchanges, of crazy ranting."[38] Unless it is properly regulated, it can easily become yet another destructive force in the lives of children and an additional burden for parents. The history of attempts to regulate television underscores the difficulties of regulatory control in our market-driven age.

Back in the 1950s, television played a relatively benign role in the lives of children. The networks broadcast twenty-seven hours of squeaky-clean family entertainment per week. In the daytime, children had their choice of *Kukla, Fran and Ollie, The Mickey Mouse Club, Mr. Wizard,* or *Captain Kangaroo,* and primetime television was dominated by the likes of *Father Knows Best* and *Ozzie and Harriet.*

During the 1960s, there was a gradual increase in the amount of violence, crime, and sex shown on television screens. Programs such as *The Untouchables* and *Mission Impossible* were far more violent than any TV fare in the 1950s. This trend prompted a great deal of public discussion, and in 1964 the Senate set up a subcommittee to explore the link between crime and violence on television and juvenile delinquency. This was followed in 1968 by the establishment of a National Commission on the Causes and Prevention of Violence. Studies and surveys were commissioned, and the accumulated research evidence pointed to a "pattern of positive association between the viewing of television violence and aggressive attitudes and behavior" in children.[39]

In the wake of these findings, the FCC warned the television industry that children's programming would be strictly monitored. The networks responded by agreeing to a measure of self-regulation. By 1974, each broadcaster was required to make a "meaningful effort" to provide special programs for preschool and school-age children in the late afternoon hours. In addition, restrictions were placed on the amount of advertising allowed during children's programs, and host selling (using program characters to promote products) was prohibited. These measures had some effect, but in 1979 the FCC got tougher, issuing a "Notice of Proposed Rulemaking" that alerted broadcasters to the fact that in the future they would be expected to provide a minimum of seven and a half hours a week of educational children's programming.

Before the networks had time to respond, however, Ronald Reagan was elected president, and an administration committed to deregulation and a greater reliance on free enterprise came to power. Mark Fowler, the new chairman of the FCC, believed that "consumer sovereignty" should be the guiding principle in television programming and that American families would be best served by allowing the networks to show whatever attracted the largest audiences. According to Fowler, if millions of schoolchildren wanted to watch *Montel Williams* or *Geraldo* instead of doing their homework, they had an absolute right to do so. In his words, "The marketplace will take care of children."[40]

By 1984, the FCC had removed virtually all guidelines on general program content and had abolished the previously established limits on advertising in shows targeted at young people. As a result of these decisions, children's programming became much more market-driven. By the end of the 1980s, the networks were airing entire programs whose sole purpose was to sell products. *GI Joe*, *Thundercats*, and *Maxie's World* are examples of this genre. In

1980, ABC, CBS, and NBC averaged over eleven hours a week of children's educational programming. By 1992, they averaged barely an hour.[41]

During the 1990s there have been numerous advocacy and legislative efforts to make television more family-friendly, but few concrete gains. In 1990, a Democratic Congress passed the Children's Television Act, which required the FCC to reinstate restrictions on advertising during children's programming and to enforce broadcasters' obligations "to meet the educational and informational needs of the child audience."[42] This seemed promising, but it was 1996 before the FCC got around to creating rules for implementing the Children's Television Act, and then they were hardly worth the paper they were written on. Broadcasters were instructed to do their best to air at least three hours of educational television per week. Not surprisingly, such weak rulemaking has had very little effect on programming. According to the *Washington Post,* "The Children's TV Act was supposed to encourage the TV industry to develop alternatives to the usual Saturday morning ghetto of violent animated fare and toy-related programs," but broadcasters instead engaged in the "creative relabeling of programs with dubious educational value."[43] Did you know that *Yogi Bear, Sonic the Hedgehog,* and *The Mighty Morphin Power Rangers* are now officially categorized as educational programs?

Most commentators believe that President Clinton missed a golden opportunity when, in the spring of 1997, he decided to give away, with no strings attached, a large block of new frequencies, which broadcasters needed for the new digital technology. The spectrum in question was worth approximately $70 billion on the open market, and if Clinton had auctioned it off, at least some of the proceeds could have been used to underwrite educational programs for children.[44] Alternatively, he could have made the giveaway contingent on broadcasters' coming through with significant new educational programming—a strategy favored by FCC Chairman Reed E. Hundt. At one point Hundt advocated that broadcasters turn over a full 5 percent of the new digital channels to public-interest programming. In the event, "yielding to enormous pressure from broadcasters who control local stations in each congressional district," the new spectrum was just given away.[45] The sad fact is, in an age where elected officials rely on corporate contributions to fund their campaigns, neither Clinton nor Congress was able to face down the National Association of Broadcasters.

When it comes to regulating television—or the Internet, for that matter—Washington has produced a great deal of talk but little in the way of concrete action. Presidents Reagan, Bush, and Clinton have all paid lip service to the need to protect young people from the worst excesses of the media, but when push comes to shove, they have simply backed off, yielding to pressure from the entertainment industry. And this is despite the fact that we now know children are damaged when they are exposed to the full blast of an unregulated media. For instance, an increasing weight of evidence links television and movie violence to aggressive, even criminal behavior among children.

Television, Videos, and Violence

Television has enormous power. In modern America, many children—particularly disadvantaged children—spend the bulk of their waking hours in front of a television screen. The average American teenager watches twenty-two hours of TV per week, while spending five minutes alone with his or her father and twenty minutes alone with his or her mother.[46] In terms of both its depth (the amount of time spent watching it) and its breadth (the number of people who watch it), television is the most powerful cultural force this world has ever seen. It is sobering to realize that "never before have societies left it almost completely to the commercial marketplace to determine their values and their role models."[47] Consider the following facts:

- Children who watch an average amount of TV see 8,000 murders and more than 100,000 other acts of violence during their elementary school years.
- By renting just four videos—*Total Recall, Robocop 2, Rambo III, and Die Hard III*—a child would witness 525 deaths.
- MTV music videos average twenty acts of violence per hour. Indeed, 60 percent of programming on MTV links violence to degrading sexual portrayals.
- Saturday morning children's programs average twenty to twenty-five violent acts per hour.[48]

Since 1960, more than 3,000 studies have evaluated television's effects on children and teenagers. The studies themselves have been juried, reviewed, compared, and revisited, and the experts are in agreement. In the words of a leading researcher, Leonard Eron, "The scientific debate is over": the relationship between viewing violent programming and subsequent aggressive behaviors, including criminal activity, is real and it is causal.[49] That is not to say that televised violence is solely to blame for young people's aggression; it is to say that TV's role is a verified factor. The Hollywood producer Lawrence Gordon puts it another way: "I'd be lying if I said that people don't imitate what they see on the screen. I would be a moron to say that . . . [people] would imitate our dress, our music, our look, but not imitate our violence or our other actions."[50] None of this comes as a surprise to a young mother who recently wrote to the Federal Communications Commission, protesting TV violence: "I have seen my children voluntarily clean their room after watching *The Big Comfy Couch*. But after watching a single episode of *Power Rangers,* my four-year-old ran off to her room to 'pow, bam, bang' her dolls."[51]

Despite the evidence, many people within the entertainment industry—with tactics reminiscent of tobacco industry apologists—persist in denying the negative effects of violent programming. This is a disingenuous stance, given that the industry's lifeblood is advertising, which it sells with the explicit understanding that TV has enormous power to influence learning and behavior. How else could the media convince advertisers to spend billions on commercials? As Senator Paul Simon has noted, "They are essentially claiming that exposure to a twenty-five-minute program has no impact, while exposure to a thirty-second commercial has great impact."[52]

Copycat Violence

Over the years researchers have shown how a particular movie or television drama can inspire imitative or copycat behavior. In 1979, for example, bombing and extortion threats followed the airing of the TV movie *Doomsday Flight;* a few years later *The Burning Bed* led to at least one copycat killing of a young woman by her husband. A teenager was run over and killed and two others were seriously injured while playing chicken in imitation of a stunt in the 1993 movie *The Program*. John Hinckley's shooting of Ronald Reagan was inspired by *Taxi Driver* and the murder and mutilation of a prostitute by *The Silence of the Lambs*.

The 1994 movie *Natural Born Killers*, however, is in a class by itself, having inspired at least eleven copycat murders. This film transmits a particularly destructive set of values, because it both glamorizes violence and plays it out in a moral void. Mickey and Mallory, the drug-ingesting thrill riders portrayed by Woody Harrelson and Juliette Lewis, are not in the end brought to justice. Instead, they become celebrities as their murder toll climbs. In the final scenes they are arrested by corrupt cops, break out of jail, and ride away into the sunset, ready to murder again. The message of this movie does not seem to be cluttered up with uncomfortable consequences or painful accountability.

The extraordinary series of copycat crimes began almost as soon as *Natural Born Killers* reached theaters in the summer of 1994. In Texas, a fourteen-year-old accused of decapitating a thirteen-year-old told police he wanted to be "famous like the natural-born killers." In Georgia, a teenager accused of shooting to death an eighty-two-year-old Florida man shouted at television cameras, "I'm a natural-born killer!" Four other young people in Georgia were charged with killing a truck driver and fleeing in his vehicle after watching the movie nineteen times. And in Massachusetts, three youths aged eighteen to twenty were accused of killing an old man by stabbing him twenty-seven times. "Haven't you ever seen natural-born killers?" one bragged to his girlfriend.[53]

In the case of the crimes allegedly committed by Sarah Edmondson and Ben Darras, the links with the movie seem to be particularly clear-cut.

"At nineteen, Sarah looks like a sorority sister. Her long reddish blond hair neatly brushed; her eyes friendly behind gold-rimmed glasses." The only jarring note is that she is wearing an orange jumpsuit, standard issue at the Tangipahoa Parish jail in Amite, Louisiana.

Despite her pedigree—her grandfather was a congressman and her great-uncle a governor of the state—Sarah Edmondson stands accused of walking into a convenience store in nearby Ponchatoula at 11:50 on March 8, 1995, and shooting the clerk on duty through the spine, paralyzing her for life. Sarah and her boyfriend, Ben Darras, are also implicated in the killing of a man the previous day in Hernando, Mississippi. Before their grisly road trip, the two had "watched the movie *Natural Born Killers* again and again and again."

Sarah met Ben during her first semester at Northeastern State University, at a house off-campus where druggies hung out. They called it the commune. In February 1995, *Natural Born Killers* came out on video. A friend from the commune rented the movie as soon as it arrived at the local video store. That first day they played it three or four times. After that, it was on "like all the time." Everyone was crazy about it.

The evening of March 5, Sarah and Ben went on a binge. First they took several tabs of acid. Then they decided to go to Sarah's family's vacation cabin at the Wauhillau Outing Club. They took a video of *Natural Born Killers* with them, which they watched on the Edmondsons' VCR four or five times. According to Sarah, "Ben really loved this movie."

The next morning, the two set out east in Sarah's white Nissan. Sarah took along her father's .38 Smith & Wesson revolver, which had been lying around the cabin. Between Memphis and Hernando, Ben started talking about finding an isolated farmhouse and doing a home invasion—that is, robbing a family and killing them, leaving no witnesses. As Ben talked, it was clear to Sarah that his fantasy was directly inspired by *Natural Born Killers*. Sarah pulled off the highway at Hernando for gas. Ben told her to drive on out of town. When they came to a warehouse, he got out of the car and asked a man inside for directions to I-55. Ben then pulled out the .38 and shot the man.

The next day the two walked around New Orleans as tourists. Ben kept saying things like "It's your turn" and "We're partners," phrases directly borrowed from *Natural Born Killers*. They drove northward after dark, and Ben came up with the convenience store idea. They pulled off the road in Ponchatoula and parked in front of Time Saver No. 8. When the coast was clear, Sarah went in.

"I got a candy bar and walked up to the counter," she recalls. "A woman was working. As I looked at her, I did not see her, but I saw the demon. [In *Natural Born Killers*, Mickey has the word "demon" superimposed on his chest.] I shot it. She fell. I ran out of the store to the car and got in. I was crying and screaming. Ben asked me did I get the money. I didn't. Ben told me I had to go back inside and get the money. So I did."[54]

It would be much too simple to blame Sarah and Ben's murderous spree on the deregulation of the entertainment industry. But clearly, the fact that government has gotten out of the business of judging what is appropriate for children to watch on television or rent at the movie store has contributed to the violence of our age. It has also added to the parental load. Although parents have recently armed themselves with parent locks, parent blocks, and new rating systems, all too many are simply overwhelmed by the sheer size and scope of the task at hand. Like Karen Sinclair, they feel they are "shoveling shit against the tide."

Conclusion

The zeitgeist of contemporary American culture has become profoundly antagonistic toward parents. Moms and dads are attacked, blamed, disparaged, and undercut to a degree that is quite staggering, and our all-encompassing media are on the leading edge. But their role is not deliberately destructive in any obvious sense. Movies and talk shows do not set out to bash parents or undermine families. In the absence of effective regulation—and subsidies for educational fare—the media simply follow market signals and dish out whatever sells, whatever maximizes profits.[55] The entertainment industry both reflects and refracts the dominant values of our age. Thus when Hollywood feeds off psychobabble, narcissistic individualism, and market-driven hedonism, it serves to deepen the parent-hurting currents of our culture and makes the work of parents that much harder.

So far we have been talking about hostility against parents, but even at its worst, this antagonism ascribes a certain importance to the parental role. After all, even fools and monsters have to be reckoned with in some way, shape, or form. But when it comes to fathers, the cultural battles turn into a rout, as large numbers of men simply disappear from sight. Whether we are talking about *Murphy Brown* or *Thelma and Louise,* husbands and fathers simply aren't in the loop. As we will see, a powerful slice of media offerings portrays men as totally expendable, an irrelevancy in modern American life.

PART III

Fathers Under Siege

SIX

....

The Disabling of Dads

IN THE LATE 1990S, millions of American children deal with father absence—and father hunger—as an achingly painful condition of their childhoods. Indeed, the yearning for Dad can be so very fierce and deep that many children—particularly male children—clutch at whatever they can get. In an interview, seventeen-year-old Juan told us how much his dad means to him despite the fact that his father has spent most of Juan's childhood in prison.

When I was three, my dad committed a crime, and he was sent to prison. He has stayed there ever since, but he has always been part of my life. My mom didn't let me forget him. He and my mom are still together. We visit him like every weekend. My view is that jail has been good for him. Before he went inside, he always had a good heart, but the way he was brought up was like real bad. He robbed, he got into fights, he hurt people.

When I was a baby, I was his pride and joy. He gave me everything and took me around everywhere. I was spoiled. When he was put in jail that stopped, but he still tried to be part of my life as much as he could. I have to give credit to my mom. Because now she had all the responsibility. She was my mother and my father. She had to provide everything for me. It has been hard.

My father and my mom are like totally different people. My dad, he's more with the heart. He would tell me, "Go with your feelings, do what you want, have fun." My mom's old-school—she knows what she needs to do in her life and she just does it. They clash a lot. My dad says, "Don't worry about your mom—I'll talk to her later. I'll sweet-talk her."

My dad grew up a lot in jail. At first he got into fights. But he avoids trouble now. I've got to say he's helped me. Even though he's in jail, he's supported me out here. I let him know about my life every chance I had, like my first kiss, my first girlfriend, the first time I had sexual feelings. He gave me all the information he could. He never lied to me or kept anything from me. One time I was wondering what does a penis do. He told me flat out what it does. He told me little tricks about girls, how to pleasure them and stuff. I thank him for all of this. He's like my best friend.

Now, with my mom—well, I used to fight with my mom a lot. Because since my dad was my best friend, and anyhow he was in jail, my mom had to play the adult role. My dad would say, "Don't worry if you cut school, a couple classes don't matter as long as you pass." And my mom would say, "No way." I try to understand that my dad doesn't want to tell me no. He feels in the back of his mind that if he says no, I won't want anything to do with him. It's easy not to have anything to do with him, he being in jail and all. But I would never do that.

My dad is getting out in fifteen months. That's going to change everything. I don't know what to think. Sometimes my mom and dad fight so bad when we go on trail visits. Those are like jail visits for three days straight. Overnight—me and my mom and my dad. They argue about stupid things like the remote control.

Besides, I feel I've got to show him how to handle himself out here. If a friend of mine curses at me, just to say hello, he's probably going to get pissed and start a fight or something. But he can surprise me. I play handball with him on the trail and it turns out he beats me. He still can show me a lot of stuff. He tells me he's saving it till he comes out. So I see him as a friend. I've always seen him as a great friend. But that scares me a little bit. He doesn't understand about this college stuff. I'll be a senior next year and I'm going to have to study and study and he's coming out and thinking he's going to be with me every day.

I feel sorry for him because he's missed like my whole life, and he has regrets. I don't regret anything, though. As far as I'm concerned, everything turned out for the best, because if he hadn't gone to jail, he would either be dead or I wouldn't have a father anyway because him and my mom would have probably broken up. As it was, I got to have him in jail and my mom raised me right. I'm proud of who I am right now. I think I've got the best parents, because I've got a little bit of both. I have the street smarts of my father—my mom doesn't know a blunt from butt; I have to tell her about slang words and stuff. But then she teaches me about how to present myself for job interviews and how to do well in school. So it's good.[1]

This young man's voice is searingly honest. Wise beyond his years, Juan bears witness to the extraordinary importance of a dad, even one doing time as a convicted killer. It is a sad commentary on the father-scarcity of our times (particularly in the black community) that a seventeen-year-old who has struggled for fourteen years to maintain a relationship with a dad in prison should think he has a good deal. But given the contemporary reality, he does. As Juan points out, if it had not been for jail, his father would more than likely either be dead or have disappeared years ago. And this would have been a great loss for Juan, for his dad has made a difference, grounding and sustaining him in an enveloping love despite the constraints of prison. (Of course, none of this would have happened without the determined efforts of his wise and loving mother. Think of the energy involved in fourteen years of weekly prison visits!) At age seventeen, Juan is surprisingly intact—and college bound—and a huge amount of credit must go to his mom and dad.

The Fatherhood Problem

Until recently, fathers were always considered essential. In the words of the social analyst David Blankenhorn, "The fatherless family of the United States in the late twentieth century represents a radical departure from virtually all of human history and experience."[2] Through time and across cultures, fathers have been identified, connected to their children, and encouraged to play a significant role in their children's upbringing.

Societies have always struggled with the issue of how to tie a specific child to a specific man. In almost all cases this connection has been made through the institution of marriage and the establishment of the legitimacy principle, which holds that a child born to a married couple belongs to the husband and not to some other man. Legitimacy is an extraordinarily important concept because it establishes paternal certainty, which is the most important precondition for paternal investment, and paternal investment, in turn, is an essential determinant of child and societal well-being—a line of reasoning that is particularly relevant today. Given the complex demands of contemporary child-raising, the time, energy, and resources that fathers are willing to give to their children have never been more important.

Enforcing the principle of legitimacy is often a struggle; indeed, cross-culturally, fatherhood has often been problematic in a way that motherhood has not. As sociologist David Popenoe has pointed out, while mothers the world over bear and nurture their young with a ready acceptance of their role, fathers are often filled with ambivalence.[3] This gender difference can be explained by the elementary facts of human reproduction. Biologically speaking, the link between mother and child is incontrovertible. Fatherhood, in contrast, is inherently uncertain, which is why societies have tried so hard to connect children to their fathers. One thing seems clear: when legitimacy is "culturally unregulated"—when society fails to enforce it—"men's sexual behavior can be promiscuous, their paternity casual, their commitment to families weak." In memorable language, social critic George Gilder reminds us, "As a physical reality, the male sexual repertory is very limited. Men have only one sex organ and one sex act: erection and ejaculation. Everything else is guided by culture . . . The most important and productive roles—husband and father—are a cultural invention, necessary to civilized life, but ultimately fragile."[4]

In recognition of the problem that fatherhood is enormously important but also somewhat difficult to establish, societies have often created sanctions and imposed stigmas to enforce paternal investment. The main cultural carrier of sanctions is the institution of marriage, which in all societies serves to hold a man accountable to his children and to their mother. An important function of the vows of fidelity and permanence that are almost universally part of the wedding ceremony is to hold the man to the union.

As we are all aware, in modern America the institution of marriage has greatly weakened. Divorce has become both much easier and much more socially acceptable than it used to be, and there is now virtually no stigma attached to bearing a child outside marriage. As an inevitable result of these two trends, there has been an enormous increase in absent fathers. Today, almost 40 percent of American children live apart from their biological father.[5]

If the disappearance of fathers is clearly one of the most dramatic social trends of our time, the big question is, of course, does it matter? Is there something new and different about the late twentieth century that makes single parenthood a reasonable option and makes modern societies immune from the age-old condemnation of illegitimacy?

American society certainly seems to think so. Over the past three decades, important segments of public opinion have become convinced that fathers don't matter—a point of view encouraged by modern feminism, which for all its enormous value has indulged in some excesses. Most damaging has been a set of attitudes that center on the expendability of men. Ideas that women don't need men, women can do whatever they want without men, men are responsible for all the evil in the world, children need only a loving mother, and men only teach children how to be patriarchal and militaristic have become standard fare on the cutting edge of the women's movement.

Clearly, in some important ways times have changed. Since most women today hold jobs and bring home paychecks, a significant number of mothers can now afford to raise children by themselves. The television character Murphy Brown is just one example. In addition, AFDC/TANF has made single parenthood an option for poor women. But if single motherhood has become a self-conscious choice for many women, life without Dad can be devastating for children, as recent suicides in South Boston make all too clear.

"On the last afternoon of his life, Kevin Geary seemed upbeat. After finishing his work-study shift at Massachusetts Institute of Technology, the Boston High School junior borrowed his mother's car and headed from the Old Colony public housing development toward a friend's house in Dorchester. He wanted to play basketball, but he did not get far."

Boston police sergeant David Allen stopped Geary for driving through a flashing red light outside his apartment at Old Harbor Street and Columbia Road. Allen handed out an $85 ticket; the citation read, "1:05 P.M., Dec. 30."

"Less than an hour later, Geary, seventeen, was dead. The teenager hanged himself with a belt from a rod in his bedroom closet."

Geary was found by his mother, Linda Reid, a single mom. "I'll never forget picking up my six-foot-two son, cutting him down, and doing CPR on him," Reid said, tears turning to sobs.

Geary was the first of six young men to commit suicide in

"Southie," a fiercely proud, mostly Irish South Boston neighborhood, in the eight months between December 1996 and August 1997. "Kevin was the first," said his mother. "It's like he showed a way out." After Kevin came Duane Liotti (twenty-one), Jonathan Curtis (sixteen), Tommy Mullen (fifteen), Tommy Deckert (fifteen), and Kevin Cunningham (seventeen). A thick thread of despair runs like an electric current through Southie. It is not just the six suicides that have staggered the community's residents. Since January 1997, about seventy teenagers, most of them male, have been hospitalized for attempts at suicide.

For well over a century, Southie was a place where Irish immigrants, and later Italians and Lithuanians, climbed the ladder from poverty to middle-class success. "Southie was especially proud of its men. They were known as priests and politicians, as policemen and firemen, as longshoremen, fishermen, and factory workers."

But today Southie's problems are not too different from those of other urban neighborhoods. The blue-collar jobs that once created security for men with high school diplomas are disappearing, and the community is suffering from a lack of jobs—and a lack of fathers.

Jimmy Connolly (twenty-six), a Southie resident and high school dropout, spoke about his community to a reporter: "Around here you don't hear no one talking about college . . . Half my friends didn't even finish high school." Connolly, who recently spent six months in jail for aggravated assault with a weapon, said he knows only one man from his neighborhood who has gone to college. That man had an advantage, Connolly explained: "He had a mother and a father his whole life." This is an advantage that the young men who hanged themselves mostly did not have.

Each of the suicides is inexplicable in its own way, "shrouded by the mystery of each young man's personality and family history." But these suicides also fit a pattern. Five out of the six young men had been abandoned by their fathers. Weighed down with a bitter load of father hunger, they were struggling to grow up without a dad.[6]

The Face of Fatherlessness

The United States has the highest divorce rate in the world; it also leads the world in percentage of children born out of wedlock. The net result is that nearly two fifths of American children now live apart from their biological fathers, a figure that has doubled over the last twenty-five years.

Of the 15 million children without fathers, almost 10 million are the products of marital separation and divorce, and the remainder are the products of out-of-wedlock births, still primarily concentrated in the poor black population. Divorce, on the other hand, crosses class lines with impunity and now wreaks havoc throughout society. In 1950, one out of every six marriages ended in divorce; by 1995, the figure had risen to one in two marriages.[7] Divorced fathers often lose all contact with their children, as the data show. Two sociologists at the University of Pennsylvania, Frank Furstenberg and Kathleen Mullan Harris, for example, followed a representational national sample of 1,000 children from divorced families between 1976 and 1987 and found that 42 percent had not seen their fathers at all during the previous year. Only 20 percent had slept over at their father's house in the previous month, and only one in six saw their fathers once a week or more. According to Furstenberg, "Men regard marriage as a package deal . . . they cannot separate their relationship with their children from their relations with their former spouse. When that relationship ends, the paternal bond usually withers."[8]

But divorce is only part of the problem. The other face of fatherlessness is the rapidly growing number of out-of-wedlock births and the virtual absence of men in these new single-mother families. The statistics are dramatic. Although births among teenage girls have declined over the last thirty years, the proportion of unmarried teenagers who have children has risen sharply. There are now close to half a million live births to unwed teenagers every year. In 1960, 15 percent of teenage girls who gave birth were unmarried; by 1996, this figure had reached 76 percent. Teenage unwed motherhood is rising among whites, but it is still much more common in the black community. One out of every three black mothers is an unwed teenager, and a third go on to have a second child while still in their teens. "Marriage has become an almost forgotten institution among black teens . . . in whole sections of the black community, children are being raised exclusively by very young mothers."[9] Fathers are simply not in the picture.

Whether the concern is divorce or out-of-wedlock birth, research in the field—much of it very recent—shows that father absence has a devastating impact on children. The social scientific evidence is now extremely clear on this point. According to David Popenoe, "I know of few other bodies of evidence whose weight leans so much in one direction as does the evidence about family structure: on the whole, two parents—a father and a mother—are better for the child than one parent."[10] The work of Sara McLanahan and Gary Sandefur is particularly powerful. These two researchers recently examined six nationally representative data sets containing 25,000 children from a variety of racial and social class backgrounds and found that "children who grow up apart from a parent are disadvantaged in many ways relative to children who grow up with both parents"; they are twice as likely to drop out of high school, 2.5 times as likely to become teen mothers, and 1.4 times as likely to be out of school and out of work.[11]

But what of the poverty factor? Perhaps these outcomes are a result of one-parent families' being poorer? Not true. McLanahan and Sandefur show that loss of economic resources accounts for about 50 percent of the disadvantage associated with single parenthood. Too little parental supervision and involvement and greater residential mobility account for most of the rest.[12] It is also important to bear in mind that poverty itself is correlated with single motherhood. If fathers were to reconnect with their families, a significant proportion of all single-mother households would be lifted out of poverty.

We are not only talking about the tangible, measurable repercussions of fatherlessness—school drop out, teen pregnancy, and the like—we are also talking about the emotional consequences of life without Dad. Psychologists have documented how the partial or complete loss of a father produces long-lasting feelings of betrayal, rejection, rage, guilt, and pain. Judith Wallerstein, for example, in her research on the long-term effects of divorce has shown how children yearn for their fathers in the wake of divorce, and how this longing is infused with new intensity at adolescence. For girls, the peak years are early adolescence, twelve to fifteen; for boys, the need for a father crests somewhat later, at ages sixteen to eighteen. Father hunger seems to be particularly deep and painful among boys. According to the psychiatrist Alfred Messer, the yearning for a father among boys is often overwhelming and can lead to depression and even suicide.

There are, of course, qualifications to the general rule that fathers are valuable and two parents are better than one. We are all acquainted with a two-parent family that is a family from hell. And a child can certainly be well raised by a single mother—or father—who is devoted to that child's well-being. But overall, children living in single-parent homes (nearly always single-mother homes) are more at risk than children living with both parents. Consider the following facts:

- Children in single-parent homes are five times more likely to live in poverty.
- Children in single-parent homes are twice as likely to drop out of school.
- Eighty percent of adolescents in psychiatric hospitals come from broken homes.
- Three out of four teen suicides occur in single-parent homes.
- Seventy percent of the juveniles in state reform institutions grew up in fatherless homes.[13]

One point made time and again by scholars is that the missing ingredient in the single-parent family is not simply a second adult who can provide supervision and involvement but the biological father. Occasionally he can be replaced by a boyfriend, a stepfather, an uncle, a grandparent, or a mentor, but in general, males biologically unrelated to children do not have the same dedication to raising those children as males raising their own biological offspring. Boyfriends and stepfathers, for example, are much more likely to be implicated in cases of child abuse than biological dads.

Father Absence and Child Abuse

A number of studies have found that cross-culturally, a child is far more likely to be physically abused by a boyfriend or a stepparent than by a biological father. In a study of child abuse in single-mother households, Leslie Margolin found that 64 percent of nonmaternal abuse was committed by mothers' boyfriends. This was especially surprising given the fact that these boyfriends were infrequent caregivers.[14]

Stepfathers can be as dangerous as mothers' boyfriends, underscoring the threat posed to children by resident unrelated males. One recent study demonstrated that children under two years old are one hundred times more likely to be killed by stepparents than by genetic parents. And statistical analysis indicates that this greater risk factor cannot be attributed to differential poverty rates, family size, or race.

It does seem that marriage creates safer conditions for children, in that a child is least likely to be abused growing up in a stable family with both biological parents. The more society departs from this ideal, the more likely it is that abuse will occur. Despite the recent increase in overreporting of child abuse cases, child abuse has undoubtedly risen over the past twenty years. In 1996, there were over 3 million reported cases of child abuse and neglect—a figure that is up 367 percent since 1976.[15] This figure has moved in lockstep with our escalating rates of divorce and single parenthood.

Should we be surprised by the connection between father absence and child abuse? Probably not. Recent work by a group of scholars called the New Darwinians reminds us that as a species, we are grounded in genetic self-interest. Biological parents have unique genetic investments in their children and as a result will care much more profoundly for them than substitute parents. Even the best-intentioned stepparents (and boyfriends) tend to see stepchildren (and girlfriends' children) as a drain on resources. Because these children take money and time away from biological children and from a mate, they nearly always provoke resentment, and in a minority of cases this resentment spills over into abuse. Thus, a society that relies increasingly on substitute parents is one that veers increasingly toward violence.

It is important to point out that at least some stepfathers do a splendid job by their stepchildren, and these men deserve our admiration and respect. However, the deeper point is that overall, biological dads do a better job. Fatherly love is not something that can be easily replicated.

The violence and abuse produced by father absence spreads well beyond the home, enhancing the likelihood of crime in society at large. Juvenile crime, for example, is committed disproportionately by youths in single-mother households and in other households where the biological father is not present. Seventy-two percent of adolescent murderers and 70 percent of long-term prison inmates come from fatherless homes.[16] O.J. Simpson had a large load to deal with on the father absence front, with some of the predictable consequences. Not only was he abandoned by his father when he was three years old, but he had to cope with the fact that his absentee father was a homosexual in a day when this was not cool. In the tough neighborhood of San Francisco where O.J. grew up, his father was known as "Sweet Jimmy" Simpson.[17]

A considerable body of evidence points to the fact that fathers are critical in keeping their sons on the right side of the law. They are important for maintaining authority and discipline. And they are even more important for helping their sons develop self-control and feelings of empathy toward others, character traits that are found to be lacking in violent youth. In his book *Family and Nation,* Senator Daniel Patrick Moynihan draws one unmistakable lesson from American history: "A community that allows a large number of young men to grow up in broken families . . . never acquiring any stable relationship to male authority . . . asks for and gets chaos."[18] We increasingly invite this type of chaos. In the black community, for example, more than 70 percent of all children now live apart from their fathers.

The Impact on Fathers

Contrary to popular images, children remain a precious source of duty and delight to millions of American males. Most men crave fatherhood. They want children not simply to perpetuate their names but, more important, to feel as if they matter in the world. They seek the intangible benefits of parenting—the indescribable sense of affirmation that comes from attachment to a child.

Charles Ballard, the president and founder of the Institute for Responsible Fatherhood and Family Revitalization, believes that learning how to be a good father can be a transformative power in a man's life. This belief is born out of his own experience.

Ballard was three years old when his father left. He describes his subsequent childhood and adolescence as characterized by "deviant behavior"—he stole, got into fights, dropped out of school. As a teenager he fathered a child out of wedlock and then walked out on his girlfriend and new baby, unconsciously wanting to abandon them as he felt he had been abandoned by his own father. Ballard then joined the army and eventually wound up in jail, charged with a crime he had not committed. There he met an older man who gave him affection and guidance.

Through the kindness of this man, Ballard learned to recognize in himself a strong desire to find his son, who was then five years old, and "be the kind of father my own father could not be to me." As soon as he was released from prison, he went to the house of his son's mother. When he walked in the door, three children were playing on the floor. The oldest, a boy of about five, looked up at him and said, "Daddy!"

Ballard readily attributes his son's recognition and acceptance of him to his ex-girlfriend's generosity. She had shown the child a picture of Ballard in his army uniform and told him that his father was "a hero who was fighting to keep this country safe."

Ballard subsequently adopted his son and committed himself to being a good father. "I couldn't get a decent job on account of my prison record, but I had a child who belonged to me," he says, "so I did whatever it took to support him—I washed dishes, I scrubbed floors, I worked two jobs." His son's love for him and the imperative of supporting the boy brought out the best in Ballard. He eventually got his life back on track: he went to school at night, landed a decent job, got married, and raised two more children. He is now convinced that "the more a father nurtures his child, the more his child nurtures him." Ballard's retrospective on his own life is simple: "Becoming a father saved my life."[19]

Unfortunately, the great flowering of constructive energy that many men experience when they become loving, attached parents is increasingly imperiled by our fragile family structures. In modern America, too many men must deal with the fact that their children are growing up in someone else's home. Escalating rates of divorce and out-of-wedlock birth mean that close to half of all fathers lose contact with their children, and this has left a deep emotional void in the souls of men. As was true in Ballard's early life, this void fosters profound feelings of worthlessness and can trigger antisocial behavior. Despite a large body of research on the fallout of fatherlessness on children, the expert community has paid little attention to how child absence affects fathers. Not surprisingly, the misery of the adult often mirrors that of the child.

The father's rights movement is filled with embittered men who yearn for lost children. A large number are divorced and living apart from their children, and at least as they tell it, many of them never wanted their marriages to end. Their wives divorced them, a decision that caused these men to forfeit their families, their homes, and a large chunk of their income. Many of them feel "irreparably aggrieved," and their anguish and anger is particularly intense over "losing what matters most to them: their children."[20] Moreover, they are all but helpless to do anything about it, for when push comes to shove, the ex-wife almost always gets custody, and the custodial mother exercises effective control over the children.

Given the anguish wrapped up in separation from children, it is hard to understand why so many divorced fathers eventually choose to sever all ties with their kids. According to psychologist John Munder Ross, many divorced fathers are simply "overwhelmed by feelings of failure and self-hatred." Visiting their children only serves to remind these men of their painful loss, and they respond to this feeling by withdrawing completely. The tendency then is for divorced men "to invest their energies elsewhere, disengaging from a family that is no longer really theirs."[21]

Unattached men, whether divorced or simply never married, can be very destructive, both to themselves and to society. For decades we have known that wives and children are a strong civilizing force in the lives of men. A century ago, Emily Durkheim made the point that married men experience a "salutary discipline," because marriage forces them to master their passions and encourages the regular work habits required to meet a family's material needs. Indeed, the data show that single men are much more likely than single women to die prematurely from disease or accidents caused by self-neglect. More important, across cultures and throughout history, single men have been responsible for a disproportionate share of societal violence. In recent years the New Darwinians have stressed the difference in the propensity for violence between single and married men and have developed a theory of the "pacifying effect of marriage." Robert Wright, for example, has demonstrated that "an unmarried man between twenty-four and thirty-five years of age is about three times as likely to murder another male as is a married man the same age."[22] An unmarried man is also more likely to rob, rape, and abuse drugs or alcohol.[23] The harrowing story of John P. and John J. Royster is instructive.

While "a thunderstorm was gathering in the late afternoon of June 4," 1996, a thirty-two-year-old piano teacher was walking through a section of Central Park generally regarded as very safe. At about the same time, John J. Royster was entering the park nearby, at West 72nd Street. Their paths crossed, and Royster set upon the 110-pound woman, brutalizing her and attempting to rape her.

At his arraignment in Manhattan Criminal Court ten days later, Royster stood accused of four crimes, the attack in Central Park on June 4 and three others that followed close on the heels of the first. On June 5, fifty-one-year-old Shelby Evans was badly beaten at the heliport at 63rd Street and Second Avenue. Two days later, a twenty-six-year-old woman was beaten and sexually assaulted in Yonkers. The final crime occurred on June 11, when sixty-five-year-old Evelyn Alvarez was beaten to death outside her dry-cleaning store on Park Avenue and 88th Street.

As the life story of John J. Royster was pieced together in the weeks after these horrendous crimes, two themes stood out: his rage against women, and the extraordinary ways in which he patterned his relationships—and his crimes—after his father's.

The father, John P. Royster, was born in Brooklyn in December 1949 to a single mother. He was an altar boy and attended Bishop Loughlin High School. After graduating, he enrolled at Manhattan College, and he received an accounting degree in 1971.

In 1973 he got married. The next year his son, John J., was born. "He was the love of my life," John P. told a reporter. "It was my mental attitude in conceiving him to love him more than life." A short time afterward the parents split up. According to John P., his ex-wife instigated the divorce and subsequently tried to prevent him from visiting his only child. They fought a custody battle that raged for six years.

"The child loved me and I loved the child," says John P. "The child was a weapon to hurt me, because it was obvious to all that there was a love relationship . . . I fought tooth and nail to have the times I saw him."

When John J. was six years old, his mother moved with him to the Morris Park section of the Bronx. After the move, John P. visited his son only sporadically, and eventually not at all. According to John P., the tensions with his ex-wife escalated, and eventually she "cut me off forever." John P. began to spiral down. He went from job to job and from residence to residence. He was in turn an insurance salesman, a real estate agent, and a financial consultant. He seemed to have a hard time staying in one place. In 1982 he began a relationship with a woman named Willye Jean Dukes. In 1987 Ms. Dukes left him, and a few months later she obtained a court order barring him from going near her. She charged that John P. was threatening to kill her. In January 1988, while Ms. Dukes was waiting with her sisters on a crowded subway platform, John P. appeared with a twelve-gauge shotgun, killed her, and wounded one of her sisters.

Meanwhile, despite all his family troubles, John J. prospered in school. His friends characterized him as smart and nerdy. He collected comic books and developed an interest in the martial arts. In seventh grade he was president of his junior high school class. John J. was fourteen when his father gunned down Willye Jean Dukes and was sent to jail. At this point, his school performance became more erratic, but he was still able to do well in some subjects. According to Danny Schott, an English teacher at Samuel Gompers High School who was close to him, John J. liked English best and was an A student in this subject.

John J. left home after high school and fumbled for a footing. Like his father, he moved from address to address, at one point living at Covenant House, a home for troubled teenagers. He became obsessed with the martial arts, and his interests now extended to meditation and Eastern religion. Women tended to rebuff him. According to a neighbor, he spent entire days watching violent and pornographic movies, especially movies of men hurting and raping women.

Despite his rootlessness, John J. was able to find work, although he had trouble hanging on to a job for any length of time. His longest employment was at The Gap, where he worked as a part-time stock clerk for four months in 1992. Three years later he was working as a sales clerk at Software etc., a computer store on Sixth Avenue, but he quit in December 1995, saying that he had family problems. It was about this time that he fell in love with a Japanese woman who was temporarily in New York visiting family. John J. told a friend, "She's the one," but in January she returned to Japan. John J. was devastated. A detective who spoke to him after his arrest reported, "He said he loved that girl . . . he felt powerless when she left."

In April 1996, John J. got a job at Staples on 86th Street. In May he was dismissed. A coworker reported that "he was very nasty to women, especially white women . . . Out of nowhere, he would make ugly comments." A couple of weeks later, John J. went on his brutal rampage.[24]

The story line running through the lives of John P. and John J. Royster is poignant and frightening. The damage done to the father by the loss of his son was exceeded only by the damage done to the son by the loss of his father. In the end, both father and son wreaked a brutal—and unforgivable—vengeance on women. In John P.'s case, the target was the woman who had left him. In John J.'s case, the targets were randomly chosen, anonymous women who merely stood for the women who had spurned him and kept his father from him. In his written confession to the police, John J. said, "I was thinking of my girlfriend" when he saw the woman he attacked in Central Park. The father, interviewed on June 14, 1996, in the prison where he is serving a life sentence for killing Willye Jean Dukes, summed it all up: "He's like a chip off the old block."[25]

Fatherhood and Society

In our society, as in all others, parents teach their children to trust in and care for others. These values, which are the building blocks of civic virtue, are precisely those that we are losing in late-twentieth-century America. Children are not born with such qualities as commitment and compassion; these virtues must be purposefully taught and reinforced by mothers and fathers. Children learn most things, including values, through imitation and modeling. The more caring and trustworthy a parent is, the more likely it is that the child will acquire these attributes. Generally speaking, if such virtues are not taught within the family, they are not taught at all.

Given this fact, it is easy to see how the disappearance of fathers makes it much harder to develop civic virtue or build strong families and communities. In the wake of losing Dad, most children become bitter—or at least skeptical—about such values as responsibility and commitment. If a child needs to wonder why Dad took off, leaving him or her in the lurch, or if a child goes to bed at night not knowing whether Dad will be there in the morning, or if a child needs to ask, "Who is my father?" it becomes exceedingly hard to build the reservoir of trust that is essential if a child one day is to be a good spouse or a responsible citizen. Thus, if we are to maintain our rich and complex democracy, a major national objective should be to increase the proportion of children who live with and are nurtured by their fathers, and to decrease the proportion of children who are not.

The bottom line seems to be that fatherhood and fathering are enormously important, and when fathers are crippled and cast aside, serious repercussions are felt throughout the nation. A withering of the father-child bond devastates children, stunts men, and seriously erodes our social capital. For make no mistake about it: fatherlessness is much more than a private agony. It creates an open, festering wound that saps the strength of the entire nation.

The great challenge is to understand how and why this has happened. We now know the data and realize that there are many fewer attached fathers than there used to be. But this trend is not etched in stone. We are not talking about some inevitable evolutionary momentum. In recent years, fathers have been the subject of a tidal wave of critical thinking and punitive action. If the past few decades have seen a systematic war against parents, the battles waged against fathers have been particularly ugly and fierce.

Devalued in the Workplace

On the economic front, the story is a simple one. As we saw earlier, men are dealing with a far-reaching deterioration in the terms and conditions of employment. Wages have fallen dramatically over the last twenty-five years, and the rate of decline has been much more rapid for men than for women. Indeed, up until the early 1990s, sagging wages were entirely a male phenomenon. According to Lester Thurow, at no other time in history have the median wages of American men fallen for such a sustained period. Wages of white men have fallen slightly faster than those of black men, and young men have suffered disproportionately. Overall, wages are down 25 percent for men twenty-five to thirty-four years of age.[26]

Falling wages significantly undermine the ability of men to shoulder family responsibilities. For example, a third of all men in the twenty-five-to-thirty-four age group now earn less than the amount necessary to keep a family of four above the poverty line.

And it's not just wage levels we are talking about, but the entire web of securities that used to be tied up in a job. Men are being evicted from a working world that used to sustain them by giving them not only wages but health care, seniority, a pension, and, most important, an identity. Work was their clan or tribe. They were Sears men, or IBM workers proud to be part of the Big Blue family. These attachments and securities are increasingly a thing of the past. In the late 1990s, laid-off, throwaway workers scramble for a footing in shifting corporate sands.

If white-collar workers are being downsized and discarded, poorly educated minority workers are failing to find any kind of a foothold in the labor market. In 1993, for example, over 40 percent of adult black males were unemployed, had stopped looking for work, were in prison, or simply could not be found by the census.[27] This extraordinary rate of joblessness has severely affected the ability of black men to support a family. William Julius Wilson has related the dramatic decrease in marriage among blacks to an equally dramatic fall in the number of marriageable men— that is, those who hold jobs. According to Wilson, in 1960 there were seventy employed civilian black men for every hundred black women. By 1990, this figure had dropped to forty.

In recent years, the problems of shrinking wages, joblessness, and insecurity have been compounded by a sharp rise in inequality. As wealth trickles up to an ever more glittering elite, ordinary Americans have become bewildered, even angry. Increasingly, they see very little justice in who gets what in our society.

Over the last twenty years, the tide has risen (real per capita GNP went up 29 percent between 1973 and 1993), yet 80 percent of the boats have sunk. Equalizing trends of the period from 1930 to 1970 reversed sharply in the early 1980s, and the gap between the haves and have-nots is now greater than at any time since 1929. The 1980s were extravagant years in which privileged Americans built themselves a good life. McCoy, the main character in Tom Wolfe's novel *The Bonfire of the Vanities,* is in many ways the ultimate symbol of this decade. The biggest producer on the trading floor of a Wall Street firm, McCoy is an immensely successful cad with terrific curb appeal who spends his time "baying for money on the bond market."[28] However, the boom years only existed for those at the very top of the economic ladder. During this decade, the top one percent of the population enjoyed fully two thirds of all increases in financial wealth, and the bottom 80 percent ended up with less financial wealth in 1989 than in 1983.[29]

Whether the immediate problem is a pink slip or a boss who has just bought himself a Gulfstream jet, the cumulative impact of these economic trends has been hard on male egos. Not only have some of these developments been particularly negative for men—compared to female wages, male wages have plunged more sharply and for a longer time—but male self-confidence and notions of personal worth remain heavily vested in earning power. Even today, thirty years into the modern women's movement, men continue to judge themselves and one another by their ability to come through as breadwinners. In extensive focus group research conducted for his 1995 book, *Fatherless America,* David Blankenhorn found that men gave priority to being a good and steady provider when they defined manhood. In the words of one participant, "I think first you have to provide for your family financially. Probably everybody will agree on that one."[30]

Abandoned by Government

Increasingly devalued in the workplace, men have also been discounted and pushed aside by government. The fact is, in recent decades the political establishment has not come through for husbands and fathers. Take the case of disadvantaged men. However one judges the results of the war on poverty, it clearly created a social welfare system that focuses on women. Men, especially poor men, have been largely ignored. As we have seen, TANF, the program that now provides income support for poor families, was set up in such a way so as to deliberately exclude fathers.

The seeds of what came to be called AFDC and then TANF were sown during the Great Depression. With over a quarter of the labor force out of work, the federal government became newly involved in the provision of welfare. Aid to Dependent Children (ADC), which gave widows cash subsidies so they could stay home and look after their children, was part of the Social Security Act of 1935. The rolls quickly expanded to include mothers who were divorced or who had never married.

Over time there was a growing disparity between the benefits of the ADC program, which grew quite rapidly, and the benefits for unemployed heads of households, which remained stagnant. As this gulf widened, it became difficult for mothers and fathers to stay together. On strictly economic grounds, an employed father would do better by his family if he deserted his wife and children so they could obtain ADC, with its higher levels of financial assistance.

To make matters worse, in the 1950s and 1960s various states decided to crack down on unqualified ADC recipients; government agents staged announced midnight raids to make sure that mothers really had been deserted and that there was no "man in the house."[31] If a man was found on the premises, the mother lost her ADC benefits. The effect of these raids was to further discourage fathers even more from living with their families.

In 1988, as part of the Family Support Act, AFDC (as the program was now called) was finally extended to provide assistance to two-parent families in which the principal earner—either the father or the mother—was unemployed. However, benefits under this new program, AFDC-UP, were limited to six months in most states, and they have not been widely used.

Given this history, it is not surprising that a substantial body of research now links welfare benefits to high rates of out-of-wedlock births, low rates of marriage, and long-term poverty. C. R. Winegarden estimates that fully half the increase in black out-of-wedlock births can be attributed to the effects of welfare.[32] While Jodi Sandfort and Martha Hill, at the University of Michigan, have demonstrated that the higher the cash benefit provided to an unwed mother, the lower the probability that that mother will get married after the birth of her child. Furthermore, unwed mothers who subsequently get married are significantly less likely to remain in poverty than those who do not. Thus, as cash welfare to an unmarried woman increases, the odds that she will marry decrease, which in turn decreases the prospect that she will escape either poverty or welfare.[33]

One thing we can be sure of: by encouraging out-of-wedlock births and discouraging marriage, welfare has encouraged fatherlessness among poor families. Indeed, in the mid-1990s, 90 percent of all families receiving cash benefits did not have a father living in the home.

Over the last few years, the antifather bias in our public policies has found its clearest expression in the demonization of deadbeat dads (fathers who fail to pay child support). During the 1996 political conventions, vilification of these "deadbeat dads" won enthusiastic applause from Republican and Democratic audiences alike. In his campaign, President Clinton repeatedly promised to give this country the toughest child support enforcement it has ever had. Cracking down on deadbeat dads is about all our political leaders have to offer on the fatherhood front—thin stuff in a country that leads the world in fatherlessness. Where did this punitive policy perspective come from?

At least some of the anger over deadbeat dads was spurred by a widely quoted Census Bureau report, *Child Support and Alimony: 1989*, which seemed to point to a widespread failure on the part of noncustodial fathers to come through for their children. In the words of the report, "Five million women were supposed to receive child support payments in 1989. Of the women due payments, about half received the full amount they were due. The remaining women were about equally divided between those receiving partial payment and those receiving nothing."[34]

This report, which is still extensively quoted, triggered a great deal of public outrage. However, its meaning is much less clear than has been commonly supposed. First of all, an overlooked fact is that almost 38 percent of "absent fathers" have neither custody nor visitation rights and therefore no ability to connect with their child. It seems strange to call them by the pejorative term "absent" when they have no right to be present.

Another overlooked fact is that these statistics on child support payments were based entirely on interviews with custodial mothers. No attempt was made to interview noncustodial fathers, yet there is reason to believe that this might change the numbers. A pilot survey of absent parents conducted in the mid-1980s, which is in fact the only study concerned with the noncustodial parents' point of view, found a 30 percent discrepancy between what noncustodial fathers said they paid and what custodial mothers said they received. After all, women on AFDC have a powerful incentive to underreport their income.

Another fact worth mentioning is that according to a little-known 1991 DHHS study, noncustodial mothers have a far worse record of child support compliance than noncustodial fathers do. "Among parents who are due child support, fathers are less likely to receive a payment [than mothers], with 47 percent of fathers and 27 percent of mothers receiving nothing."[35] Of course, when confronted with this particular fact, we do not immediately conjure up images of "deadbeat mommies"; rather, we strive to find sympathetic explanations of what must be going on with these women to cause them to deprive their children of needed economic support.

In a recent article, journalist Jack Kammer invites us to indulge in a little sensitivity training by reversing roles. What would fatherhood would look like if dads had the same rights and prerogatives currently reserved for mothers? Imagine the scenario: A father becomes pregnant and faces the following choices. If he doesn't want to become a parent at this point in his life, he can have an abortion. If he wants the child, he can force the mother to become a mother, even against her will. After his child is born, he can still change his mind about being a parent and put the child up for adoption or place it in foster care, thereby absolving himself of all further responsibility. If he decides to keep the child, he will receive a government check, medical insurance for himself and the child, food stamps, and, of course, a primary relationship with his offspring. The mother will receive an order to fulfill her traditional female role by going to the father's home three days a week to cook, clean, and shop for him and the child, but she must leave before the kid returns from school. (She is on a fixed schedule of how often she can visit the child). If she fails to cook, clean, and shop for the father and the kid, she will be rounded up, hounded, and harassed, and might even be thrown in jail. If the father interferes with her scheduled visits, nothing happens. No one cares about her desire to be a parent to her child. The authorities only care about the father's desire to see her cook, clean, and shop. ("You owe it to your child," they tell her gravely.) Fully aware of his superior power, the father treats the mother any way he wishes. If she starts seeing another man, for instance, he cuts off her visits with her child. Fully aware of her powerlessness, she becomes frustrated, angry, resentful, and uncooperative. She might fake an injury to avoid having to cook, clean, and shop. She might even skip town.[36]

It is easy to feel a rush of sympathy for a mother living under such conditions. We certainly don't warm to the idea that we need to crack down on her. Probably we recognize the need to change a system that is capable of turning a loving and valuable parent into a despised scofflaw. We begin to understand the craziness of imagining that it is possible to keep in place all the obligations of traditional parenthood without its main reward—loving contact with a child. Jack Kammer, for one, is of the opinion that it is our treatment of fathers rather than male nature per se that is the cause of our child support problem.

Our entire panoply of attitudes and policies toward noncustodial parents reeks with hostility to fathers. One new measure stands out as an example of extreme insensitivity. As a result of recent changes in child support collection procedures, fathers whose children receive AFDC/TANF no longer send their money to their children directly; instead, they are expected to repay the government for its check. The implications are not lost on the men who must live with this: according to a recent report, "The men were keenly aware that payments to children on AFDC do relatively little to improve the children's welfare . . . The idea of paying child support to discharge a welfare debt does not sit well with some fathers, and has little to do with their sense of themselves as providers for their children."[37]

To visualize what this means to an individual, let's return to Kammer's imaginary scenario. Because of new legislation, women are no longer ordered to cook, clean, and shop for their own kids. Now a government-supplied domestic worker is dispatched on a regular basis to take care of that. The mother is now ordered to repay the government by joining a crew that cooks, cleans, and shops for the residents of a state college dormitory or military barracks. Knowing that her efforts have absolutely no bearing on the health, happiness, and well-being of her child, she has even less motivation to comply with the government's child support order, while her resentment and frustration are elevated yet another notch.[38]

No wonder the collection of child support is such a stubborn problem in modern America. We've been cracking down for years, but despite serious federal and state efforts to strengthen child support enforcement mechanisms and punish delinquent fathers— sometimes with prison terms—the number of deadbeat dads has declined only slightly since 1978. The fact is, we don't need a bigger crackdown—we need a new approach.

Demoralized by the Media

ELAINE: Will they live here after they get married?
ROBIN: Who?
ELAINE: Holly and that nice young man—what is his name?
ROBIN: Oh, Abe. Well, I'm not too sure she wants to marry him.
ELAINE: A pregnant girl. What's she, crazy? She should grab him.
ROBIN: Well, it's not really his baby.
ELAINE: So what? She still should grab him. Believe me, I know what she's going to have to go through. You know, I'm a feminist too. I was a single mother after your father left. You think that was easy? I even voted for Carter twice. But you can't fight nature. God knows, you girls keep trying. Treating your men like side dishes you stick your fork in when needed, just like they used to treat us.
ROBIN: Mother, who am I treating? Do you see a man here anywhere?
ELAINE: No, I don't, and I think it's a problem.[39]

Popular culture increasingly portrays men as redundant and expendable. Movies such as *Thelma and Louise, Boys on the Side,* and *Waiting to Exhale* show strong, vital women battling the odds—moving to new cities, coping with professional setbacks, dealing with AIDS, having babies—and in the process shedding a series of unappealing, inadequate men. Listen to Savannah, one of the main characters in *Waiting to Exhale:* "A long time ago I asked God to send me a decent man. I got Robert, Cedric, Daryl, and Kenneth. God's got some serious explaining to do. So my prayers got more detailed, like how about some compassion, could he have a sense of purpose, a sense of integrity, could he listen, and the truth is most men are deaf. They'd prefer to guess what you need, but they don't guess worth shit. They live without a conscience. What they're best at is convincing us that we should feel desperate. Thank God I don't fall for that shit."[40]

Given the messages coming out of the media, it is increasingly difficult for men to derive much self-esteem or security from the roles of husband and father. Sitcoms and celebrities remind men of how very superfluous they have become. In a famous 1992 episode, the television character Murphy Brown joyously chose single motherhood. Around the same time, the movie star Michelle Pfeiffer gave an interview in which she explained why she had decided to adopt a child on her own: "Men are like pinch hitters. So what's the deal?" Should she conceive or adopt? She reviewed the pros and cons: "I thought about all my options, and certainly one of those options was to just have a baby with somebody, which I guess is the obvious option. But when it came right down to it, I just couldn't do it. I thought, I don't want some guy in my life forever who's going to be driving me nuts."[41]

At least in the entertainment industry, men are often not considered valuable as either husbands or fathers but as irresponsible "side dishes" whose presence is largely irrelevant to real life. Gloria Steinem's quip that "a woman needs a man like a fish needs a bicycle" has become part of conventional wisdom in Hollywood.

Black Men: The Special Targets

The war against dads has been particularly hard on black men. African Americans are still living in the shadows of slavery, which utterly demolished the male protector/provider role and the pride, dignity, and strength that came with it. Black males are thus especially susceptible to the belief that they are disposable and dispensable. Black boys growing up are used to hearing that "black men ain't shit, they ain't never going to be shit, and you are just like your daddy."[42]

It is important to remember that slavery, like its modern descendant, AFDC/TANF, had distinctly different effects on men and women. Even under slavery, females were able to fulfill their most elemental gender-specific role: they could be mothers and nurse their babies. Males, however, were completely stripped of their identity as men. One of their basic roles—to provide—was assumed by the white master. Their other basic function—to protect—was something they were utterly powerless to do against the white man's overwhelming force. As a society, we have never "focused on the gender-specific, for-men-only psychological devastation of these facts."[43] Many of the emasculating features of slavery were perpetuated under Jim Crow and carried over into the modern era courtesy of AFDC/TANF. We rarely recognized how "welfare," a set of programs that render men redundant and cut husbands and fathers out of the loop, recalls and renews the deep wounds of slavery.

Slavery and its aftermath show us what can happen if we do not attend to the anguish of husbands and fathers. The unique trajectory of black males has produced a rich tradition of dignity and strength under adversity, but it has also encouraged fragile men to ward off obliteration through a mix of posing and posturing, machismo and gratuitous violence. It is hard for wounded egos to deal with pain and loss. To admit hurt is to succumb to weakness. To lay bare one's sorrow is to let down one's guard on treacherous terrain.

In the 1990s, white men are beginning to understand what it means to be irrelevant and redundant, what it feels like to experience invisible pain. As employers, government, and the culture increasingly move against husbands and dads, men everywhere are being crippled. When it comes to husbands and dads, the African-American experience prefigures the contemporary mainstream experience—and the results are devastating.

In Search of Comfort

So what are these crippled men doing with their despair? In the 1990s, millions of demoralized, displaced dads understand what the score is. Increasingly alienated from a secular culture that denies the legitimacy of their pain, they are newly convinced that no one is listening except God. This helps explain why we are seeing such an explosive growth in movements of male spirituality and solidarity. Well over 800,000 men attended the Million Man

March, sponsored by the Nation of Islam, in October 1995, and in that same year, 825,000 men attended Promise Keeper events in sports stadiums around the country. In huge numbers, men are seeking solace in brotherhood and turning inward to their gods. Jesus or Allah might just come through for them in a way that is increasingly problematic for employers, government, and the media.

The political arena has not always been so bereft of support or succor. Earlier in this century, men turned to Congress and to trade unions for help, and help was forthcoming. Government policy—specifically the Works Project Administration and the GI Bill—put men back to work, and the labor movement both protected the family wage and effectively increased the share of national income going to workers.

Times have clearly changed. In modern-day America, fathers are either ignored or reviled by those who wield power. In some instances, dads are scorned or even demonized, but more often they just don't figure in our national conversation, as they are no longer seen as relevant. In movies such as *Boys on the Side,* husbands and fathers are most definitely shoved to the side. This is a film that celebrates a much more fashionable theme: solidarity among women. Similar messages can be found in government policy. President Clinton's 1996 welfare reform bill hardly mentioned fathers, except as the source of additional monies. They are simply not regarded as being "in the loop," and they are therefore treated as extraneous to the serious issues at hand.

When the anguish of crippled men is not addressed in the public square but is siphoned off into spiritual movements, it makes for a risky future. The needy men who are drawn to Promise Keepers and the Nation of Islam are ripe for the picking. As we shall see in Chapter 7, both movements are tremendously isolated from the mainstream culture and are therefore susceptible to extreme political elements. This is not good for our democracy. It therefore behooves those of us committed to democratic processes and progressive agendas to pay attention to the enormous load of pain borne by men in contemporary society.

We see the male yearning of men connectedness as a tremendous window of opportunity, and we are particularly aware of the potential inherent in mobilizing these men in a national parenting movement. If we can create the conditions that allow many more men to become loving, attached fathers, we can underpin the lives of children, anchor men much more firmly in productive lives, and greatly enhance our store of social capital. In the last chapters of this book, we turn to the challenge of crafting a Parents' Bill of Rights that both creates a huge level of new support for adults raising children and pulls fathers in as equal and honored partners.

But first let us take a look at the movements in which men are seeking solace, for they can teach us a great deal about what moves men's souls. They also point to the dangers posed by forcing men to take their agony—and their need for comfort—to a space on the margins of our democracy.

SEVEN

Escape Routes:
Promise Keepers and the
Nation of Islam

IN NOVEMBER 1995, we spent a day talking with a small group of fathers who belonged to Promise Keepers and the Nation of Islam, in order to explore what membership in these movements meant to these men. As the day wore on, we found ourselves interacting intensely with two of them: Marcus Glover, a twenty-eight-year-old graphic designer who joined the Nation when he was a student at Howard University, and Jim Papathomas, a thirty-four-year-old first-generation Greek American who became involved in Promise Keepers some two years earlier. These were the highlights of a remarkable four-way conversation.

CORNEL WEST: Marcus, why did you join the Nation?

MARCUS GLOVER: Because I felt that Minister Farrakhan had great expectations of me as a black man and that my community was counting on me. He was able to show me that God's standards, not the mediocre standards of the world, should be the focus of my life. The strong sense of community in the nation was very compelling and helped me figure out how to be a black man in a treacherous age. The solidarity and support are deep. Take the Million Man March. It was like nothing else I have ever experienced—it was one of the happiest days of my life. Visually, the impact was incredible. The eye is simply not used to it. Endless ranks of black men stretching far into the distance. It was unreal, especially when I got to mingle and noticed how these men were treating one another. Men were smiling and hugging when they did not even know each other's name. It got me thinking about what we are used to: the tension, the animus, the naked violence between us black men. This is what we expect to see.

What I mainly saw at this gathering was black men trying to hold themselves to different standards—to higher standards. Black men newly willing to hold themselves accountable—to their god, to their women, to their children. I guess this is what the Nation means to me.

CORNEL WEST: The march was extraordinary. I will never forget standing on that podium, looking out at this great surging river of black humanity. The scars and bruises these men bore on their souls showed in their faces. Upturned, uplifted faces, drinking in the spirit of the speeches, hungry for hope and vision.

SYLVIA ANN HEWLETT: How about you, Jim—why did you join Promise Keepers?

JIM PAPATHOMAS: I am pulled in as a Christian, and I am pulled in as a father and a husband. What I mostly get from Promise Keepers events is support from other men. It's hard to describe the power of it. Last time, sitting in front of me was this fellow with a ponytail and a Harley jacket. I probably would not have run into him any other place. I was so inspired, I picked up my cell phone right then and there and called my wife. I said, "Listen to this—fifty thousand men singing their hearts out, joining hands and praising God." I met a few men there—a student from Lynchburg, Virginia, a pastor from New York—whom I pray for every day now.

CORNEL WEST: What is going on out there in the world that makes affirmation and solidarity so important right now?

JIM PAPATHOMAS: This movement helps me find a way to build a strong family in an age where everything seems to be disintegrating. It's a jungle out there. The downsizing, the layoffs—they get to you. My company's going through it, and no one's job is safe this time around.

MARCUS GLOVER: I share with my brothers in Promise Keepers this fear about what is happening in the workplace. There is a huge level of insecurity out there. Now, being a college graduate, I have a good job working in the graphics department of a publishing company. But it's a small department, and just this year there have been several layoffs. Coworkers that I know well, real productive people, have just been pushed out. There is no good reason I can see, since the company's doing well. Anyhow, the effect on me is lots of stress and anxiety. Will my job be there tomorrow when I walk into the office? What will I do if I lose my job, what with a new baby and Tracy not working? Out of choice, that is—we made the decision that she be at home for the first few years of our son's life.

SYLVIA ANN HEWLETT: Are the top managers at your company also getting fired?

MARCUS GLOVER: Are you kidding? The perks are getting more ridiculous, not less. Just last week when I was parking my car in the office parking lot, the chairman just happened to pull in right alongside of me. He was driving a brand-new $200,000 Bentley. He has also recently moved into a $4 million home. It makes no sense that a few can live in such incredible luxury when so many people are hurting.

CORNEL WEST: Are the battles out there mostly economic, mostly centered in the workplace?

JIM PAPATHOMAS: I guess not. Most of us guys are dealing with a strong anti-male bias in the secular culture. There's a broken record out there: men are part of the problem, men should be more like women, men are no good, men are expendable. I think that a lot of guys—and I'm one of them—have learned to hate these messages.

SYLVIA ANN HEWLETT: Part of the problem is that feminists—and I include myself here—have a deep suspicion of religion, because throughout history it has been used to control and terrorize women.

JIM PAPATHOMAS: But that's not what this movement is about. Listen, this is what Promise Keepers tells men to do: show your feelings, communicate a lot, treat your wife with love and respect, spend a lot of time with your kids, say you're sorry when you make a mistake, keep your commitments, and remember that the real important place is in the home, not the workplace or the athletic field. Does this sound oppressive?

SYLVIA ANN HEWLETT: No, it sounds a lot like what women in the feminist movement have been telling men to do for a long time. But how do we know there isn't some other agenda?

CORNEL WEST: It could be that this is cloaking language to cover the fact that what this movement is about is reasserting male control: I own my woman, my children, my home.

JIM PAPATHOMAS: I can't say anything official for the Promise Keepers, but I can speak for myself, and I'm not trying to control or own anyone. Right now I'm struggling with how to be a good husband and father and remain a strong man, and I think servant-hood is the key. Let me tell you a story. Just last week I was talking with two coworkers, both divorced women in their forties. I tried to explain how a man could both head up his family and serve his family. They started off pretty suspicious of my whole approach, saying, 'Don't tell me that. Don't tell me that the man has to be the boss.' But what I explained to them over the course of half an hour was that as Christ is head of the Church, so a man is head of the family. What was Christ? Christ was a servant. He came and he provided. He came and he died. He came and gave himself for the betterment of humanity. That is what we Promise Keepers mean when we talk about male leadership: we men are supposed to be man enough to give our best energies to our families. We are sup-posed to put our wives and children first. We're committed to finding out what our wife's expectations are and then doing every-thing in our power to meet them—not just physical and financial needs, but also spiritual and emotional needs. It's a small example, but if my wife has had a frustrating day at work, I take a step back and really try to listen to her and respond to her needs, regardless of how tough my day has been.

CORNEL WEST: I, for one, am sympathetic to this servanthood model of male leadership. It can be profoundly different from a patriarchal one. The notion that the strongest man is the one who serves the most is powerful.

MARCUS GLOVER: But in trying to be strong men, we are not only up against the culture, we are also up against the government. I can't help but see a connection between government policies and what's happened to the African-American family, particularly husbands and fathers.

First there was slavery, with its practice of breaking up black families, selling off the kids one by one, splitting up the parents. Now, this system wasn't imposed from outside, it was sanctioned and supported by our own government.

In the modern age we have welfare, not slavery, but it serves the same purpose. The government hands out some benefits to needy families, but only on one condition: that husbands and fathers leave the home. I know mothers who are forced to deny that they have husbands, forced to pretend that their children don't have fathers, in order to survive. This crazy system was set up and paid for by our government. It doesn't make any sense unless you believe, as I do, that it has another purpose—to keep us black folk weak and divided against one another.

Politicians don't seem to focus on these problems. Is it that they don't see the patterns or they don't value the victims? Whatever the reason for the blindness, it is difficult to deny the results. It's as though this country has had an official policy, one that goes back two hundred years, to break up the African-American family and destroy African-American men.

CORNEL WEST: So how can the Nation undo this damage?

MARCUS GLOVER: We look to ourselves. The key to the Nation is self-discipline. When you join the Nation, you have to stop all kinds of bad behavior: drinking, smoking, fornication. When I was rootless and confused, this helped ground me. It helped me become a responsible person, and it can help others.

These two young people had never met before—indeed, before this meeting they knew very little about each other's organization—yet the commonalities are striking. Job insecurity and managerial greed were a drumbeat in our conversation, and so was the hostility of the wider society. Marcus Glover stressed the onslaught on government, while Jim Papathomas stressed the onslaught of the culture. These men and others in the group seemed thoroughly in touch with the all-out war our society has waged against husbands and fathers. They also shared another sentiment: the only refuge in these treacherous times is their faith—and their brothers. They have given up on politics and on our democracy.

Shea Stadium, 1996

Bill McCartney's voice is hoarse and urgent as he addresses the crowd in Shea Stadium. Sometimes he bellows, sometimes he whispers. But whatever the decibel count, he holds this audience of 35,000 men in the palm of his hand. A hushed fervor fills the stadium. Men are weeping openly, linking hands, and hugging one another. Men with tears streaming down their faces unashamedly shout out, "Jesus, Jesus, we love you!" Others, raising their arms in an ecstasy of praise, attempt to touch the face of God.

This is a guy thing. No women are allowed, except in the press box and as volunteers on the concession stands. Guys are doing all the things they normally do at a game—eating hot dogs and performing the wave cheer. And they are doing stuff guys normally don't do, like weeping and listening to sermons. The Reverend Thomas Goodhue, of the United Methodist Church of Bay Shore, is impressed. "These Promise Keepers get guys to pay sixty dollars a head to be told they need to shape up as husbands and fathers. I take my hat off to them."[1]

The theme of this September event was "Breaking Down the Walls" between men and women, between blacks and whites. And at least one of the speakers had hands-on advice. At two-thirty on Saturday afternoon, Bishop Washington Boone dealt with the issue of "Coming Through for Your Family." His session began with a film clip shown on a huge screen deep in the outfield. The ingredients were all too familiar. A husband, preoccupied with a stressful job, ignores his wife. He rarely listens to what she has to say and fails to find time to do anything with her. Her frustration escalates. When she finally loses her cool and screams at him, he doesn't know where her anger is coming from and can't deal with it. Husband and wife retreat and withdraw. The next incident pushes them even further apart. They seem headed for a divorce.

As the film clip faded away, Boone, an African-American minister from Atlanta, strode up to the podium and challenged the men in the audience. "When last did you spend a whole day with your wife? Does your son see you as a role model? Does your daughter want to marry a guy like you? If your kids won't listen to you and your wife feels ignored, more than likely you're just not putting in the time. Your walk needs to match your talk when it comes to family. How you relate to your wife and kids is the first fruits of your relationship with God, and you need to hold yourself accountable."

At this event, Bill McCartney, the founder and CEO of Promise Keepers, handled the issue of race himself. In a noontime interview, he spoke with passion of his desire to commit his ministry to reconciliation between the races and how this challenge is "near and dear to the heart of God." He told us how he was going about his mission: "I figure that you can't generate trust through the mail or on the phone, so this last year I visited forty-seven cities and sat down and talked to clergy who are men of color and tried to listen and learn. I now believe that the central problem is not blatant racism—that is relatively rare—but rather a pervasive spirit of racial superiority on the part of white folk and a profound insensitivity to the pain and the damage this has wrought. Persons of color need to understand Anglos in order to succeed. Anglos, for their part, have no need to understand black and brown folks. And when men and women of color fail to become comprehensible—or fully human—to white folk, it becomes easier to hold them down."[2]

If one emphasis of the Shea Stadium rally was interracial unity, the attendees reflected that goal. Men of color made up about a quarter of the crowd, and portions of the program were conducted in Spanish and in Korean. A high point of the rally was the Saturday press conference that McCartney conducted with forty African-American and Latino pastors from the New York area. Together they pledged to confront racial hatred by changing the hearts of men and seeking forgiveness and reconciliation. Jerome Green, a pastor from the Bronx, was both elated and depressed by the press conference: "Hey, man, this is historic. These cats have taken this issue of racism by the horns. I'm proud to be here with my brothers, black and white. Getting these guys together ain't easy. But how come the press didn't show up at this press conference? I'll tell you why. It's because something good is going on. The press is only interested when we're acting up as predators or hoodlums."[3] Green was exaggerating—a little. The religious press was there, as were a smattering of reporters from local newspapers. But there was no sign of the *New York Times,* the major TV networks, or the national newsmagazines—all of which are based in the Big Apple.

The Super Bowl of Christianity

Despite the fact that over the last six years close to 3 million men have participated in Promise Keepers events, the establishment continues to have a hard time taking this movement seriously. Accounts of Promise Keepers meetings have filtered through to the mainstream press, but there is a tendency to dismiss them as anti-abortion, anti-gay happenings on the lunatic right, a reaction that is condescending and simplistic. It may also constitute a major political blunder, for progressive groups need to take Promise Keepers seriously. Not only has this organization grown by leaps and bounds—membership has leveled off recently, but between 1991 and 1996 Promise Keepers was the most rapidly growing movement of our times—but it is remarkably supportive of parental energies.

Eight years ago, Promise Keepers did not even exist; its first conference, in July 1991, drew a mere 4,200 men. But its growth has been exponential. The organization now has an annual budget of $87 million and 360 paid staff members.[4] During 1996, 1.5 million men attended Promise Keepers conferences in twenty-two cities. These conferences, two-day gatherings of song, sermonizing, prayer, and meditation, for which attendees pay $50 to $70, are the focal point of the organization's activities. They are described as "The Super Bowl of Christianity," or as "equal parts religious revival, inspirational pep talk, and spiritual support group."[5]

Promise Keepers conferences are usually held in giant outdoor football stadiums and incorporate elements of traditional Christian worship as well as activities more commonly found at college ball games. The biggest event to date, "Stand in the Gap," held in Washington, D.C., on October 5, 1997, involved approximately 700,000 men in a religious happening that stretched a mile along the Mall from the Capitol past the Washington Monument. Observers described the power of the scene: hundreds of thousands of Christian men hugging, singing, and repenting for their own sins and those of a secular and socially troubled America. "They fasted and confessed to one another inside canvas prayer teepees set up on the Mall . . . The throng fell almost silent as one speaker directed the men to prostrate themselves while holding photographs of family members they had mistreated . . . The first of many prayers from the stage came from a messianic Jew who blew a traditional ram's horn or shofar. He was followed by gospel choirs and Indian, African-American, Asian, and Hispanic preachers."[6]

Promise Keepers aims to use religious faith to restore and revitalize personal relationships, and its leaders are committed to teaching men how to be newly responsible to God and to their wives and children. At the heart of the movement is the mission of creating "men of integrity" who will commit to living more godly lives by keeping seven promises: honoring Jesus Christ through worship, prayer, and obedience; pursuing vital relationships with a few other men; practicing spiritual, moral, ethical, and sexual purity; building strong marriages and families through love, protection, and biblical values; supporting the church by giving both time and resources; reaching beyond racial and denominational barriers to demonstrate the power of biblical unity; and influencing the world through being obedient to the commandments of Christ.

Promise Keepers bears the unmistakable stamp of Bill McCartney, a former University of Colorado football coach. McCartney, a deeply religious man of passionate intensity, was raised Catholic but in 1974, at the age of thirty-four, was "born again" as a Protestant fundamentalist. In 1982 he became Colorado's head coach, and in less than a decade he turned what had been a losing, deeply troubled football team into national champions. However, the long hours and relentless demands of big-time collegiate football took their toll on his personal life. As he wrote in his autobiography, *From Ashes to Glory,* "My obsession with winning at football caused me to often neglect the important things in my life—my wife, my kids, and my relationship with God."[7] By 1990, his marriage was on the rocks and his daughter had recently given birth to the first of two out-of-wedlock children. Such personal anguish could not have been far from McCartney's mind when the idea of Promise Keepers first occurred to him, while he was driving with a friend to a Fellowship of Christian Athletes meeting one afternoon in March of that year. He had a vision of Folsom Field, the stadium in Boulder where the University of Colorado plays its home games, filled to capacity with men honoring Jesus Christ and learning how to become "men of integrity."

McCartney's personal history helps explain his commitment to reconciliation, both between men and women and between blacks and whites. As a football coach, he worked in one of the few truly integrated areas of American life. For years he recruited heavily among the poor and minorities, and his two grandchildren are interracial, born of his daughter's relationships with football players who were men of color, one black and the other Samoan. McCartney's family problems also help explain the emphasis on rededication to marriage and family that is so central to the Promise Keepers message.

Promise Keepers has undeniably changed the lives not just of the men who attend the rallies but of their families as well. As Alethea Bickell of Wichita, Kansas, says, "Before [my husband] went to Promise Keepers, I had filed for divorce—it was that bad. But something dramatic occurred. I sent a frog [to the conference] and got back a prince."[8]

Much of the thinking behind this magical transformation is contained in a slim volume by Glenn Wagner called *Strategies for a Successful Marriage: A Study Guide for Men,* which is widely used by Promise Keepers. The central premise of this book is that most divorces are predictable and avoidable. It challenges "men of integrity" to head off marital breakdown with its attendant agonies by adopting the following principles:

1. Love your mate *with total commitment.* God intended that "a man leaves his father and his mother and cleaves to his wife, and they become one flesh." (Genesis 2:24, Ephesians 5:31). Marriage entails forsaking all other loves—including self-love. Try to become a man who actively and unashamedly glues himself to his wife. God puts this responsibility for stick-to-itiveness upon the husband.

2. Love your mate *with complete acceptance.* Christ sees men and women as holy and blameless, "without stain or wrinkle or any other blemish" (Ephesians 5:27). This is how we should view our mates—we should accept them without reservation. There is no greater need among wives than to know their husbands accept them unconditionally—no matter how they look or cook, how they walk or talk, or how many wrinkles, layers or pounds they have gained.

3. Love your mate *with no strings attached.* God's love is delivered to us without demanding readiness or reciprocity on our part. This is how we should love our wives—we should give affection and support freely, without thought of what we will receive in return. Men should find out what their wife's expectations are—financial, physical, spiritual and emotional—and then commit to doing everything within their power to meet them. Discern what she wants and then subjugate your desires to hers.

4. Love your mate *with generous praise.* Tell your wife you love her on a daily basis. Praise her publicly, praise her privately, praise her in front of the children. Be creative in your praise. Be specific and concrete in your praise.
5. Love your mate *through explicit action.* Husbands tend to believe that it is enough to demonstrate love through hard work, by bringing home the paycheck. But our wives are looking for little acts of consideration. For example, do chores no one likes: fold the laundry, clean the bathtub.
6. Love your mate *by spending time together.* Time is a gift from God entrusted to our care for us to invest wisely. Pay tribute to the importance of your wife by giving her the gift of time. Make space for her, make room for her, every day of your life.[9]

This kind of advice sits well with many wives. According to John Reinhart, a Promise Keeper from Minnesota, "My wife is really behind [this movement]. We've been married nineteen years, and after this last year there are things that she saw me make a priority which she would like to have seen nineteen years ago. They're finally there."[10] Brad Kammerzelt, a forty-one-year-old Oregon logger and veteran of several Promise Keepers events, credits the movement with improving his relationship with his wife: "[Promise Keepers] taught me to look out for [my wife's] needs, to address her needs rather than just thinking about my own. And the more I give to her, the more she wants to give back to me."[11] And Madeleine Cialella, of Waterbury, Connecticut, noticed a comparable transformation in her husband after he attended a Promise Keepers conference: "My husband came home [from the conference] with a patience he never had, listening and understanding. I give God the glory."[12]

The Appeal of Promise Keepers

What is it about Promise Keepers that both attracts such large numbers of men and provokes such profound responses among many of them? First and foremost, the movement speaks to the deepening insecurities of men's lives. Jim Papathomas described how he struggles "with new types of risk at home and at work," contrasting his situation with that of his father. "Work was hard for Dad, even backbreaking, but he could count on his boss, and his position in the family was unchallenged. It didn't matter that he wasn't the most sensitive guy in the world. He showed his love through being a good provider."[13]

For Papathomas, the securities of this traditional world have crumbled. His sister and two cousins have recently divorced—the first divorces in the history of his family—and holiday get-togethers are sprinkled with talk of embittered ex-husbands and abandoned children. At the same time, the workplace has ceased to be a safe haven. For the last ten years, Papathomas has worked in the marketing department of an insurance firm. His sales figures look great and he has given loyal service, yet he's running scared. His company has downsized in recent years, and the sales force has shrunk from 20,000 to 8,000. Every day he deals with the anxiety that he might be the next person in line to be fired.

Papathomas described how becoming a Promise Keeper has helped him deal with the uncertainties of his life: "I use the energy generated by this movement, particularly the male bonding, to reaffirm my faith and reconnect to God." He talked about how he and four other Promise Keepers formed a prayer group in his workplace. "There are just five of us in my company, me and four other brothers in Christ. We are of different racial backgrounds and belong to different churches and would never have found each other had it not been for Promise Keepers. We often meet midmorning and say a prayer together. It takes just a few minutes, but it soothes and uplifts the soul." According to Papathomas, this spiritual bonding with other men "gives me the wisdom to value my wife and children in ways that strengthen my relationship with them. That is a measure of security."[14]

Criticism of Promise Keepers

Over its short lifespan, the Promise Keepers movement has attracted virulent criticism. Some of the attacks have been directed at McCartney, an outspoken opponent of both gay rights and abortion. McCartney publicly supported Amendment 2, a 1992 Colorado state ballot proposal that would have overturned any state or local law protecting homosexuals from discrimination; he has also been a frequent speaker at pro-life rallies. However, the Promise

Keepers organization takes no position on abortion, and although its literature does maintain that homosexuality is a sin that "violates God's creative design for a husband and a wife," it also states that gays are "included and welcomed in all our events."[15]

McCartney's stance on these sensitive issues is not ours (we align ourselves firmly with progressive folk who have fought recent attempts to diminish or destroy homosexual rights or the legal right to an abortion) but it does help explain why Promise Keepers is generally thought to be heavily involved with right-wing politics and politicians. Indeed, an undercurrent of intense suspicion often runs through news reports in the liberal press. For example, a 1995 article in the *Washington Post* described Promise Keepers as part of "the pantheon of conservative Christian, morally absolutist cultural and political groups converging in this country." It also claimed that most of the speakers selected to preach at Promise Keepers rallies "are very conservative. A large number would be Republican in their political inclinations, or, if they are not Republican, they would be fiscally conservative."[16]

But the men involved in Promise Keepers take umbrage at the notion that it is anything other than a spiritual movement. "Politics is simply not part of it," said Jeff Metzger, a New Jersey pastor. "Speaking from personal experience, it's not part of what I take from it. If you go looking for that bias, you might find a few statements along the way that resonate to a right-wing sensibility . . . but that is not what this movement is about for me." Jim Papathomas agreed, arguing that "the seven promises are ways of helping and solving problems that politicians cannot touch. The bias of the media might be to describe spiritual movements in political terms, but it's not helpful to describe this movement as Republican or Democrat. It's discouraging to hear commentators talk that way."[17] Indeed, even the *Post* article grudgingly concluded that the men at the Washington event "talked not of politics but about personal struggles to change careers, overcome addictions, handle their anger, or to remain disciplined Christians."[18]

Another charge in the early days of the movement was that it was a platform for angry white men with a thinly disguised racist agenda. Back in 1993 and 1994, the vast majority of those who attended the stadium events were white. But as we found out at Shea Stadium in September 1996, one thing Promise Keepers does now emphasize is reconciliation between the races. The organization's board of directors is headed up by an African American, and nearly half of Promise Keepers' roster of keynote speakers in 1997 were black or Hispanic. Furthermore, at the staff level, the record of the organization in hiring minorities is impressive. At a special Promise Keepers conference for pastors and ministers held in Atlanta in February 1996, the organization paid the expenses (registration fee, hotel bill, and airfare) of 2,000 African-American ministers in an effort to ensure adequate representation from poor black churches. This persistent focus on healing racial divisions seems to be having an effect within the Christian community. In 1994, at the urging of Jack Hayford, a prominent southern California minister who frequently speaks at Promise Keepers events, the all-white leadership of the Pentecostal Fellowship of North America dismantled itself and re-formed as an interracial body.

Charges of right-wing extremism and racism have surfaced fairly regularly, but perhaps the most common criticism of the Promise Keepers movement concerns attitudes toward women. Feminists and their allies on the left are offended by the idea of any group's encouraging men to reassert leadership within the family. But exactly what that term implies for Promise Keepers is a matter of some dispute. To Bill McCartney and many men within the movement, "Leadership is servanthood. For the guy to be the leader means he outserves his wife."[19] But feminist groups find fault with this explanation. According to Rosemary Dempsey, a vice president of the National Organization for Women, "The message . . . that men must take back control of the family, be the head, the boss . . . is a not-very-well-cloaked misogynistic message."[20]

The most frequently cited evidence that the movement is pushing a patriarchal agenda is contained in a book by Dr. Tony Evans entitled *Seven Promises of a Promise Keeper.* In a section called "Reclaiming Your Manhood," Evans writes, "I'm not suggesting that you *ask* [your wife] for your role back, I'm urging you to *take* it back. If you simply ask for it, your wife is likely to say, 'Look, for the last ten years, I've had to raise these kids, look after the house, and pay the bills . . . You think I'm just going to turn everything back over to you?' Your wife's concerns may be justified. Unfortunately, however, there can be no compromise here. If you're going to lead, you must lead. Be sensitive. Listen. Treat the lady gently and lovingly. *But lead!*"[21]

It is difficult to read this passage without picking up a strong undertow of male arrogance, and it is this passage that has caused women's groups to protest Promise Keepers conferences. Over the past year, feminists have upped the ante. At its national convention in Memphis in June 1997, the National Organization for Women announced a campaign against Promise Keepers. Members attending the convention overwhelmingly passed a resolution declaring Promise Keepers to be "the greatest danger to women's rights." At the same event, NOW announced the development of an action kit to unmask and publicize the group's "deceptively innocuous agenda." Patricia Ireland, the president of NOW, declared, "I see the Promise Keepers and I am afraid . . . it's a modern-day Women Hater's Club, its he-man members are bent on padlocking women to the stove."[22]

On the face of it, it seems that NOW might find a worthier target than an organization that is working to help men be more virtuous and come through as better husbands, fathers, and citizens. Promise Keepers clearly does call on men to lead their families, but according to many men within the movement (and their wives), the leadership model it offers is not that of a domineering master. As Jim Papathomas pointed out in our round-table discussion, this conception of leadership "comes directly from the example of Christ, who led not by domination but by service and sacrifice." It is a model patterned after the foot-washer from Galilee who said he came "not to be served, but to serve."[23] This notion of servanthood is deeply appreciated by the wives of men in the movement. Cissy Wong, of Houston, Texas, says she lived in a miserable, destructive marriage with her husband, Larry, for fourteen years. After a particularly violent episode, the family pastor took Larry to a Promise Keepers meeting, and today Cissy says that her husband is a reformed character. Indeed, sometimes he is so romantic and attentive that she finds it disconcerting. "Once, he came home and apologized for treating me so badly over the years and said he wanted to wash my feet," she reports. "I let him, but I really thought he had lost it."[24]

But what really is at stake here is not fine-grained distinctions between different models of leadership. The sticking point for liberals resides not in the concrete details of the Promise Keepers movement but in its cultural surround. An influential group on the left balks at any set of ideas that is rooted in religious passion and at any system of beliefs that emphasizes family loyalty over and above individual rights and freedoms.[25] Thus, underlying much of the hostility toward this movement are the huge issues of religiosity and individual identity, particularly women's identity.

If a feminist—or any liberal person, for that matter—were to talk with men like Jim Papathomas, however, she would undoubtedly acquire a richer view of the Promise Keepers movement. Still, it is unclear that such a person would come away with any real empathy or enthusiasm, especially for the notion that Christian servanthood could work for women. Feminists can be intensely secular in their orientation, for understandable reasons. As a result, it is extremely difficult for progressive folks to wrap their minds around the notion that God could be a benign, let alone beneficial, inspirational force in the lives of men and women. At the end of the day, feminists are quite simply not interested in seeing men become more "godlike" in their attitudes and in their relationships.[26]

It is also hard to move away from concepts of individual rights to concepts of family interdependence. Feminism is grounded in a commitment to equal rights and equal opportunities, and it is easy to see how a person who is focused on achieving equality might construe the roles of wife and mother as part of the problem rather than part of the solution. Ever since the early 1960s and the publication of Betty Friedan's *The Feminine Mystique,* an important strand of feminist thought has seen women's family roles as inherently oppressive. For at least some modern feminists, the route to liberation has been bound up with the task of separating from men—and even from children—and establishing autonomous existences. How can we now expect these women to turn around and become vested in the project of establishing a new and better form of interdependence with men?

These questions constitute fundamental barriers that prevent leftists from even listening to what Promise Keepers have to say, let alone establishing any common ground. This is a great pity, for if we are interested in enhancing this nation's store of parenting energies, there is much to work with in the Promise Keepers movement. Despite the best efforts of feminism, single moms are overburdened and struggling; single-mother families are poorer and more violence-prone than two-parent families, and children in these families are at risk in a variety of ways. Even if a mother has constructed a strong independent identity, she is simply better off when living in a stable, loving relationship with the father of her child. It therefore makes sense to work on producing more of these stable, loving relationships. This project may well involve giving a little support and legitimacy to aspects of the Promise Keepers movement that enhance men's willingness to come through for their families.

As columnist Kathleen Parker of the *Orlando Sentinel* points out, "If half a million white guys commit each year to work for racial harmony, to spend more time with their kids, to pray instead of striking out, to work on an imperfect marriage rather than seeking solace on Sunset Boulevard, who's worse off? Maybe I'm missing something, but this sounds like progress to me."[27] One thing is for sure: if liberals, feminists, trade unionists, and other progressive people fail to reach out and respond to the anguish of estranged, isolated men, other groups surely will. And we can probably rely on the fact that these other groups will be on the extreme right. By spurning this movement, the liberal left will push it in the wrong direction.

The Nation of Islam

Promise Keepers is not the only escape route for disaffected husbands and fathers. A measure of the deep alienation felt by contemporary men is that there are now two major movements that respond to their yearning for connection. In recent years, the Nation of Islam has provided solace and inspiration for black men in much the same way as Promise Keepers has for white men (and for an increasing number of men of color). At its best, the Nation serves to affirm the value and integrity of black men and strengthens their resolve to take responsibility for their wives and children.

We first met Marcus Glover at our roundtable discussion. A part-time minister in the Nation's Harlem Temple as well as a graphic designer, Marcus grew up in suburban Westchester County, New York, and went mostly to white schools. Membership in the Nation gave him a sense of identity and self-worth he had searched for but been unable to find elsewhere. "Right from the beginning I loved this notion of being proud of our heritage, of digging into the past and discovering that black people had an impressive history," he says. "I also appreciated the discipline of the Nation. I joined the movement at age nineteen, a point in my life when I desperately needed someone to set firm parameters. In the Nation you are persona non grata if you are caught drinking, lying, or getting bad grades. This was good for me. It was good that someone cared enough to say, 'Get up at five in the morning and pray' or 'Work hard and earn good grades.' The fact is, you can't be a member of the Nation and carry a bad average. What are you in school for if not to better yourself and better your people? This kind of philosophy was something I needed."[28]

Marcus downplays the political component of the Nation's teachings. "The Nation of Islam is not a political organization," he stresses. "It's a religious organization." Asked about the rhetoric of separation that leaders of the Nation frequently employ, he says, "I like to compare it to a problematic marriage. Perhaps the wife feels she has never been listened to, or perhaps she has been abused. But it's not until the woman threatens to leave that the man really focuses and says, 'We can work this out!' It is then that he comes through with the compassion and support. Well, when black people talk about the idea of a separate nation, it is just a threat. The hope is that this will provoke dialogue and responsive action."[29]

Three years ago, Marcus met his wife-to-be, Tracy, and introduced her to the Nation. Since then they have married and had a son. Tracy has an extremely clear sense of what she owes to the Nation. She credits the Nation's support of the traditional family with breaking a pattern of single motherhood in her family that goes back several generations: "I come from three generations of single moms—my mom, my grandmother, and my great-grand-mother all raised their children on their own. So I know how tough it can be—the backbreaking labor, the lonely anxieties. I also know that without the teachings of Elijah Muhammad, Minister Farrakhan, and our own Minister Conrad, we would not have this union, Marcus and I, and I certainly wouldn't have the ability to stay home and care for my baby. Because of the Nation, my husband is motivated to go out and work two jobs so that I can raise our son properly. I am eternally grateful."[30]

The Father of the Nation of Islam

The Nation of Islam was founded in 1930 by W. D. Farad Muhammad, a silk salesman in a poor neighborhood of Detroit. Farad, who claimed to be an Arab born in Mecca, began his ministry by incorporating proselytizing into his door-to-door silk peddling. He urged his customers to adopt certain dietary practices, lecturing them about the Asiatic and African origins of black people and railing against "blue-eyed devils." In 1934, Farad suddenly and mysteriously vanished, and his associate, Elijah Muhammad, took over his fledgling ministry.[31]

Elijah Muhammad, a Georgia-born sharecropper's son with only a third-grade education, led the Nation of Islam until his death, in 1975. Over that time, he accomplished the feat of turning the Nation from a small cadre of believers into a nationwide social and religious movement that had approximately 35,000 followers and ran a variety of business ventures with combined assets of as much as $100 million. Today, followers of the Nation consider Elijah a divinely appointed messenger of God, sent to deliver his word to African Americans.

Although Elijah remained the Nation's leader throughout his life, during the 1950s and early 1960s his national spokesman, Malcolm X, was the figure most often publicly identified with the group. However, Malcolm gradually drifted toward more orthodox Islam and eventually broke with the Nation. Seven months after leaving the group, in 1965, he was assassinated. A number of people have accused the current Nation of Islam leader, Louis Farrakhan, of involvement in the murder, and Farrakhan has admitted that his public condemnations of Malcolm may have encouraged the assassins. But he adamantly denies any involvement and now celebrates Malcolm's genius.

Shortly before his death, Elijah designated one of his sons, Warith Deen Mohammed, as the heir to the leadership of the Nation. Within a year, Warith broke with his father's teachings. Declaring that Elijah was not a divine prophet, he oriented the group toward a more orthodox observance of Muslim rituals and ceased preaching the doctrine of the white man as a conspiratorial oppressor. Eventually, Warith changed the group's name to the American Muslim Mission, and today he still leads what has become the largest African-American Muslim group in the country.

This sharp turn away from the teachings of Elijah Muhammad enraged such followers as Louis Farrakhan, who headed the Nation's Harlem Temple after the departure of Malcolm X. Farrakhan quickly broke away from Warith, taking the group's name and a number of its followers with him. Today he leads a Nation of Islam of approximately 100,000 members.

Elijah Muhammad's teachings, which still inspire the new reform views of the Nation, are infused with highly politicized convictions regarding race. Indeed, some claim that Elijah's "primary mission was not religious conversion. His main goal was to develop a group solidarity that could become strong enough to overcome the oppression by whites."[32] He believed that blacks belong to the tribe of Shabazz, which came from space 66 trillion years ago, and that the white race was created 6,000 years ago by a black scientist named Yakub. Yakub, through genetic manipulation, created a number of races that were lighter, weaker, and genetically inferior to the black man. The lowest of this order of races is the Caucasian. The white man turned out to be a liar and a murderer— Elijah Muhammad called such men white devils—but according to Elijah, Allah allowed the Caucasian to dominate the world as a test for the black race. Elijah Muhammad also taught that blacks are Allah's chosen people and will inherit the earth. Naturally enough, white people—and Elijah Muhammad often specified Jews—are anxious to stop black people from achieving this goal. He believed the way out of repression was not integration but self-sufficiency and separation.

In preaching this doctrine, Elijah, like the current ministers of the Nation, drew from both Muslim and biblical sources. For example, he claimed that the tribe of Abraham described in the Old Testament referred not to the ancient Israelites but to modern-day blacks.[33]

It seems safe to assume that many of the more elaborate and fantastical of Elijah's beliefs were intended to be symbolic and allegorical rather than factual in nature. Nevertheless, these beliefs have had a real political effect. Separation from white American society, for example, remains a stated goal of the Nation. The fourth point of "The Muslim Program," printed in the Nation's weekly newspaper, the *Final Call,* reads in part: "We want our people in America whose parents or grandparents were descendants from slaves to be allowed to establish a separate state or territory of their own—either on this continent or elsewhere . . . We believe our contributions to this land and the suffering forced upon us by white America justifies our demand for complete separation in a state or territory of our own."[34]

Despite these ambitious demands, it would be wrong to describe the Nation's aims as purely or even mainly political. Elijah's teachings have immense practical ramifications. He stressed the importance of strict moral conduct and respect for self and family. He prohibited the Nation's members from using drugs, alcohol, and tobacco as well as from eating pork. He preached reverence for the traditional family structure, emphasized personal responsibility and ethics, and urged members to remember that Islam "dignifies" and to take pride in themselves and their race. In other words, the separatist message of the Nation was delivered in conjunction with a powerful appeal to personal morality and responsibility. At least one prominent African-American commentator, Boston University professor Glenn Loury, argues that whatever one thinks of Farrakhan, he is a *religious* leader, speaking to a flock desperate to hear an explicitly spiritual appeal. In fact, the Nation of Islam has a track record of "turning the souls" of a great many underclass men, especially in prisons. In contrast, liberal black political leaders, ironically "drawn substantially from the clergy, have checked their religious fervor at the door of the Democratic party. In coalitions with feminists, gays, and radical secularists, and in reaction against the politics of the religious right, they have muted their voices on spiritual issues, leaving a void in black public life that Minister Farrakhan has adroitly filled."[35]

This brings us to the critical issue of Farrakhan and racism, the primary focus of the mainstream white media. Farrakhan's spiritual and practical contributions to the Nation of Islam and to the larger black community are seriously compromised in the eyes of right-thinking people by anti-Semitism and other forms of racial hatred. (We unequivocally reject any form of racism or anti-Semitism; these sentiments simply have no place in civilized society.) Two examples of incendiary remarks are particularly well known. In November 1993, a Farrakhan aide named Khalid Abdul Mulammad delivered a speech in which he referred to Jews as the "bloodsuckers of the black nation" and called the pope a "no-good cracker." He also urged blacks in South Africa to murder all of that country's whites. Bowing to a storm of public criticism, Farrakhan announced in February 1994 that he had stripped Khalid of all his official duties.[36] However, the banishment appears to have been temporary. In August 1995, an article in the *Final Call* identified Khalid as a minister and representative of the Nation.[37] Then, in a

Reuters interview a few months later, just before the Million Man March, Farrakhan referred to Jewish, Korean, and black business owners as the "bloodsuckers" of inner-city neighborhoods.[38] Such utterances make it difficult to give credence to Farrakhan's positive initiatives.

The Million Man March

When Louis Farrakhan and former NAACP leader Benjamin Chavis, Jr., announced their plans in 1994 to convene a Million Man March in Washington in October 1995, media coverage was generally limited to denunciations of various racist and anti-Semitic public comments that Farrakhan had made. Indeed, in the days leading up to the march, many black public figures and organizations, including Colin Powell and the NAACP, withheld their support, arguing that it was impossible to separate the message from the messenger.

Yet such criticisms were largely swept aside in the wake of what turned out to be an overwhelmingly uplifting event. Between 700,000 and one million black men (depending on whose numbers one believes) gathered together with such a sense of spiritual purpose that only one arrest was reported throughout the day, and those who attended described the experience in a gush of emotional superlatives. As marcher Michael Nelson, a forty-seven-year-old lieutenant-colonel from Virginia, put it, "I was taken in, heart and mind and soul."[39] It turned out that the message did manage to eclipse the messenger. "This event is not about Louis Farrakhan," a thirty-one-year-old Citibank marketer named Rob Bostick explained on the day of the march. "It's about African-American males getting together to talk about issues."[40]

The march was officially billed as "A Holy Day of Atonement and Reconciliation." As Farrakhan explained in August 1995, this atonement was primarily religious, and it was necessary in order to lay the moral foundation among black men for the task of rebuilding the black community: "Our failure to accept the call of Allah (God) to be the responsible heads of our families and community is our principal failure. Therefore, we as a people must atone to Allah (God) for our failure to accept the call to freedom. We, as men, must atone for the abuse of our women and girls, and our failure to be the leaders of and builders of our community. We must atone for the destruction that is going on within our communities; the fratricide, the death dealing drugs, and the violence that plagues us. Our atonement is first to Allah (God) that He may return to us power and dominion to take control of our lives, destiny, and our community."[41]

Reconciliation was something of a secular corollary to atonement—an apology for and a laying aside of grievances between black people and black groups. Farrakhan also saw reconciliation as a means of unifying the black community under a common purpose: "We must reconcile our differences one with the other so that we may face our oppressors as a solid wall of unity."[42]

With this unity in mind—and taking into account the wide range of faiths represented at the march—Farrakhan couched the religious aspects of his appeal in nonsectarian terms. In his speech to the crowd, he urged that "moral and spiritual renewal is a necessity. Every one of you must go back home and join some church, synagogue, temple or mosque that is teaching spiritual and moral uplift . . . The men are in the streets, and we got to get back to the houses of God."[43]

Atonement, reconciliation, and spiritual renewal were not meant to be ends in themselves; rather, they were seen as first steps toward enabling the black community to rebuild itself through the application of personal responsibility, hard work, and discipline, without waiting for assistance from the government or others. As marcher Andre Bundley, a Baltimore middle school principal, put it, "When we look at the ills in our community, if they are going to be corrected, they are going to be corrected by us."[44]

Thus a doctrine of self-help was the key message of the march, one which, as at least a few commentators noted ironically, could as easily have been uttered by a conservative Republican as by Farrakhan. In the words of thirty-four-year-old marcher Joseph Williams, "The message is for black men to hold themselves accountable."[45] Farrakhan wrote in August 1995 that the march was designed in part to show the world a "vastly different picture of the Black male." But he was even more interested in showing black males a different picture of themselves. Self-help is impossible without a measure of self-respect, and while television, movies, and music may contribute to racist stereotypes of black males as "thieves, criminals, and savages," the stereotypes are unlikely to change until black males realize in themselves the capacity for improvement.

Judging from the comments of those who participated, the march may indeed have helped provoke such a transformation. Samuel Herbert, a cancer research technician from Buffalo, summed up the experience in terse words: "A million black men. Not one Uzi. Not one fight. Crying joyful tears. Embracing each other. I have never been so proud as I am today."[46] Deloyd Parker, Jr., the executive director of the Shape Community Center in Houston, put the matter in more collective terms: "We left as one million black men. We returned home as one million black brothers—there's a big difference. This whole thing has helped us conquer the fear of each other and the fear of ourselves."[47]

So powerful was the effect of the march on those who took part in it that Glenn Loury, who initially refused to support it because of Farrakhan's involvement, found himself moved to conversion after spending time mingling among the marchers as they trickled into the capital on the day before the event.

Here were young black guys, the same ones occasionally mistaken by belligerent police officers or frightened passersby for threats to public safety because of the color of their skin and the swagger of their gait, scrambling up the steps and lounging between the columns of the National Gallery building, some even checking out the "Whistler and His Contemporaries" show on display inside. And there were others, sharing an excited expectancy with Japanese tourists and rural whites as we all waited in line to tour the White House. Taking in these various scenes, an obvious but profound thought occurred to me: this is their country, too. So, embarrassed that I needed to remind myself of this fact, I wept.

The next day, as I beheld hundreds of thousands of black men gathering . . . I would be even more deeply moved. Everything that has been said about the discipline and dignity of the gathering, and the spirit of camaraderie that pervaded it, is true. It was a glorious, uplifting day, and I was swept up in it along with everyone else. It almost did not matter what was being said from the podium.[48]

It is still an open question whether the lasting impact of the Million Man March will be as strong as the emotions it initially provoked among the participants. In the days following it, the media—which a week before had been choked with denunciations of Farrakhan—were filled with anecdotes of, if not changed lives, then certainly changed intentions.

Carlotta Pinto, of Los Angeles, reported that her husband, George, called on the night of the march "and began telling me how much he loved me and how much he wanted to make what we had work. He hadn't said that to me in years . . . I haven't heard him this happy in a long time. You wouldn't think one day would do that, but it did."[49] James Stokes III, of Chesapeake, Virginia, told a similar story: "I went home and told my wife that from this day forward I am going to be a better husband and that no matter what, through thick and thin, we are going to be together. I meant it from the bottom of my heart."[50]

An Atlanta businessman, Thomas J. Miller, the owner of a successful tea-distribution company, turned over management of his company to his wife in the wake of the march and volunteered to work full-time at the Southern Christian Leadership Conference, performing public relations duties for the group's gun buy-back and teen mentoring programs.[51] George Blue III, a twenty-four-year-old from Montgomery, Alabama, wasted no time applying his new resolve: in the week after the march, he asked his girlfriend to marry him, enrolled in Tuskegee University, joined the Urban League and the NAACP, and registered to vote.[52]

On a larger scale, the mayor of Detroit, Dennis Archer, used the momentum generated by the march to recruit more than 15,000 volunteers to help prevent violence and arson and enforce a municipal curfew during the Devil's Night unrest that plagues the city every Halloween. For his part, Louis Farrakhan announced after the Million Man March that he would launch a nationwide voter registration drive in conjunction with other black organizations, including the National Coalition on Black Voter Participation.[53]

Common Threads

At first glance, Promise Keepers and the Nation of Islam seem strange bedfellows, but they share a surprising number of attributes, some more obvious than others. First and foremost, both groups understand themselves as spiritual movements, helping men answer such questions as How do I renew myself? How do I transform myself into a more virtuous person? And how do I gain access to the inner strength that will enable me to do that?

Second, both groups seek to affirm men as responsible people, particularly in their roles as providers and protectors of their families. Atonement is a key concept for both Promise Keepers and the Nation. Men are required to recognize their own brokenness and ask forgiveness—for example, to tell their wives they are sorry —before they can expect a renewal of the spiritual energy necessary to reconnect with their god and their families. In their other-directed, religious sensibilities, these movements are profoundly countercultural. This emphasis on atonement and servanthood couldn't be more different from the "rights talk" we are so used to in contemporary America.

Other common threads take us into deeper and more dangerous territory. Both Promise Keepers and the Nation are responding to the huge loss of power experienced by so many men today. The enormous devaluation of men in their family roles and their yearning to reconnect with their wives and their children are the fuel that has fed the fire in both movements. Downsized in the workplace, demonized by government, and brushed aside by the media, millions of American men feel bewildered and bereft, newly in need of consolation. Economic and cultural marginalization is at its most extreme in the black community, where a large portion of young men are either hustled into prisons or lowered into graves. Unfortunately, the black male experience prefigures what is happening to a broad swath of men. Increasingly frustrated by a political establishment that denigrates or denies their pain, millions of regular guys reckon no one is listening except God. These are the men who are turning to Promise Keepers and the Nation for help in repairing their souls and rebuilding their lives. These movements are therefore dealing with needs that are deep and desperate: they are wrestling with nothing less than salvaging male capability in the face of the onslaught of history.

Can Promise Keepers and the Nation of Islam meet this enormous challenge? At the very least, these movements would seem to need help from progressive forces in our society, for how can any spiritual movement bolster blue-collar wages or shorten the work week? As we have seen, structural economic problems are a large part of what disables men. Although these movements need outside energy, however, they are unlikely to get it—or unlikely to get the right kind. In the late 1990s, both Promise Keepers and the Nation of Islam are tremendously isolated. The political mainstream—and in particular, the left—either mocks or reviles them.[54] Thus the desperate energy of the men in these movements is likely to be captured by illiberal, anti-democratic forces on the fringes of our society.

We are not suggesting that the potential for an easy alliance between the reformist left and these two groups exists. But if the leaders of Promise Keepers were to affirm homosexual and women's rights and stay out of the abortion wars, and if the leaders of the Nation of Islam were to repudiate anti-Semitism and patriarchy, it would be a giant step forward. Then it might be possible for progressive folk to pay attention to what is really going on in these movements and to respond constructively. For if we continue to look at Promise Keepers and the Nation of Islam and see only patriarchy reestablished or gay-bashing celebrated, we lose out on a rare opportunity to take the agony of crippled men and turn it into something good: a new commitment to husbandhood and fatherhood. Our nation urgently needs many more men who are willing and able to come through for their families.

We are determined that this precious energy should not be allowed to escape. As we describe in the final section of this book, our dream is to honor the male yearning to reconnect with wives and children and to harness this energy in a parents' movement that gives new value and dignity to both mothers and fathers.

PART IV

Reweaving the Web of Care

EIGHT

....

What Do Parents Want?

DESPITE ALL THE RHETORIC about family values, there are virtually no hard data on what parents, as a constituency, expect or need from government and the community at large. This is surprising, to say the least. Given that we live in an age where Republicans and Democrats expend enormous amounts of energy outshouting each other in a competition to be the "real" proponents of family values, it is astonishing that no one has bothered to ask the views of those on the front lines: mothers and fathers. So we decided to begin our parent empowerment initiative by doing precisely that. Politicians spend a great deal of time talking *about* and *at* parents. We thought it would be a good idea to actually *listen* to them.

In the summer of 1996 we undertook the first ever nationwide poll of parents' political priorities. This survey, which was carried out by the independent pollsters Penn & Schoen under the aegis of the National Parenting Association, was conducted just before the presidential election and targeted the mainstream of American parents—those whose household income falls in the $20,000 to $100,000 range. As an accompanying project, we conducted a series of focus groups among subsets of parents to enrich our understanding of the attitudes and perspectives underlying the survey data. The results of these two exercises are powerful.

The first surprise is that both our poll and our focus groups revealed a remarkable degree of consensus among parents. This is contrary to popular opinion, which tends to see American parents as a group rent by schism. Such a perception is encouraged by politicians, who like to use parents as political footballs in their ideological games, magnifying differences and dividing a constituency that is already weak and vulnerable. Working mothers are set against at-home mothers, moms against dads, urbanites against suburbanites, blacks against whites, and welfare mothers against everyone else (welfare moms are portrayed as a particularly heavy burden on regular American families, pushing taxes up, pulling living standards down).

Despite this conventional wisdom, our data show that once we get away from "hot button" issues such as abortion, there is impressive agreement among parents. On the critical issues that underpin and condition daily life—workplace policy, tax policy, school schedules—there is *enormous unity across race, class, and gender.* It seems that in these central areas, blue-collar and professional parents, African-American and white parents, mothers and fathers, share a set of urgent concerns and are ready to rally behind a common agenda.

What is important to parents is not abortion, gay marriage, prayer in school, or kicking poor mothers and immigrants off the welfare rolls. When push comes to shove, parents are concerned with practical rather than ideological issues and display a great deal of solidarity. For example, middle-class parents want to help rather than hinder those less well off than themselves. Fully 81 percent of moms and dads in our survey are prepared to support policies that would raise wages so that all full-time working parents are able to earn an income above the poverty line. In today's market-driven America, this is a startling, even radical finding.

Given this shared perspective, what are the key pressure points in parents' lives? And what kind of support do they feel will most help them do a better job by their children? We found that across the face of this nation, parents' central and increasingly desperate concern revolves around a time crunch—often provoked by intense economic pressure—which seriously limits their ability to come through for their children. Mothers and fathers battle with what they call "a parental time famine" as they strive to balance the competing demands of work and family in a world newly dominated by shrinking paychecks, lengthening work weeks, and single parenthood. They think it's high time that government and employers stepped in to help them. They don't see why raising children has to be such a lonely and thankless struggle.

The Highlights of Our Survey

The poll results, which are confirmed by our focus group findings, show at the top of parents' wish list a set of policies that deal directly with the parental time famine. (For detailed results, see appendix.) Together, these policies produce the external supports that parents feel would lighten the load and significantly improve their ability to produce more and better time for their children. Parents do not need a policy wonk or a social worker to explain to them that three-week-olds should not be in kennels and that seven-year-olds should not be in self-care. They don't need to read the expert literature to understand that teenagers who are home alone watch trash TV, eat junk food, experiment with sex and drugs, and definitely do not do their homework. But however perceptive their insights or strong their motivation, parents know they cannot solve the problems thrown up by the time crunch and the wage squeeze without the following kinds of support.

Time-enhancing workplace policies

Mothers and fathers, professionals and blue-collar workers, understand that work pressure is at the heart of their struggle to be loving and attentive parents. They would like government and employers to be much more imaginative in creating flexible work arrangements that provide the "gift of time" in an age when they increasingly do not have the option of staying home with the kids. By huge margins, parents want

- Government tax incentives to encourage employers to adopt family-friendly policies that target the time crunch. Fully 90 percent of parents—the vast majority of fathers as well as mothers—would like access to compressed work weeks, flextime, job-sharing, and benefits for part-time work.

- A law guaranteeing three days of paid leave annually for child-related responsibilities such as attending a parent-teacher conference or taking a child to the dentist (favored by 87 percent).

- Legislation allowing workers to take time off instead of extra pay for overtime (favored by 79 percent) and allowing workers to trade two weeks' pay for an extra two weeks of vacation time per year (favored by 71 percent).

- Legislation requiring companies to offer up to twelve weeks of paid job-protected parenting leave following childbirth or adoption (favored by 76 percent). Companies with fewer than twenty-five employees would be exempt.

Relief from the economic burdens of child-rearing

Parents believe that the high cost of raising the next generation—who will, after all, ensure America's future competitiveness and pay our collective social security bill—should not be wholly borne by moms and dads. They understand that the work they do contributes to our national well-being and that it is reasonable to expect some significant support from the public purse. In our focus groups, parents talked a great deal about sagging wages, but they also stressed the importance of job security. In the heartfelt words of one father, "Job security would make a huge difference, instead of having to always worry about whether there will be a job the next day. It would probably make me a better father."[1]

To cope with these crucial problems, parents want, by overwhelming margins,

- Tax breaks to help underwrite a child's education. Ninety-four percent of parents favor federal tax deductions/credits to help pay for schooling (particularly preschool and college) for families earning less than $100,000.
- Tax breaks on children's necessities, such as diapers, car seats, school supplies, and learning tools (favored by 82 percent). This could be done by eliminating state and local sales taxes on these items.
- A tripling of the dependent deduction for children in families with annual incomes under $100,000 (favored by 82 percent). This would bring this deduction up to $6,500 per child, almost precisely the level it was at in the early 1950s.
- The raising of wages to pull all full-time working parents above the poverty line (favored by 81 percent).

A longer school day and school year

Parents are deeply aware of the lack of fit between their own work schedules and children's school schedules. The typical American school is in session six hours a day for at most thirty-two weeks of the year, while Mom and Dad are typically at work nine hours a day for more than fifty weeks a year. This dramatic lack of synchronicity between work and school—which is only getting worse as work weeks lengthen and paid vacation shrinks—produces a situation where more and more kids go home to an empty house. As one working mother described it, the pressures on both parent and child can be intense: "He comes home by himself now, and he's ten. That's a decision I had to make, because I don't get off work until six. He's got his key, his bus pass is attached to his pants, he calls me right away. It's kinda working out, but it's frightening for me."[2] To cope better with circumstances such as these, by large margins parents want a longer school day and school year. Seventy-two percent of parents would like schools to be kept open longer for classes, supervised homework, or extracurricular activities so that school schedules better match the working day.

Overall, the data from our survey are replete with good news. In both the poll results and the focus group findings, parents display a vision that is extremely responsible. They have no desire to offload their kids; on the contrary, they are struggling to take back territory and function. Without necessarily knowing the theory or the jargon, they understand that the parent-child bond is precious and that it is imperiled in new and serious ways. They also realize they need meaningful help if they are to come through with additional effort and energy. They know how much they are overextended, and they are ready to reach out for new kinds of external support.

In addition, parents display a pragmatism that greatly bolsters their case. They are not reaching for the moon but have a measured take on what constitutes the art of the possible in the late 1990s. They recognize, for example, that it might be more acceptable to develop subsidies for parents through the tax code than to create other, more intrusive options that smack of greater government interference in family life. They also understand that in order for middle-class parents to develop a stake in such social supports, it might be necessary to include families with incomes up to $100,000 per year.

Table 1. Parents Unite Across Gender, Race, and Income

		Percent who supported each measure					
	TOTAL	GENDER		RACE		INCOME	
		Men	Women	White	Black	Under $35,000	Over $35,000
Time-pressure measures							
Working flexible hours	91	85	95	90	90	89	90
Matching school and work day and year	72	71	73	70	79	73	73
Economic-pressure measures							
Tax breaks for parents with kids	86	86	85	87	90	82	89
Raising wages above poverty level	81	74	88	78	100	84	80

An Emerging Consensus

But perhaps the most positive piece of news contained within these new data is the dramatic level of unity and consensus among parents, as shown in Table 1.[3] The set of policies described above elicits not lukewarm but overwhelming support from moms and dads; approval rates range from 70 percent to 95 percent. This has enormous implications. If parents across the usual income and demographic divides can unite behind an agenda that addresses the time crunch and the wage squeeze, they have immense potential as a political force. There are, after all, 62 million parents in America, and if they were to come together and speak with one voice, they could wield great influence in the corridors of power.

Specific Concerns and Priorities

Beyond the overarching worries triggered by the time crunch and the wage squeeze, parents share some specific anxieties. Crime, drugs, and the quality and cost of education are at the top of the list. Although parents are somewhat concerned about a decline in "family values," a rather small proportion of them worry over the high-profile items on the conservative agenda: abortion, homosexual marriage, and the like.

The survey sought to probe parental opinion on specific issues in

Table 2. Parental Concerns

QUESTION: Speaking as a parent, what are your biggest concerns or worries for your children? (Open-ended—up to three responses allowed)

	Percent mentioning concern
Crime/violence/gangs/safety	30
Drugs	21
Quality of schooling	17
Paying for preschool/schooling & college	15
Declining family/moral values	14
Providing opportunities	7
Health/AIDS	5

two ways, by asking open-ended questions and by requiring parents to rank-order a list of issues. To find out what was on their minds, the survey asked respondents, "Speaking as a parent, what are your biggest concerns or worries for your children?" To ensure a broad range of ideas, up to three responses were allowed. Table 2 lists the concerns that were mentioned by at least 5 percent of respondents.

Just as significant as what is on the list is what is not on it. A whole array of issues often identified as family values simply do not appear. These include teenage sex and pregnancy (mentioned by 3 percent), TV and movie sex (mentioned by 1 percent), and welfare (mentioned by 1 percent). What is more, not a single parent in the sample spontaneously brought up abortion or homosexuality as a major problem area when asked about significant concerns for his or her children.

To arrive at the second measure of parents' concerns, the poll asked respondents to consider whether two groups of ideas would be helpful or not to American parents (see Table 3). The first group focused on crime, the workplace, and education. Laws limiting the accessibility of guns are considered extremely helpful by more than two thirds of parents and helpful by over four fifths—responses that are in line with our findings about the centrality of crime and violence in parents' worries. Turning to the workplace, some 60 percent say flexible hours would be very helpful; this measure also receives the highest absolute level of support, 91 percent. Raising wages to put all full-time workers above the poverty level is also seen as extremely helpful by 81 percent of parents. On the tax front,

Table 3. Parents' Priorities

QUESTION: For each idea, please tell me whether you think it would be extremely helpful, helpful, not very helpful, or not at all helpful to American parents and families.

	Extremely Helpful %	Helpful %	Not Helpful %
Group 1			
Laws to keep guns away from children	69	81	17
Letting parents work flexible hours in their jobs	60	91	8
Raising wages so that all full-time workers are above the poverty level	60	81	17
Increasing tax deductions/credits for parents with children	45	86	13
Making the school day and year more in sync with the work day and year	38	72	25
Group 2			
Banning marriages among people of the same sex	29	40	51
Making divorce laws punish adultery in awarding support and child custody	22	55	39
Using tax dollars to help parochial schools	22	53	43
Cutting off welfare payments after two years to mothers who can't find a job	20	44	50
Making abortion illegal	15	28	61

an overwhelming majority (86 percent) would like to see increased tax deductions/credits for parents with children, while on the education front nearly three fourths approve of making the school day and year better in sync with the working day and year.

The results were quite different for the second group of issues, which contained items often stressed by advocates of family values. Only 29 percent of parents think banning homosexual marriage would be extremely helpful for families. In fact, the parents who think it would be unhelpful (51 percent) substantially outnumber those who consider it helpful (40 percent). Only about one fifth are strongly in favor of reconstituting our divorce laws to take "fault" into consideration when awarding support and child custody, although more than half do support such a measure. In a similar vein, just over one fifth find the idea of using tax dollars to underwrite parochial schools extremely helpful for families, although a majority find this helpful. Turning to welfare reform, only 20 per-

Table 4. Parents' Priorities

QUESTION: In general, which set of ideas do you think would be more helpful to parents and families, Group 1 or Group 2?

	Group 1 %	Group 2 %
All parents	77	16
Gender		
Men	74	17
Women	79	15
Race		
White	76	17
Black	75	13
Income		
Under $35,000	72	20
$35,000–$75,000	79	16
$75,000 +	78	13
Religion		
Born-again Christian	68	28
Other Christian	84	10

cent of parents are strongly in favor of cutting off welfare payments after two years to mothers who can't find a job, though twice as many support this idea. Banning abortion draws even less favor as a measure that would help families. Just 15 percent of parents think it would be extremely helpful and 28 percent think it would be helpful, whereas a huge 61 percent of parents say that making abortion illegal would not be helpful. All in all, it seems that the items listed in this second group tend to polarize parents, as the high negative responses indicate.

After rating each group of issues, parents were asked to rate the two groups against each other (see Table 4). The results are extraordinarily clear-cut: 77 percent think the first group would be more helpful to parents and families, while just 16 percent think the second group would be more helpful—a margin of almost five to one. Particularly impressive is the extent to which this preference is shared across the usual income and demographic divides. The first group of issues is preferred by a huge margin whatever the age, sex, educational level, income, race, or religious identification of the parent. Even among conservative Baptists, the first group of issues is preferred by 73 percent and the second by only 25 percent.

The survey findings thus show a clear consensus among American parents about what kind of political agenda they will rally behind. When moms and dads are asked about their deepest concerns for their children, the issues that come spontaneously to mind are safety and education. These are not the issues that dominate the divisive contemporary debate over family values. And when asked about their own political priorities, parents make it abundantly clear that a focus on practical issues such as income support, tax breaks, and the creation of workplace policies that would enable them to give more and better time to their children would be most helpful. The priorities of the family-values advocates—banning abortion, outlawing same-sex marriage—simply do not register with American parents when they are asked how government and the wider community can best help families with children.

Policies Parents Would Vote For

How does this consensus translate into a willingness to vote for specific policies? The survey teased out a series of specific proposals and solicited individual responses.

At the top of the list are four proposals favored by 60 percent or more of parents polled. In the number-one slot is legislation requiring gunmakers and gun sellers to put trigger locks or safety catches on guns to prevent children from using them. This proposal is strongly favored by 78 percent of parents. Next comes federal income tax credits or deductions to help pay for college for families earning $100,000 a year or less, which is strongly favored by 71 percent of parents, making it the most popular of several tax changes suggested in the poll. The high level of support for these measures underscores the fact that violence and education are the issues that generate most anxiety for parents. Number three on the list is legislation to ensure three days' paid leave a year for child-related responsibilities such as attending a parent-teacher conference, strongly favored by 68 percent of parents. In fourth place are tax incentives to companies to ensure that all full-time workers earn wages above the poverty line, strongly favored by 61 percent of parents. Policy items three and four reflect a deep desire to help relieve the time crunch and wage squeeze experienced by so many parents. We should point out that in addition to receiving high levels of strong support, these four measures have impressive levels of broad support, with at least 80 percent of parents in favor and at least a five-to-one ratio of support to opposition.

Five additional proposals enjoy strong support from at least half of all parents polled. Some 59 percent strongly favor a ratings system for sex and violence on TV. Almost as many—58 percent—strongly favor doubling the existing $1,000 annual federal tax credit for child care and preschool expenses. Some 56 percent strongly favor eliminating state and local sales taxes on children's necessities such as diapers, school supplies, learning tools, and car seats, and 52 percent strongly support tax incentives for family-friendly workplace policies. Some 50 percent strongly favor tripling the dependent tax deduction. Thus, a set of proposals that aim to ease financial burdens on parents, make the workplace more responsive, and help parents promote sound values among their children also enjoys broad popularity, with at least 75 percent of all parents in favor and a support-to-opposition ratio of at least three to one.

A Voice for Parents

Finally, parents want a collective voice, an organization that reflects their urgent concerns and can produce new clout for moms and dads in Congress, in state assemblies, on school boards, and in the private sector.

By an overwhelming 89-to-9-percent margin, parents are in favor of the creation of a parents' organization similar to the American Association for Retired Persons (AARP). About half say they are strongly in favor. Support is most intense among women, those aged twenty-five to thirty-four, people with high school or some college education, residents of larger cities, northeasterners, southerners, Baptists, and Catholics, with clear majorities in each of these categories. However, substantial numbers of parents in most other demographic groups—over 40 percent—strongly support the creation of such an organization, and an overall majority are in favor.

The Meaning of This Poll

The great task facing us in these waning years of the twentieth century is to end the war against parents and reweave the web of care that will allow us to rebuild our families and communities. The huge missing piece is figuring out how to conjure up the political will. As we now understand, the virulent antiparent sentiment in our nation did not materialize out of thin air. Moms and dads have an impressive array of economic, social, and cultural forces pitted against them, which is why the results of our poll and our focus groups are so very powerful. Finding a political platform that elicits such deep and broad support across an interest group of 62 million people is an enormously important step in the right direction.

Our survey tells us that America's parents have clear ideas about what they want—concrete support from government and the private sector to help them deal with the time crunch and the wage squeeze—but they do not think that anyone in power is listening to them, let alone helping them. So perhaps the time has come to consider creating a national organization for parents that would give mothers and fathers real leverage with those who make policy, winning them the social supports they so urgently need. The story of the emergence of the AARP contains important lessons for parents seeking stature and standing in the public square.

Gray Power

The AARP got off the ground in the mid-1950s, when a retired high school principal, Ethel Percy Andrus, was turned down by dozens of companies in her efforts to obtain health insurance for the members of her association of retired teachers. In desperation, she formed her own insurance union, which she called the American Association of Retired Persons. Its purpose was to enhance the quality of life for older persons. Over time, the AARP, along with the Gray Panthers and the National Council of Senior Citizens, became politically active, organizing the elderly vote on issues of common concern. By 1994 the AARP had 34 million members, a figure that includes half of all Americans over age fifty, or one in four registered voters. Indeed, the AARP is now twice the size of the AFL-CIO and has more members than any voluntary organization in America other than the Catholic Church.[4] These kinds of numbers translate into tremendous clout in Congress. Whatever the state of the budget deficit, virtually no elected politician will talk seriously about cutting social security or Medicare, the two programs that together account for over a third of federal spending. Anyone mentioning cutbacks quickly earns the label "grannybasher" and more often than not is kicked out of office.

By dint of mobilizing huge numbers of seniors in the political arena, the AARP turned a previously downtrodden group into a hugely powerful electoral force capable of winning generous entitlements. In 1960, fully 35 percent of the elderly fell below the poverty line; today, only 10.5 percent do. And in 1996, social security payments alone totaled $349 billion.

Seniors have brought off an extraordinary feat, one which demonstrates that even in our mean-spirited, market-driven age, it is still possible to persuade government to underwrite generous programs of social support. The story of gray power is one of electoral clout, but it is also one of moral suasion, for we should not forget that social security has profound ethical underpinnings in the eyes of most Americans. The vast majority of retirees believe—erroneously, it turns out—that they have earned this benefit by dint of paying social security taxes throughout their employed lives.[5] But the payoff is not seen as narrowly economic. Most people, and not just the elderly, see social security as fair and just, the legitimate reward for a lifetime of work on the job and at home, not simply as some kind of return on investment.

The Challenge Ahead

This brings us to a critical question: is the AARP a credible or appropriate model for a nascent parents' movement? Unfortunately, political trends among parents since the 1950s have created a number of obstacles to an AARP-type organization. As political analyst Ruy Teixeira has demonstrated, the political power of parents has diminished in recent years.[6] Demographic shifts—particularly the increase in the number of elderly people—have reduced the proportion of parents in the eligible electorate from 55 percent in 1956 to 35 percent in 1996, and the low turnout of parents at elections is an additional disadvantage. Teixeira has shown that in every election since 1956, there has been a poorer turnout among parents than among nonparents, and that this gap has widened dramatically over time. Back in the 1950s there was a one-percent-age-point gap between parents and nonparents in terms of voting behavior, but by 1996 this gap had widened to twelve percentage points.

On the face of it, these figures are not encouraging for those of us interested in mobilizing parents—they seem to be a weak and declining presence in the political arena. Appearances notwithstanding, these trendlines do not negate the enormous potential of parent power. Moms and dads may make up a smaller proportion of the voting population than they used to, but they still compose more than one third of the electorate—62 million people. If parents actually got out to vote, they could produce a great deal of clout. Which brings us to the question of voter apathy. There is nothing immutable about this reluctance to vote—after all, a much larger proportion of parents used to vote. It is a question of giving mothers and fathers something to vote for. The fact is, if parents are less than enthusiastic on the voting front, who can blame them? In recent years, neither Congress nor the White House has come through with an agenda that deserves their support. President Clinton talks up a storm about wanting to help regular moms and dads, but so far he has come through with a thirty-five-cent increase in the minimum wage, an FCC ruling that "encourages" broadcasters to air three hours of educational television a week, a $500 child tax credit, which brings the dependent deduction up to half of its value in the 1950s, and a huge cut in the provision of section 8 rental vouchers. For most parents, this does not amount to a hill of beans.

The problems of mobilization are clearly daunting, but at least on the organizational and strategic front, the AARP constitutes a powerful model for parents. Millions of moms and dads across this nation are facing an urgent set of unmet needs and an unresponsive political establishment. If they can band together and find collective strength as senior citizens have done, they stand a much better chance of persuading a politician—or a party—to provide the serious support they so desperately need.

But strategy may be the least of our problems. Even more difficult than figuring out how to mobilize parents is forging a new public morality that will put parents front and center in the national conscience. Harvard historian Theda Skocpol reminds us that while Americans don't like welfare, they have "always favored social benefits for those who contribute vitally to the national community."[7] If we are to give moral heft to the parenting role, we need to do a much better job of making sure that fellow citizens understand the scope and reach of the social benefits contributed by moms and dads. To do this we lean on the G.I. Bill of Rights—the most successful policy initiative of recent times, and one whose underlying values very much fit the spirit and purpose of a parents' movement.

The GI Bill is a powerful model for parents because it encompasses several important principles. First, it was constructed as a set of *universal benefits* that were available to all veterans—women as well as men, blacks as well as whites—who had fought for their country during World War II (and, later, the Korean and Vietnam wars). Second, these benefits were *enormously generous.* The idea was to pay homage to the significance of what these veterans had done by risking their lives for their country. Third, the individual benefits that made up the programs were tremendously *enabling and empowering:* the educational benefits enhanced earning power, and the housing benefits encouraged veterans to buy their own homes. GIs were not warehoused in public projects; instead, they were given the tools to build lives they could be proud of. Finally, when all was said and done, the GI Bill was a stunningly successful investment that immeasurably *boosted the nation's economic well-being.* In concrete terms, the government received eight dollars back for every dollar spent, and who can quantify the value of ten Nobel prizes?

These principles comprise the heart of any parents' movement. These are the essential elements that will give a parents' movement moral suasion and take support for such a movement beyond self-interest and narrow interest-group concerns. This is why we use the GI Bill as a model when we craft our Parents' Bill of Rights. Surely we can learn from the AARP—seniors have, after all, been enormously successful—but we look to the GI Bill of Rights for deeper meaning as we embark on building a movement that needs both strategy and soul.

NINE

....

A Parents' Bill of Rights

IN OCTOBER 1995, our Task Force on Parent Empowerment set out to gather the testimony of experts and parents from diverse communities across America. The goal was ambitious: we wanted this group to help us create the building blocks of a new parents' movement. For more than two years this task force deliberated, examining the research evidence, weighing policy options, and listening to the voices of mothers and fathers on the front lines. In the winter of 1997–1998 it completed its work and presented us with some important levers for change: a set of policies capable of relieving the parental time famine, lightening the intense economic pressure on parents, and rewriting our cultural script to give new value and dignity to the parental role. We then put this work together with the insights gained from our nationwide survey and crafted a blueprint for supporting parents, which we call a Parents' Bill of Rights.

This Parents' Bill of Rights owes much to the GI Bill of Rights: it deals in the currency of generous universal benefits; it is impressively enabling and empowering; it adds tremendously to our economic well-being; and it rests on the same ethical foundation— service to our country. The GIs who fought in World War II were vitally important in maintaining America's national security, risking their lives to defeat fascism and in so doing making the western world safe for democracy. In less obvious though equally important ways, the parents who fight our domestic wars are essential in maintaining our national security. By giving over large chunks of their lives to cherishing children, they contribute to the happiness of the next generation, but they also generate the social and human capital essential for the healthy functioning of our democracy. This parallel between soldiers and parents is understood in other nations. Charles de Gaulle, president of France in the 1960s, once said that motherhood should be regarded as "a social function similar to military service for men, that has to be financially supported by the whole community." This statement dramatizes the distinctive French view that the honor and sacrifice inherent in the parental role entitles parents to the support of the larger society.

Constructing our Parents' Bill of Rights over the past two and a half years has been a highly interactive and parent-driven process. The policy options may have been fine-tuned by scholars and policy analysts, but they are couched within a framework that has been determined by the needs and desires of parents. Even our final blueprint is far from being a top-down directive; rather, we present a list of options—sometimes overlapping, sometimes less than comprehensive—for the serious consideration of parents. We mean for mothers and fathers in communities across America to try our Parents' Bill of Rights on for size and then mold and add to it as they see fit.

A PARENTS' BILL OF RIGHTS

Mothers and fathers are entitled to

1. TIME FOR THEIR CHILDREN

- Paid Parenting Leave
- Family-Friendly Workplaces
- A Safety Net

2. ECONOMIC SECURITY

- A Living Wage
- Job Opportunities
- Tax Relief
- Help with Housing

3. A PRO-FAMILY ELECTORAL SYSTEM

- Incentives to Vote
- Votes for Children

4. A PRO-FAMILY LEGAL STRUCTURE

- Stronger Marriage
- Support for Fathers
- Adoption Assistance

5. A SUPPORTIVE EXTERNAL ENVIRONMENT

- Violence-Free Neighborhoods
- Quality Schooling
- Extended School Day and Year
- Child Care
- Family Health Coverage
- Drug-Free Communities
- Responsible Media
- An Organizational Voice

6. HONOR AND DIGNITY

- An Index of Parent Well-Being
- National Parents' Day
- Parent Privileges

1. Time for Their Children

As we discovered in our national survey and in our focus groups, mothers and fathers are desperately worried about the parental time famine. This is the number-one problem in their lives. Across the usual divides of race and class, they yearn for the ability to spend more and better time with their children. Parents know full well that newborns should not be in day care, that seven-year-olds should not be home alone, and that unsupervised teenagers wreak havoc in the late afternoon hours. And while they understand that quality child care and an extended school day can help, they also understand that much of what they do to inculcate character, competence, and compassion in their children cannot be delegated. But where will they find the time to come through on all these fronts? Fully 90 percent of the parents we polled—the vast majority of fathers as well as mothers—feel impossibly stretched and squeezed as they deal with long work weeks or two or three jobs. At the very least, they would like employers, government, and the community at large to help them deal with the time crunch.

Paid Parenting Leave

Paid parenting leave is of enormous significance to moms and dads. Practically speaking, if parenting leave is not paid (and our current legislation is limited to unpaid leave), those who need it the most—overburdened low-income parents—are least likely to take it. Childbirth is surely a joyous and miraculous event, but it is also life-bending and backbreaking. For most parents it is a time of profound vulnerability. In Europe, childbirth triggers a generous benefits package that includes prenatal care, obstetrical care, generous hospital stays, five months' leave at full pay, home visits, baby equipment subsidies, and so on.[1] Compare this with the United States, where out-of-pocket expenses for childbirth amount to several thousand dollars and most working women are constrained to be back on the job six weeks after birth. Other rich nations seem to understand that the stakes are enormously high. If a family can successfully negotiate the magical first months of life, all kinds of good things will happen: a newborn will bond with his or her parents, a family will cohere, and a child will get off to a good start in life.

Paid parenting leave is also of great symbolic importance. It sends a message to moms and dads that the nation at large values this new child and intends to give its parents time to nurture and nourish it. It sends a signal that a child is not just another private possession but a social blessing of enormous import. These messages and signals give honor and dignity to parents, and in so doing help individual moms and dads steel themselves for a lifetime of nonmarket work.

We therefore recommend government-mandated, *paid, job-protected parenting leave for twenty-four weeks*—thought by many experts to be the minimally adequate period of time for a parent to bond with a new child. This would significantly expand the scope of the Family and Medical Leave Act of 1993. Paid parenting leave would be offered to all working parents for the purpose of looking after a newborn baby, a newly adopted child, or a seriously ill child. Workers who cannot obtain income replacement through company benefits policy or disability insurance would be entitled to the minimum wage for this six-month period. The Social Security Trust Fund should cover the wage replacement costs, thus ensuring that employers would not suffer financial hardship or be tempted to discriminate against young parents. In the case of small firms (fewer than fifty employees), government would also pick up the expenses involved in carrying health insurance and other employee benefits while a worker is out on parenting leave.

Paid parenting leave can be used entirely by one parent or shared between them. Leave can be used to stay at home full-time, or it can be combined with part-time employment. And the 120 days that make up the twenty-four weeks can be taken until a child's sixth birthday. If government creates a parenting entitlement that is both generous and available to both sexes, sexual stereotypes may well break down. The Swedish experience is relevant here. In 1974, when parenting leave was first introduced in Sweden, only 3 percent of fathers took advantage of it. But by 1990, 26 percent of those drawing this benefit were fathers.[2]

Family-Friendly Workplaces

Government should encourage the private sector to address the parental time famine. Public policy plays a critical role here, because of the potential divergence of interest between what is good for the employer and what is good for children. Both want more of a parent's time. Government should therefore weigh in and create incentives for firms to provide time-enhancing policies as part of a family-friendly benefits package. These policies have proven highly effective. Companies as different as Hewlett Packard, Price Waterhouse, and First Tennessee Bank have shown that it is possible to create a fluid, less rigid workplace that gives workers with family responsibilities significant discretion over how they structure their careers, how many hours they work each week, and when and where work is performed.[3] In some states, companies that offer on-site child care already qualify for tax concessions. Why not expand these provisions?

We recommend *carefully tailored tax incentives for companies* that offer flexible hours, compressed work weeks, part-time work with benefits, job sharing, career sequencing, extended parenting leave, and home-based employment opportunities. We also recommend *the four-thirds solution,* an idea developed by child psychologist Stanley Greenspan.[4] Under this plan, each parent works two-thirds time to pursue career goals, and together they provide four thirds of a single income. Thus one third of each parent's time is left for direct baby and child care. The provision of prorated benefits and the creation of part-time career tracks would help make this a realistic option for large numbers of two-parent families.

A Safety Net

It is our belief that a Parents' Bill of Rights will create a situation in which many fewer families depend on welfare to make ends meet. Measures such as paid parenting leave, wage subsidies, and school-to-work programs (discussed below) should enable many more poor parents to enter the mainstream economy. However, although the welfare population will undoubtedly shrink, there will always be at least some poor parents who fail to meet the challenge of self-sufficiency.

We therefore recommend that government *reinstate the right to income support* for poor parents with children under six, with the provision that *unmarried teenage mothers be required to live in a home* under the strict supervision of experienced mothers.[5] This arrangement would both make sure that these young mothers acquire some parenting skills and detract from the lure of unwed motherhood as a way of life.

This recommendation involves amending key elements of the 1996 Welfare Reform Act, which capped lifetime cash benefits at five years per recipient, whatever the age of the child.[6] The problem with this cap, which is designed to force welfare mothers into the labor force no matter how bad the conditions, is that it also forces those mothers to spend most of their waking hours away from their children, who, "already fatherless, will now not even be raised by their mothers."[7]

At the crux of this matter are issues of class and race. Far too often our political leaders talk about how desirable it is for middle-class parents to spend more time with their children and in the same breath recommend that as many welfare moms as possible join the workforce and leave their children in substandard care. This double message is deeply offensive. It is hard to believe that white middle-class kids need parental attention while black disadvantaged kids do not.

2. Economic Security

According to our survey, after the time crunch, economic insecurity is the most worrisome problem facing parents today. The two problems are obviously related: economic pressure often translates into longer hours or an additional job, which in turn creates the parental time famine we have just been talking about. In other words, it is impossible to provide mothers and fathers with the gift of time without directly confronting the terms and conditions of employment. Thus, a central goal of our Parents' Bill of Rights is to address the sagging wages and mounting insecurity that have so seriously debilitated moms and dads over the past twenty-five years. Although the GI Bill boosted earning power through greatly expanded access to higher education, we emphasize more direct measures. In an age of weak labor unions and out-of-control managerial greed, we cannot assume that enhanced productivity will translate into higher wages for workers.

A Living Wage

Government and the private sector should underwrite a series of *subsidies that bring wages up to at least $7 an hour,* a level that would enable every full-time worker to keep a family of three above the poverty line.[8] Specifically, we recommend a series of subsidies for low-wage workers as proposed by Columbia University economist Edmund Phelps. In the Phelps plan, subsidies are limited to full-time jobs for low-wage employees, and they are graduated—the lower the wage, the higher the subsidy.[9] Phelps proposes that the wage subsidies be paid for by a tax on companies in the sector receiving them. Since these subsidies would replace the earned income tax credit (EITC), the money currently used to finance the EITC would help defray their cost. Despite these savings, this would undoubtedly be an expensive program. Phelps estimates that initially it would cost $100 billion a year, but he is convinced that since these subsidies would create healthier families and communities, the direct and indirect savings would quickly offset the expenditure. In his view, family breakdown, social decay, welfare dependence, and crime "can be traced to economic forces that have deprived a great many less advantaged workers of much of the power of their labor."[10] A major strength of Phelps's plan is that it comes from inside the economic establishment and is therefore being taken seriously by political leaders and the mainstream press.

Such a large-scale program of wage subsidies would force the private sector to address the issue of managerial greed. In order to meet their new tax liabilities as well as remain competitive, corporations would have to cut into executive compensation and thus reduce the income gap between managers and everyone else.

Job Opportunities

Government, in partnership with schools and the private sector, should support and underwrite *programs that improve the chances of students*—particularly disadvantaged students—*navigating the path to productive and decently paid jobs.* More than 50 percent of U.S. employers say they cannot find qualified applicants for entry-level jobs, while more than 40 percent of African-American males never make it into a mainstream job. School-to-work programs can help lower both percentages.

The framework is already in place. In May 1994, President Clinton signed the School-to-Work Opportunities Act, which provides seed money to states and local partnerships—including business, educational, and community organizations—to develop programs that emphasize more work experience in high school and more on-the-job training in the workplace. There is no single model. Using federal money, states and their partners are free to design the school-to-work system that makes most sense for them.

School-to-work programs are often successful, especially when they involve multidimensional connections with potential employers. However, they are resource-intensive, and so far the money allocated to them by the federal government has been extremely limited. Over the period 1994–1996, thirty-seven states were awarded implementation grants totaling $472 million, averaging less than $10 million annually for each participating state.[11] Given the scale of the problems we face on the joblessness front, states need a much more substantial commitment. And given how difficult it is for young ex-cons to reenter the job market after serving their time, government should also publicize recent efforts to grant tax credits to businesses and organizations that employ ex-offenders.[12]

Tax Relief

Government can do much more with tax policy to support families with children. As we have seen, the burden of taxation now falls much more heavily on low- and middle-income working households, where most children live, and much less heavily on wealthy households, which are mostly older and without children. This is mainly because of the onslaught of payroll taxes, which have risen significantly in recent years and are highly regressive (an identical 7.6 percent is levied on all workers, and income above $65,400 is exempt). We have four proposals.

First, *eliminate payroll taxes for working parents* who have children under six. During the critical early childhood years, when earning power is particularly low and child-related responsibilities are particularly heavy, the federal government should pick up the employee portion of payroll taxes (FICA). We suggest paying for this by making earnings above $65,400 subject to FICA. If more affluent folks were asked to pay payroll taxes on all their earned income, the government would take in an additional $53 billion.

Second, *extend the recently enacted child tax credit* ($500 per child per year) to low-income families who already benefit from the earned income tax credit and allow them to offset this credit against their social security taxes. Twenty-five million American children live with parents who will not benefit from the child tax credit passed by Congress in May 1997 because their incomes are not high enough.[13] They are ineligible for this credit because they already benefit from the EITC and already pay very low federal income taxes. But these low-income families are liable for payroll taxes and have a substantial tax liability at the end of each year. If anyone needs tax relief, these families do.

Third, *create a $2,000 per child family allowance.* This would apply to children under six and would be limited to families whose annual income is less than $50,000. This benefit would be paid for by the Social Security Trust Fund and could be underwritten by pushing the retirement age from sixty-five to sixty-seven. It is important to note that a child allowance does not discriminate against at-home parents. It could be used to help defray the cost of child care, but it could also be used as replacement income for parents who choose to care for their children at home.

Finally, *eliminate local sales taxes on children's necessities* such as diapers, school supplies, learning tools, and car seats.

Help with Housing

In a manner reminiscent of the 1950s, government should once again provide substantial housing subsidies for families with children. The basic problem is that in recent years, the price of housing has risen much faster than wages. Indeed, in 1996, 5 million American households paid more than half of their pretax income for housing. We recommend the following policy initiatives.

First, government should *create a mortgage subsidy* to make home ownership a realistic ambition for many more young families. This subsidy would be limited to families with incomes below $100,000 a year, and the program could be partially paid for by limiting the tax deductibility of mortgage payments for wealthy homeowners (those earning more than $200,000 a year). In addition, government should give serious consideration to spurring the development of a housing partnership market.[14]

Second, government should *increase the availability of section 8 rent vouchers* for low-income families. The Department of Housing and Urban Development has already moved away from the construction of public housing projects toward rent vouchers, which pay the difference between 30 percent of household income and the prevailing market rent. This policy shift makes sense. Vouchers have the advantage of giving mobility and choice to low-income families. Instead of confining the poor to blighted ghettos, they allow recipients to decide where they want to live.

The problem with rent vouchers is that there are not nearly enough of them. In 1996 there was no increase in the number of vouchers provided by government, yet millions of low-income families urgently needed affordable housing. At an average yearly cost of $3,500 per household, vouchers are much less expensive than paying to warehouse homeless families in shelters.[15]

Our proposed program of subsidies and vouchers would underwrite family homes as the GI Bill did. Such a program is desperately needed. The housing crunch is actually worse than the one following World War II. In the late 1940s, 5 million families were either homeless or on the brink of homelessness; today, over 6 million are.[16]

3. A Pro-Family Electoral System

We should reform the voting system so as to give more clout to mothers and fathers. As we understand from the discussion in Chapter 8, if we could somehow expand the size of the parent population and at the same time persuade more mothers and fathers to vote in elections, we would be in a much better position to fund programs of family support. It seems that modern-day parents are simply too alienated and overburdened to conjure up a large presence at the polls. We therefore propose two measures that, taken together, would increase the political power of parents and make it much easier to fund an extended school day or paid parenting leave.

First, parents should be given *incentives to vote*. The United States is an unusual democracy in that we have no incentives or sanctions that encourage citizens to vote—indeed, in recent elections fewer than half of eligible voters have actually cast their votes. According to the political scientist Ray Seidelman, "In countries as different as France and Australia government is heavily involved in making sure people vote. For example, in Italy voting is not compulsory but an individual's failure to vote is publicized. In Belgium, Luxembourg and Australia, citizens are required to vote and may have to pay a fine if they don't."[17] In these other democracies, citizenship brings with it electoral responsibilities as well as rights. Sanctions might be difficult to impose in the United States, but incentives could be very workable. For example, the government might waive the application fee for a driver's license if the applicant could prove that he had voted in a national or local election, or a welfare applicant might be eligible for a small bonus if she had proof that she had voted in the last election.

Second, serious consideration should be given to the suggestion that parents be given *the right to vote on behalf of their children*. Not too long ago, the voting age was lowered from twenty-one to eighteen. We recommend lowering it further, to encompass all Americans. A legally designated parent or guardian would then have the right to vote on behalf of a child younger than eighteen. This makes intuitive sense: today's elections will affect today's children well into maturity, and they should have an opportunity to influence that future, if only through their parents. But the measure also has immense practical ramifications: overnight it would almost double the potential size of the parent vote.[18]

It is also important to make the mechanics of voting much easier—an initiative that is particularly helpful for overloaded parents. The United States is one of the few countries where the individual is personally responsible for registering to vote; in most other countries, government assumes the task of finding and registering citizens who are eligible. For example, if a registered voter in Britain moves from one town to another, the government takes the lead in finding and reregistering that person. We recommend that parents be encouraged to register to vote when they register the birth of a child or when they register a child for school—the voter registration form could simply be attached to the forms parent fill out for these other purposes.

We also suggest that election days be designated national holidays. In most other countries, election days are holidays. Working parents in Europe do not have to vote very early or very late in the day or get special permission to leave their jobs in order to go to the polls.

These measures would have the cumulative effect of significantly increasing the size of the parent vote and would help shift the balance of political power toward less affluent, young parents—precisely those fellow citizens who are seriously disadvantaged at the present time.

4. A Pro-Family Legal Structure

If parents are to come through for their children, we need to do something about structure as well as function. Measures such as paid parenting leave and flextime are essential if a single mother is to manage work and family adequately, but these practical supports cannot substitute for a father. We are firmly convinced that most children benefit from the sustained loving attention of two parents, and the best way of ensuring an increase in the number of two-parent families is to bolster the institution of marriage.

Stronger Marriage

Two attentive, loving parents who are available on a daily basis are the greatest gifts we can give a child. It is hard to produce this gift outside of marriage. In recent years, scholars and policy analysts have avoided talking about family structure, fearing that they might somehow exacerbate racially charged divisions between dual- and single-parent families. This concern is legitimate, but we feel that progressive people do not have to adopt a morally relative stance. In the wise words of Theda Skocpol, "Most people accept that two married parents are best for children, even though each of us is personally acquainted with mothers and fathers who have to soldier on outside this ideal situation. Progressives can acknowledge the tension between ideals and second-best necessities."[19]

Thus, government should get back into the business of fostering the value of marriage as a long-term commitment. Like it or not, our laws and policies have enormous moral suasion. The adoption of no-fault divorce in the 1970s, for example, told a very powerful story: no one is to blame when a marriage breaks up, and no one has to take responsibility for the consequences. By giving a green light to much easier methods of ending marriage, these new laws produced a major shift in private decision-making. As sociologist Andrew Cherlin has shown, the liberalization of divorce laws both changed public attitudes toward divorce and, over the long haul, weakened the institution of marriage.[20] We need to undo this damage and once more direct our laws to the task of strengthening marriage, underpinning parents, and protecting children.

The first step is to *give more weight to the act of getting married.* One idea is state laws that allow couples to choose a more rigorous marriage, along the lines of a law recently adopted in Louisiana that permits couples to choose between a standard marriage and a covenant marriage. Couples who choose a covenant marriage pledge to enter matrimony only after serious deliberations, including premarital education. They also agree to try to resolve potential conflicts through counseling if either spouse requests it and to seek divorce only after a mutually agreed-upon two-year separation or under special circumstances such as adultery, abuse, or abandonment.[21] By raising the bar and creating tougher standards, the covenant option may produce more durable marriages.

A second step is to *make it more difficult to obtain a divorce,* particularly when children are involved. Parents who wish to divorce should face a three-year waiting period, during which time they would be obliged to seek marriage counseling. In addition, they should be legally obligated to safeguard their children's financial future before they are granted a final divorce decree. In the spirit of a 1990 report from the British Law Commission, we should simply "throw sand in the machinery of divorce."[22]

A third step is to *eliminate the marriage penalty* in our tax code. As we have seen, over the past three decades some basic features of our tax laws have shifted against the interests of married couples.[23] Income splitting was effectively eliminated in 1969, and the 1986, 1993, and 1997 tax reform packages included numerous provisions that further increased the code's bias against married couples. Our current tax laws particularly penalize marriages in which husband and wife both work outside the home and earn the same or similar salaries. For example, a study by the National Bureau of Economic Research finds that if a person who earns $10,000 and has a child marries another person who earns $10,000 and has a child, the marriage costs them $3,717 in taxes and lost benefits. One way to reduce the marriage penalty is to lower taxes on two-earner couples until these couples no longer pay more in total taxes then they would have paid if they had remained single. This frequently proposed reform, however, would primarily benefit higher-income couples, In addition, by shifting more of the total tax burden onto couples with at-home parents, such a change would also effectively create a new "homemaker penalty" in the tax code. For this reason, a much better way to end the marriage penalty is to restore income splitting, permitting all married couples to share their joint income equally for purposes of taxation.[24]

Support for Fathers

The significance of fathers in the lives of their children goes far beyond their paychecks. There is now a great deal of evidence showing that a sustained and loving relationship with Dad improves a whole set of outcomes for children: performance at school, emotional health, involvement with drugs and crime. Yet the United States suffers from an extremely high level of fatherlessness. As we have seen, 40 percent of children currently live apart from their fathers. We propose a set of measures that will reduce this number.

The federal government should mandate *a special ten-day parenting leave for new fathers* that is both paid and compulsory. A father is expected to take this leave even if the mother is receiving parenting benefits for the same child at the same time. Making this leave compulsory will help get rid of the stigma attached to paternity leave in many work contexts. This special leave would give new legitimacy to the father-child bond.

State laws should guarantee *generous visitation rights for noncustodial parents* and reinforce them by an appropriate set of sanctions. If a noncustodial parent (which is most often the father) has not seen his child in, say, three months, that parent should be fined or otherwise put on notice that such conduct is unacceptable. Even if it is impossible to enforce this kind of provision fully, its existence would clearly indicate that society acknowledges the importance of a father's presence and is prepared to go to considerable lengths to encourage contact between fathers and children.

Federal and state government should *restructure our system of welfare benefits to privilege two-parent families.* Particularly powerful are measures that would encourage a mother and a father to actually live together. We recommend that half of all additional section 8 rent vouchers and half of all mortgage subsidies be set aside for two-parent families. By supporting two parents who are raising children together, these policies will help right an important wrong. For thirty years our system of income support for poor families has made it extremely difficult for men to be either husbands or fathers. It is high time we destroyed a perverse incentive structure that encourages the formation of single-parent families.

Adoption Assistance

Half a million American children are currently in foster care, and many of them are doing badly. Even with a greatly improved system of family support, there will always be some cases in which a biological parent is unable to provide a safe and caring environment and the child needs to be placed in another home. Research in the field shows that children who are adopted fare as well as biological children in terms of self-esteem, mental health, and school achievement.[25] We recommend that we replace the current emphasis on foster care with an emphasis on adoption. This entails *reconfiguring the legal system to make it much easier to adopt a child.* For example, states should be required to find adoptive homes for children within thirty days of the termination of parental rights.

5. A Supportive External Environment

According to our national survey of parents, beyond the overarching worries triggered by the time crunch and the wage squeeze, parents share some specific anxieties. Concern over juvenile crime and the quality and cost of education are at the top of a list that includes inadequate child care and hostile media. Mothers and fathers feel that many elements in the external environment have become antagonistic to parents—and other caregivers—and they yearn for a more supportive societal context.

Violence-Free Neighborhoods

Issues of child safety and juvenile crime are at the top of the list of parental concerns. The fear that the community is not safe and their child might become either a predator or a victim keeps moms and dads up at night and fuels some of their worst nightmares. And they have reason to worry: juvenile crime has quadrupled since the early 1980s. Owing to a dramatic rise in single parenthood and longer hours spent at work, between 5 and 7 million latchkey children go home alone after school, and as we have seen, the data show that these kids are at significantly greater risk of truancy, poor grades, substance abuse, pregnancy, and violent crime. In the words of the criminologists James Alan Fox and Sanford A. Newman, "When the school bell rings, leaving millions of young people without adult supervision or constructive activities, juvenile crime suddenly triples."[26] The creation of an extended school day and the development of high-quality after-school programs should therefore become an integral part of juvenile crime prevention.

We propose that school districts around the nation *provide students with an extended school day and extracurricular activities after school*. Such initiatives would provide safe havens for youngsters in the late afternoon hours, keeping them off the streets but also ensuring that they are gainfully engaged. As we shall see, an extended school day has an extremely positive effect on the academic performance of participating children.

Second, school districts should *encourage the formation of parent safety patrols* to create a safety zone around each school. In many American cities, the most challenging part of getting an education may be getting to and from school safely. Each year New York City police handle 50,000 reports of petty crimes involving juveniles. Most of these crimes are committed by schoolchildren and take place in the vicinity of a school. The attacks usually occur after school as children head for their buses and trains. Twenty-five private schools in New York City have spearheaded a solution: groups of parents who patrol the streets around a school at dismissal time wearing bright orange vests to identify themselves and carrying walkie-talkies and whistles. These parent patrols act as highly effective deterrents.[27] School districts might also reach out and involve MAD DADS organization in before- and after-school safety patrols. Originally formed in 1989 in Omaha, Nebraska, and now active in eleven states. MAD DADS (men against destruction) see themselves as positive role models, concerned loving parents, and "a visible presence in our cities against the negative forces that are destroying children."[28] This organization has an extremely impressive track record in community-based efforts to reduce rates of violent behavior among young people.

Third, government should *ban the sale of handguns to all young people* under the age of twenty-one; *enact "safe storage" laws* which make adults criminally liable for failure to take specific precautions in making guns inaccessible to children; and *mandate the installation of trigger locks on guns* to make it harder for children to fire them. In September 1997, President Clinton called on gun manufacturers to install child trigger locks on a voluntary basis.[29] We think trigger locks should be made mandatory—as do 89 percent of the parents polled in our national survey.

Quality Schooling

Parents have the right to quality schooling for their children—to have their nurturing and nourishing energies reinforced by an excellent educational experience. To accomplish this goal, the federal government and individual school districts should significantly increase educational investment.

For at least ten years, politicians have been telling us that we are throwing plenty of money at education. In fact, we don't compare favorably with our competitors. A study by the Economic Policy Institute shows that public and private spending on preschool, primary, and secondary education is lower in the United States than in most other countries. America ties for twelfth place among sixteen industrial countries. Indeed, to bring the amount of money we spend on primary and secondary education up to the average level found in these other countries, we would need to increase spending by more than $20 billion annually. It is only because the United States spends a great deal of private money on higher education that we look good in the international league tables; overall, we tie for second place among these sixteen industrial countries.[30]

The education spending gap between America and the rest of the advanced world is especially wide for very young children. The United States devotes very little public money to preschool education. Of all federal, state, and local money spent on education, less than half of one percent goes to those aged five and younger. Thus, fewer than half of our three-to-five-year-olds attend preschool programs. Most nursery schools are private—and expensive—and Head Start enrolls only a third of eligible children. Many of our competitors spend much more on early childhood education, and some of them—France, for example—have made child care and preschool education universally available. In the late 1990s, France is being forced to cut welfare benefits, but subsidies to children remain sacred.[31]

The ways in which our educational budgets shortchange the very young are particularly distressing given the research evidence linking preschool education to positive outcomes later on in life. Children who receive high-quality early childhood education do much better in school and eventually in the labor market than children who miss out on this opportunity. These causal connections are particularly strong for disadvantaged children.[32] In the words of the Committee for Economic Development, it is "hard to imagine society could find a higher yield for a dollar investment than that found in preschool programs for at-risk children."[33]

We therefore recommend tilting the balance of educational expenditure to *spend relatively more in the early years.* Let's fully fund Head Start. For just under $2 billion more a year, this program could be expanded to cover all eligible children.[34] And let's make the newly created HOPE tax credits available for preschool education. At the level of $1,500 a year per student, these credits are available to help defray the cost of college; they should be extended to preschool education.[35] Parents have had little time to save when their children are young, and this is also when they would like to spend more time with their children and less time working.

Extended School Day and Year

Lengthening the school day and the school year would have important benefits for families, and the majority of parents in our national survey were enthusiastic in their support of these measures. In the first place, longer hours would help to create the framework for a more rigorous education for American youngsters. In Japan and Germany, for example, schools are in session 30 to 40 percent longer than in the United States, which is one reason why students in these countries routinely outperform American students. Second, an expanded school day and school year greatly ease the problems of latchkey children. If nine-year-old Tyrone gets home at five o'clock instead of three o'clock, he has much less of that unsupervised time that is so dangerous to children. As we have seen, children who are home alone are in harm's way. Not only does a large proportion of juvenile crime take place in the late afternoon, but most teenage experimentation with sex and drugs occurs in the parental home in those same hours.

We therefore recommend that the regular *school day run from 8:30 A.M. to 4:30 P.M. and that schools offer an enriched program of extracurricular activities until 6:30 P.M.* We also recommend that the *summer vacation be pegged at five weeks* rather than its current length of nine weeks. This framework is in line with the suggestions of the parents in our national poll and in our focus groups.

Child Care

Government and businesses should *significantly increase the quality and affordability of child care for working parents.* Low- and middle-income families face enormous barriers when they attempt to find quality care for their children. Of the 13 million children who are now in day care, somewhere between 12 and 21 percent are in care that could be considered dangerous, and another 50 to 60 percent are in care where they are safe but not really learning. Only between 12 and 14 percent of children are in care that actually enhances growth and development.[36] Many of the problems involve affordability and can be solved through policies that both boost parental buying power (through wage subsidies and the family allowance) and improve the standard of care (through regulation and subsidies to child-care providers).

We would like to stress that support for out-of-home care should go hand in hand with policies (such as the family allowance) that enable more parents to look after their own children, especially in the early years.[37] We clearly do not wish to "punish parents who want to spend more time with their children" or establish the norm that parents "are supposed to farm out care of their children elsewhere."[38] Indeed, we would like to reinforce the value of mothers and fathers' taking care of their own children, while making sure that parents have access to high-quality child care if they need it.

Our first recommendation is *tougher regulation* of the child-care industry, including background checks on workers, enforcement of licensing requirements, and so on.

Second, government should provide *subsidies that underwrite training and much higher salaries for child-care workers*. Currently the median wage for a child-care worker is a mere $6.17 an hour, which explains why there is a 50 percent rate of turnover in this industry.[39] In his recent child-care proposal, President Clinton promised $250 million for training new workers.[40] This is a small step in the right direction. Improving training will accomplish little if it does not go along with higher salaries, and this will require a much bigger commitment from government. Providing decent pay would encourage child-care workers to stay on the job, which is the only way to provide continuity for children—itself a key ingredient of high-quality care.

Third, *federal funding should be restructured* so as to cut back the dependent care tax credit for affluent families and increase child-care block grants to the states. At the moment child-care subsidies go in large part to those who need them least. Close to half the $7 billion the government spends on child care goes to families earning more than $50,000 a year via the dependent care tax credit.[41] In contrast, low-income families have been stung by federal budget cutbacks. For example, child-care block grants to the states—which fund child care for poor families—lost almost a third of their value between 1975 and 1996.

Fourth, *paid parenting leave should become a central component of child-care policy.*

Fifth, a special set of *tax credits and subsidies should target full-time moms and dads*. We feel strongly that government should reach out to help parents at home as well as parents at work. The state of Minnesota is a model in this regard. In the spring of 1994, Minnesota passed the At-Home Child Care Credit Bill, which provided a credit of $720 per child (for up to two children) for married couples who take care of their baby at home. This credit helps a mother or father "afford" to stay home for the first year of life. In January 1998 Minnesota added the At-Home Infant Child Care Bill. This allows a parent who provides full-time care for an infant child to receive a subsidy in lieu of day-care assistance. Specifically, a parent is eligible for 75 percent of the established rate for infant day care.[42]

Finally, we should *integrate child care into our schools*. This is not only cost-effective, because it uses existing overhead, but it helps both parents and children make good early connections to the educational system. One such program is the School of the 21st Century, pioneered by the Yale psychologist Edward Zigler and already in operation in some five hundred schools in sixteen states across the country. The program comprises school-based, year-round, all-day care for children aged three to five; before- and after-school and vacation care for school-age children; family support and guidance through a home visitation program for new and expectant parents; and support and training to family day-care providers in the school's neighborhood.[43]

Family Health Coverage

The year 1997 saw new legislation that provided $48 billion in federal funds over ten years to expand health insurance coverage to uninsured low-income children.[44] Annual grants are now available to states to cover children up to age eighteen by expanding Medicaid, creating new state child health insurance programs, or both. The program targets children of the working poor—families whose incomes are too high for them to qualify for Medicaid but too low for them to be able to afford private coverage.

This new funding will enable states to cover somewhere between a third and a half of the nation's 10.6 million uninsured children.[45] One attractive feature is that it is financed in part by an increase in taxes on tobacco, which both allows a higher level of funding than would be true otherwise and discourages smoking by increasing cigarette prices.

We would like to propose two additional measures: *expanding these provisions to all uninsured children,* and *expanding them so that parents are also covered.* Clearly, in many of the targeted families, both parents and children have no health benefits. If a mother has chronic asthma or a father has hypertension—both common conditions among inner-city parents—it is extremely hard to do a stellar job on the nurturing front. Separating the fate of children from that of their parents does not make sense, since the destiny of children is wrapped up in their parents' health and well-being.

Drug-Free Communities

After a decade of declining levels of drug use by adolescents, the use of illegal drugs, alcohol, and cigarettes increased significantly between 1992 and 1995. The use of marijuana by high school seniors, for example, increased 63 percent over this time period. Smoking rates among youngsters are also rising rapidly: in 1996, they were at their highest level in sixteen years.[46] To counteract these disturbing trends, we recommend four measures.

First, *an extended school day and flextime for working parents* should be an integral part of drug prevention policy, since the mere physical presence of a parent in the home after school significantly reduces drug use among adolescents.

Second, parents should demand that the schools to which they entrust their children are drug-free. For many kids, "schools are a candy store of dangerous substances—cigarettes, alcohol, inhalants, marijuana, heroin, cocaine and acid—sold by classmates on the school grounds."[47] In a 1996 national survey more than 70 percent of fifteen- to seventeen-year olds said drugs are used and sold at the schools they attend.[48]

But what to do? Rigorous programs of *drug education and prevention should be mandatory in every school.* These programs need to start in the early grades (getting the message to children early on is crucial) and need to involve parents (drug education is simply ineffective unless the message is backed up at home). In addition, communities should make a commitment to creating *Drug-Free School Zones*—extending 1,000 feet in every direction from the edge of a school's property. Promoted by the federal government in 1989 and 1991, DFSZs are designed to reduce the use of alcohol and drugs through a unified strategy of prevention and law enforcement. Some communities have carried out DFSZs to good effect—Tucson, Arizona, has achieved a 43 percent reduction in drug-related incidents—but few states have advanced their initiatives beyond posting signs.[49]

Third, *our war on drugs should focus on prevention*. This war has cost the taxpayer $300 billion over the past decade, and the bulk of the money has gone to the criminal justice system—less than a third has been spent on prevention and treatment. This disparity in funding continues in spite of research showing that drug treatment is seven times more cost-effective in reducing cocaine consumption than law enforcement.[50] We should also *eliminate the disparity in mandatory sentences* between crack cocaine and powder cocaine, and require racial/ethnic impact statements for all sentencing policy legislation.

Finally, government should *ban alcohol and cigarette advertising* on billboards and in magazines, and the media should be encouraged not to *glamourize smoking, drinking, and using drugs* (fashion ads promoting the emaciated heroin chic look is a recent example). In addition, the entertainment and advertising industries should support the *Partnership for a Drug-Free America*, a nonprofit coalition that uses television ads to get parents and kids talking about why illegal drugs are a bad idea. The federal government has contributed $195 million to this campaign, but it needs matching funds; the current budget allows the average teenage viewer to see approximately four ads a week—less than the number of Nike ads they will see.

Responsible Media

There is an urgent need to rein in the parent-bashing, children-hurting messages spewed forth by the mass media, and an equally urgent need to amplify messages that support the values parents teach. Experts in the field are convinced that "an extremely effective way of limiting the impact of trash television on children is to make available something else—something better."[51] We therefore propose the following measures.

First, government should dramatically *increase its support of public broadcasting*. PBS is the only network that treats children as learners and not consumers, but this institution has never gotten the support it deserves. Currently the United States spends a mere fifty-seven cents per person on all types of public broadcasting. Spending in other countries is of a different order of magnitude: Britain spends $18 per capita, Canada $22, and Japan $10.[52] Much of this money goes to develop educational programs for children.

Second, we recommend the creation of a *Children's Hour* on network television. The FCC should require all commercially licensed stations to broadcast an hour of children's programming each weekday from 4:00 to 5:00 P.M. as part of the implementation of the 1990 Children's Television Act (this would almost double the 1996 guideline).[53] Broadcasters would not be allowed to creatively relabel *The Jetsons* or *Sonic the Hedgehog* but would be expected to develop programs that had real educational value. The new Children's Hour might feature a fifteen-minute news segment specially pitched to nine- to thirteen-year-olds—*CBS News* (or ABC or NBC, for that matter) would do an extremely fine job if given this challenge. In Britain, a children's news program called *Newsround* is shown at 5:00 P.M. and is extremely popular—a quarter of all British schoolchildren tune in to it.

Third, *our movie and CD rating system should be made stricter* and enforcement should be more rigorous. Eight-year-olds and ten-year-olds should simply not be able to purchase CD albums with a parental advisory warning, rent R-rated videos, or see an R-rated movie in a cinema—no matter who is accompanying them. Businesses that allow underage persons to buy/rent/view this material should be hit with heavy fines.

Fourth, we recommend the *adoption of a television rating system designed for parents by parents*. This would replace the current rating system, which was designed by the networks. KidScore is a possible model. Developed by the National Institute on Media and the Family over the 1995–1997 period, this rating system has been created by parents and professionals who know a lot about kids but have no connection to the television industry.[54]

Finally, we strongly urge *parents to get involved* in monitoring television. Familiarize yourself with the rating systems and parent blocks and use them to screen out offensive stuff. Keep television sets out of kids' bedrooms—54 percent of American children have a television in their bedroom, and this undoubtedly encourages more viewing and diminishes a parent's ability to monitor what is seen. Establish clear rules—no TV before school, during meals, or before homework is finished—and provide alternative activities. In a recent survey, 70 percent of children said they would prefer to do something fun rather than watch television. Simply turning off the set is not nearly as effective as planning some other activity.

An Organizational Voice for Parents

One message that emerged loud and clear from our national poll of parents was that parents want an institutional voice, an organization that can address their urgent concerns and represent them in the political arena. As we have pointed out, an overwhelming 89 percent of parents said they were in favor of a parents' organization similar to the American Association for Retired Persons. Coming together in such a group would finally give America's parents real leverage in Congress, on school boards, and in executive suites around the nation. In the words of one mother of three, "I really don't resent those older than sixty . . . I just wish my interests and my buying power were equally valued."[55]

We therefore recommend *the creation of an AARP-style organization* that speaks to the concerns parents share across the usual divides of race, income, and gender and seeks to produce new clout in the public square. This organization should work to create social supports for parents, but it should also work to enhance the respect accorded to the parental role and function.

6. Honor and Dignity

A final task of our Parents' Bill of Rights is to trigger a moral and political awakening that gives new heft and authority to the parental role. We do not underestimate the power of symbolism in our image-conscious society, and therefore we suggest a variety of consciousness-raising ideas that together will help to create a "public morality" that puts moms and dads front and center on the national stage.

An Index of Parent Well-Being

An Index of Parent Well-Being would be a refreshing counterpoint to the Dow Jones and other Wall Street indicators.[56] It would also be deeply symbolic, signifying a new national commitment to the work parents do. Initially, the index would include measures of parents' average weekly earnings, time available for children, access to affordable housing, health insurance coverage, and the divorce rate.

National Parents' Day

We encourage communities around the nation to lend resources, energy, and enthusiastic support to National Parents' Day, a day of commemoration of mothers and fathers that was signed into law by President Clinton in October 1994 after unanimous adoption by Congress. Observed on the fourth Sunday of each July, Parents' Day is "designed to provide education and awareness of issues surrounding parenting and family challenges and problems." It is also a day to honor outstanding leaders, parents, and workers in the parenting field. Supported by an impressive list of leaders from Governor George Bush of Texas to Governor Roy Romer of Colorado to Mayor Linda Lingle of Honolulu, National Parents' Day has not yet received the recognition it deserves.

National Parents' Day could showcase the vision that permeates this book. Unlike Mother's Day and Father's Day (which are enormously valuable in their own right), Parents' Day speaks to a "we" consciousness rather than an "I" consciousness—the "we" of partners raising children together, the "we" of communities looking out for all of their children. Celebrating this day will force us, as a nation and as a people, to think continuously and talk regularly about the status of parents in this country.

We recommend that churches, synagogues, and mosques celebrate National Parents' Day and use it as a focus for a week-long exploration of the spiritual significance of parenting and the scriptural foundation of the parental role. In a nation where 96 percent of all adults believe in God, religion, and spirituality in the broader sense, are sources of succor and strength for moms and dads dealing with the challenges of contemporary parenting.[57]

We particularly encourage schools and colleges to recognize National Parents' Day and use it as an anchor for a series of classes on the practical and ethical dimensions of preparing for marriage and parenthood.

Parent Privileges

Most important on our list of parent privileges is *a specially designed education credit,* worth approximately $2,000 a year for a maximum of three years, which would enable a parent who stays at home with a young child to go back to school or college to complete his or her education. At a symbolic level, this would demonstrate that we as a society value a parent's time. It would also go some distance toward compensating a parent for the huge opportunity cost involved in spending several years out of the labor force. This particular privilege or benefit closely parallels the educational provisions of the original GI Bill.[58]

In addition, we recommend several parent privileges that are less substantive in terms of cost but equally rich in symbolic significance. State and city governments as well as schools and businesses should find ways of making our public spaces more welcoming to parents and children. For example, they might offer discounted admission charges to national parks and national monuments; discounted "family day" admission to museums, movie theaters, and restaurants; priority parking in shopping malls for pregnant women and parents with small children; and priority seating on buses and trains for parents with small children. We feel it is particularly important to allocate space in every school for a user-friendly parents' meeting room. It need not be elaborate, but some comfortable chairs, a pot of coffee, and a pile of resource material would encourage parent involvement in the life of a school, with enormously positive results for children.

So there we have it: a Parents' Bill of Rights that vastly improves the life circumstances of moms and dads and dramatically increases their ability to come through for their children. The most obvious feature of our proposed bill is that it requires a huge increase in the level of public commitment to parents. This is not a plan that tinkers at the edges or deals in incremental change. In the manner of the 1944 GI Bill of Rights, we are talking about an enormously ambitious program and a tremendous new infusion of funds: there is no way to boost the earning power of blue-collar workers or provide paid parenting leave or extended school days without coming through with tens of billions of dollars. So where do we get these resources? Obviously, the money can be found. As we have seen, huge sums are sloshing around in the system, and much of that money is trickling up to the rich and the powerful. It is also true that for the first time in thirty years, the federal government is dealing with a potential budget surplus, and a major challenge facing our political leaders is how to spend it well.[59] The fact is, if we truly wanted to help parents and children, if we wished to underwrite the kind of tax breaks, housing subsidies, and education grants that buttressed family life so successfully in the 1950s, we could. It all boils down to a question of political will.

Sparking a Parents' Movement

In the winter of 1997–1998, as our work with the task force drew to a close, we paused to take stock and gather our energies for the next stage. There is much to celebrate. Over the course of the last four years we have generated the intellectual resources to fuel a new parents' movement that crosses the divides of race, class, and gender. This movement is now poised for takeoff.

What we now need is a spark to ignite the smoldering embers of parental overload and anguish. Moms and dads are so demoralized, so beaten back by the waves of attack emanating from the economy and the culture, that they often do not grasp the profound significance of their role and function. By and large they don't expect—and don't receive—any help from the wider community. Whether they are growing a child's soul or replenishing our nation's store of human capital, parents soldier on alone, besieged, belittled, and bewildered.

We hope that this book will provide the spark to ignite a tinderbox of passion in the hearts and minds of parents—that it will give moms and dads the urgent energy to pull together, to cross those rifts of color and class and find the collective strength to ask for and take what is their due. For it is only with a groundswell of grassroots support that our Parents' Bill of Rights will become a reality. When the voices of America's 62 million parents unite and grow into a roar, then and only then will parents obtain the support they yearn for and so richly deserve.

If parents can mobilize behind our Bill of Rights, it will vastly improve the circumstances of their lives, but it will also transform our democracy, for we are not talking about narrow interest-group politics here. We are all stakeholders in this critical endeavor. If parents are not supported in their sacred and secular tasks, children will spin out of control—and so will our nation. Thus, if our political leaders can spearhead this huge project, which is nothing less than a moral awakening around the significance of parenting—they will restore confidence in government and rekindle our faith in the democratic process. This is desperately needed. Given the tarnished reputation of electoral politics, we urgently need a great and glorious national endeavor with which to reinvent government and banish the apathy and cynicism that haunt our public life.

As this century lurches to a troubled close, nothing is more important than reconnecting the passions of the American people to the democratic process. What better project to revitalize our republic than giving strength and succor to parents so that they can weave the web of care that is so vital to our nation?

Detailed Analysis of Survey Results

Parents and Work

America's parents feel overcommitted and overburdened as they struggle to balance work and family responsibilities in an increasingly hostile labor market. Some 79 percent of the parents in our survey work in the paid labor force (86 percent of the men and 73 percent of the women). Fathers are more often in full-time employment than mothers; 70 percent of men report working forty hours a week or more, compared with 43 percent of women. A dramatic measure of the new economic pressure is the number of moms and dads who hold more than one job. *Fully 20 percent of parents polled report holding two or more jobs in order to earn enough money to maintain a reasonable standard of living.* Only one in six of the mothers polled is a stay-at-home parent, a dramatic change from the situation a generation ago, when the figure was approximately one in three.

The survey findings make it clear that American parents are caught in a wage squeeze and a time crunch. Indeed, 82 percent of parents polled say that they have a tougher time balancing the demands of work and family than their own parents did, while just 16 percent disagree with this proposition.

Parents and Community

Parents attempt to remain active in their communities but are severely constrained by the demands of their jobs. The survey shows that mothers

Figure A

QUESTION: Some people say that today's parents have a tougher time balancing work and being a parent than their own parents did.

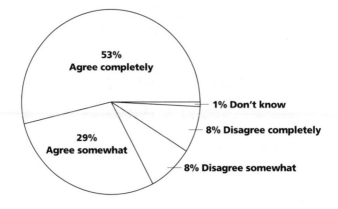

and fathers struggle to participate in community activities, although lack of time means that only a minority are able to participate on a steady basis. Parents give priority to groups and activities involving their children. For example, fully 73 percent of the parents of school-aged children report attending at least one Parent-Teacher Association meeting each year, though only 20 percent attend regularly.

In a similar vein, 62 percent of parents report spending at least some time involved in organized children's activities such as Little League and Boy Scouts, although just 22 percent are able to spend over fifteen hours a month on such activities. Some 58 percent are involved in church or religious activities, but only 11 percent spend more than fifteen hours a month doing so. Self-improvement activities, ranging from attending health clubs to joining twelve-step programs, take a back seat for parents: three in five say they have no time for such things, and only one in ten spends more than fifteen hours a month on them. This is particularly true for young parents: 72 percent of those who came of age in the nineties (eighteen- to twenty-four-year-olds) report no involvement in self-improvement activities, as do 61 percent of those who came of age in the eighties (twenty-five- to thirty-four-year-olds).

The principal factor restricting the involvement of American parents in community life is the demands of their jobs. Thirty-nine percent of those who are not involved in one or more of the three areas mentioned above say they have no time because of work commitments. Family demands are also felt, but to a lesser extent—only 19 percent mention this as the reason

Table A. Parental Activities

	Time spent per month on . . .		
	Organized Kids' Activities (school/extracurricular) %	Church/Religious Activities (besides services) %	Self-Improvement Activities (health clubs, etc.) %
None	36	41	58
Under 5 hrs.	20	26	18
6–15 hrs.	20	21	14
Over 15 hrs.	22	11	10
Don't know	2	1	1

for their lack of involvement. Disillusionment with community activities is not often given as the reason for nonparticipation; for example, lack of interest is cited by only 17 percent of respondents.

Parents and Politics

Whatever their level of involvement in organized community activities, American parents say they do participate in one important way: they vote. Fully 86 percent of the parents polled said they were registered to vote, a figure that is well above the national average. In addition, some 77 percent of them reported voting in the 1992 presidential election, compared to a national turnout of 52 percent. The principal reason cited by nonvoters for their failure to participate in elections is not having time to do so (24 percent). Not being registered to vote was cited by 20 percent. Only 18 percent said they were not interested in politics.

Which brings us to an important caveat. The U.S. Census Bureau reports that survey respondents regularly overreport their voting by 7 to 10 percent. Evidently most citizens believe they *ought* to vote. This overreporting seems to be particularly true for parents. Ruy Teixeira's analysis—presented in Chapter 8—using 1952–1996 survey data from the University of Michigan's National Election Studies, shows that parents tend to vote less than nonparents.

Although American parents say they participate in the democratic process, the survey data demonstrate that they don't feel their voices are being heard. By a margin of seventeen percentage points (57 percent to 40 percent) they agree with the statement "I don't think public officials care much about what parents like me think." A majority of both men and women hold this view, irrespective of race or party identification, in every region of the country, and in all income groups except the highest ($75,000 plus).

Figure B

QUESTION: How much do you think . . .

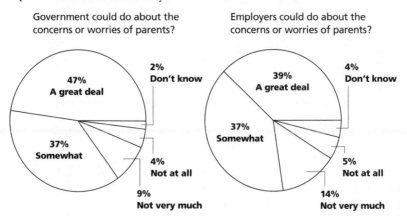

Government could do about the
concerns or worries of parents?

Employers could do about the
concerns or worries of parents?

An associated finding is that parents across the board feel that government is doing far less than it might to help them. The poll indicates that *only 6 percent of moms and dads think government at any level is doing a great deal* about the concerns and worries of parents, while 46 percent say government is doing something about their concerns and 46 percent say it is doing very little. They make it clear, however, that they feel government is capable of doing much more. Some 47 percent say government could do a great deal about parents' concerns, and 37 percent say government could do something about them. Significantly, only 13 percent say government could do little or nothing to help. These findings undercut a popular piece of conventional wisdom. In recent years, elected leaders on both sides of the political divide have become convinced that the American electorate is anti-government in principle and rejects government as an instrument for helping families (see Newt Gingrich's Contract with America and President Clinton's 1996 State of the Union Address). At least for parents, nothing could be further from the truth.

If parents are disappointed with government, they also believe the private sector could do much more to help families. *Only 6 percent of parents in our survey say that employers are doing a great deal* about the concerns or worries of parents, 37 percent say they are doing something, while a majority—53 percent—say employers are doing very little indeed. They believe that much more corporate responsibility could be shown in this area: 39 percent say business could do a great deal to help parents, 41 percent say business could do something, while just 19 percent are of the opinion that business can do very little. American parents are thus even more critical of the performance of the private sector toward families than

Table B. Policies to Help Parents

	Favor %	Oppose %	Strongly Favor %
Legislation requiring gun makers and sellers to install trigger locks or safety devices to make it harder for kids to fire them or prevent accidental firing by children.	89	11	78
Establishing federal income tax credit or deductions to help parents pay for their children's college education for families with a total income under $100,000 per year.	94	6	71
A law to ensure 24 hours' or three days' paid leave annually for family needs, like parent-teacher conferences or taking a child to the doctor.	87	12	68
Government should provide tax incentives to companies so that all full-time workers are paid a wage above the poverty line.	83	16	61
Establishing a rating system for sex and violence in TV shows like that in the movies.	82	16	59
Doubling the existing federal income tax credit for child care and preschool expenses to $1,000 per year.	89	10	58
Eliminating state and local sales taxes on kids' necessities like diapers, school materials, and car seats.	82	16	56
Tax incentives to encourage family-friendly policies by employers, such as benefits for part-time workers and flexible working hours.	90	9	52
Tripling the dependent exemption on your income tax to $7,500 per dependent.	82	14	50
Keeping schools open longer for classes, homework, or clubs to better match the typical workday.	75	24	47
Government paying for health insurance for children of parents earning under $30,000, but over the limit for Medicaid.	75	23	47
Legislation requiring companies employing more than 25 people to offer up to 12 weeks of paid family leave to mothers or fathers after childbirth or adoption.	76	23	46
Letting workers take time off instead of extra pay for overtime.	79	17	45
Letting workers take up to two weeks' unpaid leave per year in addition to their paid vacation.	71	28	38
Creating a tax incentive for marriage, by taxing married couples less than two single people with the same income.	65	32	36
Banning all handguns.	53	47	36
Requiring schoolchildren to wear uniforms.	55	44	32
Lengthening the school year by 20 days.	55	41	30

they are of government—but they also believe that business has the potential to be much more family-friendly. One of our male focus-group participants pointed out that morale would be higher if companies were more accommodating: "I think that if the company I worked for understood that we all have family and kids and were a little more lenient, they'd probably get a little bit more work out of me. That would be a whole lot better than me saying, 'You know, I'm gonna screw you every chance I get, because my kids do come first.'"[1]

Additional Policies Parents Would Vote For

Six other measures enjoy strong support from roughly two fifths or more of parents. Some 47 percent of American parents polled strongly believe that government should pay for health insurance for children in families over the Medicaid income limit but earning less than $30,000 annually. Almost as many (46 percent) strongly favor extending the Family and Medical Leave Act so that companies with more than twenty-five employees must offer twelve weeks of *paid* family leave to parents after childbirth or adoption. Allowing workers to take time off instead of extra pay for overtime work is strongly favored by 45 percent, and allowing workers to take up to two weeks of unpaid leave per year in addition to their normal paid vacations is strongly supported by 38 percent. Finally, 36 percent of parents strongly support eliminating the marriage penalty in our tax code. These six measures also enjoy broad support among parents, with at least 65 percent in favor and a support-to-opposition ratio of roughly two to one or better, so that although these policies are not top priorities for parents, they do represent areas in which parents would like to see changes.

The final group of measures has fewer strong supporters, with only 30 to 40 percent of parents strongly in favor. They are also more controversial among parents as a whole. Banning all handguns is strongly supported by only 36 percent of those surveyed, and this issue divides parents almost in half (53–47 percent). As one would expect, a complete ban on all handguns enjoys much less support than a gun control measure specifically designed to reduce children's access to these weapons. Requiring school uniforms is strongly favored by 32 percent of parents, and lengthening the school year by twenty days is strongly supported by 30 percent. A majority of parents are in favor of all these proposals, but those in favor outnumber those opposed by a margin of less than three to two. These ideas are almost as likely to generate conflict as consensus among parents.

APPENDIX B

························

Tables

Growing Together—1950 to 1978
Growth of Family Income by Quintile

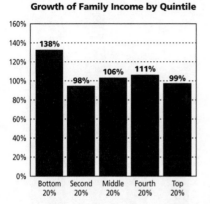

Source: Bureau of the Census, Current Population Survey. All data deflated using CPI-U-X1.

Growing Apart—1979 to 1995
Growth of Family Income by Quintile

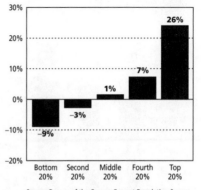

Source: Bureau of the Census, Current Population Survey. Note: Data for1995 reflect changes in top coding and the use of 1990 population weights. All data deflated using CPI-U-X1.

Cumulative Change in Real Wages Since 1980

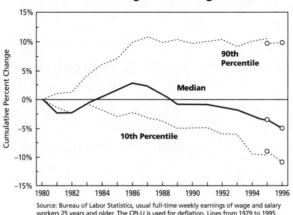

Source: Bureau of Labor Statistics, usual full-time weekly earnings of wage and salary workers 25 years and older. The CPI-U is used for deflation. Lines from 1979 to 1995 represent annual averages; lines from 1995 to 1996 are based on third-quarter figures.

Child Poverty in Rich Nations:
Where Taxes and Transfers Help Least

The UK and the US have the highest child poverty rates among the eight industrialized countries shown below—27.9% and 22.3% respectively of their children 17 years or younger live below 40% of the adjusted median family income, according to 1986 figures. France also has a high child poverty rate—21.2%, according to 1984 data. However, while France and the other continental European countries reduce their child poverty rates significantly through taxes and transfers, in the US the rate goes down only 1.9% to 20.4% after families receive all forms of cash income plus food stamps and other benefits and pay their taxes (if any). Direct comparison of income and poverty across a wide range of countries was made possible by the Luxembourg Income Study (LIS) database.

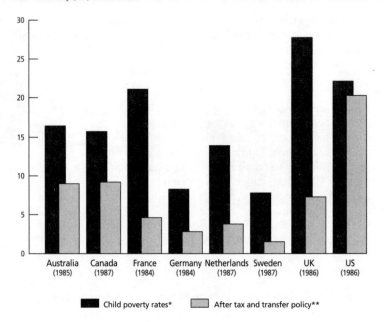

Poverty rates measured as percentages of children living below 40% of the adjusted median family income in each country.

* The ratio of the US poverty line for a three-person family to the adjusted median income was 40.7% in 1986. Thus, the 40% line is close to the official US poverty line.

**Includes all forms of cash income plus food stamps and similar benefits in other nations, minus federal income and payroll taxes.

Income is adjusted using the US poverty line equivalence scale.

Source: Timothy M. Smeeding, "The War on Poverty: What Worked?" Testimony to the Joint Economic Committee, US Congress, 25 September 1991.

Notes

1. The Partnership

1. The only policy we have in place is the 1993 Family and Medical Leave Act, which entitles eligible employees to take up to twelve weeks of unpaid, job-protected leave for specified family and medical reasons, including childbirth and adoption. More than a third (36.5 percent) of men and slightly less than a third (30.9 percent) of women are not covered by the FMLA. See Commission on Leave, U.S. Department of Labor, "A Workable Balance: Report to Congress on Family and Medical Leave Policies" (Washington, D.C.: GPO, 1996), p. xvi. As Harvard economist Claudia Goldin has shown, partly because we do not have paid parenting leave or other social supports, no cohort of college-educated American women has had a high success rate in combining family and career. The cohort who graduated in 1972 provide a guide for today's college women. In 1991, when this group was 37–47 years old, 28 percent of the sample had yet to have a first birth. Goldin estimates that 24 percent to 33 percent of this group had achieved a career. Thus *only 13 percent to 17 percent of the group had achieved family and career* by the time they were forty years old. Among those who attained a career, 50 percent were childless. See Claudia Goldin, "Career and Family: College Women Look to the Past," National Bureau of Economic Research, Working Paper Series No. 5188, July 1995.

2. Parents and National Survival

1. An index measuring the social health of children is at its lowest point in twenty-five years. See *1996 Index of Social Health* (New York: Fordham Institute for Innovation in Social Policy, 1996), p. 6.
2. National Commission on the Role of the Schools and the Community in Improving Adolescent Health, *Code Blue: Uniting for Healthier Youth*

(Washington D.C.: National Association of State Boards of Education/American Medical Association, 1990), p. 3.

3. Centers for Disease Control and Prevention, "Rates of Homicide, Suicide and Firearm-Related Death Among Children—26 Industrialized Countries," *Morbidity and Mortality Weekly Report* 46, no. 5 (Feb. 7, 1997): 101–5. According to this study, the number of child homicides in the U.S. is five time higher than the *combined* figure for twenty-five other developed countries.

4. Steve Farkas and Jean Johnson, *Kids These Days: What Americans Really Think About the Next Generation,* a report from Public Agenda, sponsored by Ronald McDonald House Charities and the Advertising Council, 1997, p. 13.

5. The language of these sentences owes much to the work of the advisers to the Task Force on Parent Empowerment, particularly Enola Aird and Nancy Rankin.

6. Megan Rosenfeld, "Father Knows Squat," *Washington Post,* Nov. 13, 1994, p. G1.

7. Even with the September 1996 hike in the minimum wage, it still has only 63 percent of the buying power it had in the 1960s. See Edward N. Wolff, "The Economic Status of Parents in Postwar America," paper prepared for the Task Force on Parent Empowerment, Sept. 20, 1997, p. 27.

8. Summarized from Kenneth House, "No. 2 at Levi's Cashed Out at $107 Million; Executive's Package Set Bay Area Record," *San Francisco Chronicle,* Nov. 12, 1997, p. A1, and Ralph T. King, Jr., "Levi's Ex-President Got 1996 Payment of $125 Million," *Wall Street Journal,* Nov. 14, 1997, p. B6.

9. David Cay Johnston, "Tracking Executives' Compensation," *New York Times,* Apr. 14, 1997, p. D6. For median wage data, see U.S. Census Bureau, Historical Income Tables—Persons, Table P29, www.census.gov.

10. Allan Carlson, president, Rockford Institute, telephone interview, Feb. 10, 1998. This $6,500 figure represents the same percentage of the 1996 median family income as $600 did in 1948. See also Ben J. Wattenberg, "The Easy Solution to the Social Security Crisis," *New York Times Magazine,* June 22, 1997, p. 30.

11. Peter Wilkinson, "Madonna on Life Before and After Motherhood," *Redbook,* Jan.1997, p. 58.

12. This figure describes the average expenditure on a child from birth to eighteen years, in a husband-wife household with an income in the $33,700–$56,700 range. See U.S. Department of Agriculture, Center for Nutrition Policy and Promotion, *Expenditures on Children by Families, 1995 Annual Report,* Publication No. 1528 (Washington, D.C.: GPO, 1995).

13. Viviana A. Zelizer, *Pricing the Priceless Child: The Changing Social Value of Children* (New York: Basic, 1985), p. 3.

14. Jane Addams, *Democracy and Social Ethics* (Cambridge Mass.: Belknap/Harvard University Press, 1964).

15. Carol Gilligan, *In a Different Voice: Psychological Theory and Women's Development* (Cambridge Mass.: Harvard University Press, 1982), pp. 149, 129.
16. Jean Bethke Elshtain, *Democracy on Trial* (New York: Basic, 1995), p. 129.
17. Gus A. Haggstrom, Linda J. Waite, David E. Kanouse, and Thomas J. Blaschke, "Changes in the Life Styles of New Parents" (Santa Monica, Calif.: Rand Corporation, Dec. 1984), p. 61.
18. Diana DiNitto, *Social Welfare: Politics & Public Policy* (New York: Allyn & Bacon, 1995), pp. 169–70. See detailed discussion of AFDC in Chapter 6.
19. Stephanie Ventura, demographer, National Center for Health Statistics, telephone interview, Dec. 10, 1997.
20. U.S. Bureau of the Census, *Child Support and Alimony: 1989*, Current Population Reports, series P60, No. 173 (Washington, D.C.: GPO, 1991).
21. Daniel R. Geyer and Steven Favasky, "Custodial Fathers: Myths, Realities, and Child Support Policy," *Journal of Marriage and the Family* 55 (Feb. 1993): 73–89.
22. For an in-depth discussion, see Jack Kammer, "What Do We Really Know About Child Support?" *Crisis* (Jan. 1994): 16.
23. Harry F. Harlow, "Love in Infant Monkeys," *Scientific American,* June 1959, pp. 68–74.
24. Willard Gaylin, "In the Beginning: Helpless and Dependent," in Willard Gaylin, Ira Glasser, Steven Marcus, and David J. Rothman, eds., *Doing Good: The Limits of Benevolence* (New York: Pantheon, 1978), p. 10.
25. Urie Bronfenbrenner, "Discovering What Families Do," in *Rebuilding the Nest: A New Commitment to the American Family* (Milwaukee, Wis.: Family Service America, 1990), p. 31.
26. James Alan Fox, *Trends in Juvenile Violence: A Report to the United States Attorney General on Current and Future Rates of Juvenile Offending* (Washington, D.C.: Bureau of Justice Statistics, Mar. 1996); Centers for Disease Control, "Rates of Homicide . . . Among Children," pp. 101–5; Select Committee on Children, Youth, and Families, *U.S. Children and Their Families,* p. 31, and National Law Center on Homelessness and Poverty, *Blocks to Their Future: A Report on the Barriers to Preschool Education for Homeless Children,* Sept. 1997; Lloyd D. Johnson et al., *National Survey Results on Drug Use from the Monitoring the Future Study, 1975–1996* (Washington, D.C.: National Institute on Drug Abuse, 1997), Table 20-1; Karen W. Arenson, "Students Continue to Improve, College Board Says," *New York Times,* Aug. 23, 1996, p. A16; Centers for Disease Control, *Morbidity and Mortality Weekly Report,* Apr. 21, 1995, and *Suicide Deaths and Rates per 100,000, United States, 1989–1995,* unpublished data; National Center for Health Statistics, *Health United States 1996–97,* July 1997, Table 73, p. 193.
27. Carnegie Council on Adolescent Development, *Great Transitions: Prepar-*

ing Adolescents for a New Century (New York: Carnegie Corporation of New York, Oct. 1995), p. 10.

28. Fox, *Trends in Juvenile Violence.*

29. Fox Butterfield, "Survey Finds That Crimes Cost $450 Billion a Year," *New York Times,* Apr. 22, 1996, p. A8.

30. Barbara M. Jones, "Guns, Drugs, and Juvenile Justice: Three Aspects of the Crisis in Youth Violence," paper prepared for the Task Force on Parent Empowerment, Apr. 17, 1996, p. 1.

31. Nancy Jo Sales, "Lost in the Park," *New York,* June 16, 1997, pp. 24–29; N. R. Kleinfield et al., "Lives Tangle in Park's Hidden World," *New York Times,* June 1, 1997, p. 1.

32. Centers for Disease Control, "Suicide Among Children, Adolescents, and Young Adults—United States, 1980–1992," vol. 44, no. 15, Apr. 21, 1995, pp. 289–90; National Center for Health Statistics, Mortality Data Tapes, "Suicide Deaths and Rates per 100,000, United States, 1989–1995."

33. Sylvia Ann Hewlett, *Child Neglect in Rich Nations* (New York: UNICEF, 1993), p. 1.

34. U.S. Bureau of the Census, *1997 March Current Population Survey,* App. C, Table 20.

35. Joe Dalaker, statistician, Bureau of the Census, telephone interview, Oct. 15, 1997.

36. *National Survey Results on Drug Use;* National Institute on Drug Abuse, "Facts About Teenagers and Drug Abuse," NIDA Capsule Series (C-83-07), 1996; "Monitoring the Future Study: Trends in Prevalence of Various Drugs for 8th Graders, 10th Graders and High School Seniors," NIDA Capsule Series (C-94-01), 1996.

37. National Center for Education Statistics, *NAEP 1994 Trends in Academic Progress* (Washington, D.C.: GPO, Nov. 1996), p. iv.

38. National Center for Education Statistics, *Digest of Education Statistics, 1997,* Table 99, "High school graduates compared with population 17 years of age, by sex and control of school: 1869–70 to 1996–97," p. 108, Dec. 31, 1997.

39. Carnegie, *Great Transitions,* p. 10.

40. David C. Rowe and Robert Plomin, "The Importance of Nonshared (E_1) Environmental Influences in Behavioral Development," *Developmental Psychology* 17, no. 5 (1981): 517–53.

41. Victor R. Fuchs, *Women's Quest for Economic Equality* (Cambridge, Mass.: Harvard University Press, 1988), p. 111.

42. Edward N. Wolff, "The Economic Status of Parents in Postwar America," paper prepared for the Task Force on Parent Empowerment, Sept. 20, 1996, p. 9.

43. Juliet B. Schor, *The Overworked American: The Unexpected Decline of Leisure* (New York: Basic, 1992), p. 29.

44. Jerome Kagan, *The Nature of the Child* (New York: Basic, 1984), p. 108.

45. J. L. Richardson et al., "Substance Abuse Among Eighth-Grade Students

Who Take Care of Themselves After School," *Pediatrics* 84, no. 3 (Sept. 1989): 556–66.
46. Michael D. Resnick et al., "Protecting Adolescents from Harm," *Journal of the American Medical Association* (Sept. 1997): 823–32; S. Jody Heymann and Alison Earle, "Family Policy for School Age Children: The Case of Parental Evening Work," Malcolm Wiener Center for Social Policy and the John F. Kennedy School of Government, Harvard University, April 1996, H-96-2.
47. James Alan Fox and Sanford A. Newman, "After-School Crime or After-School Programs: Tuning in to the Prime Time for Violent Juvenile Crime and Implications for National Policy," a report to the U.S. Attorney General, Department of Justice, Sept. 10, 1997, p. 3.
48. Howard Hayghe, supervisory economist, Bureau of Labor Statistics, telephone interview, Jan. 13, 1998.
49. Fox and Newman, "After-School Crime," p. 6.
50. James S. Coleman, "Effects of School on Learning: The IEA Findings," paper presented at Conference on Educational Achievement, Harvard University, Nov. 1973, p. 40.
51. Laurence Steinberg, "Failure Outside the Classroom," *Wall Street Journal,* July 11, 1996, p. A14; Laurence Steinberg et al., *Beyond the Classroom: Why School Reform Has Failed and What Parents Need to Do* (New York: Simon & Schuster, 1996), p. 119.
52. Michael Sandel, "Making Nice Is Not the Same as Doing Good," *New York Times,* Dec. 29, 1996, p. E9.
53. Robert D. Putnam, "Bowling Alone: America's Declining Social Capital," *Journal of Democracy* 6, no. 1 (Jan. 1995): 65–78. See also Putnam, "The Strange Disappearance of Civic America," *American Prospect* (Winter 1996): 34–48.
54. Bill Moyers, *Bill Moyers: A World of Ideas* (New York: Doubleday, 1989), p. 60.
55. "Excerpts from Tapes in Discrimination Lawsuit," *New York Times,* Nov. 4, 1996, p. D4.

3. Managerial Greed and the Collapse of Economic Security

1. Parent interview, Task Force on Parent Empowerment, Oct. 14, 1997. Pseudonyms are used throughout this book for all persons who participated in focus groups held by the task force.
2. Judith H. Dobrzynski, "New Road to Riches Is Paved with Options," *New York Times,* Mar. 30, 1997, p. 1. Increasing top executive compensation comes in the form of stock options, and as a result, the "market advance has delivered a stunning windfall to corporate chieftains almost regardless of individual performance."
3. Albert O. Hirschman and Michael Rothschild, "The Changing Tolerance for Income Inequality in the Course of Economic Development," *Quarterly Journal of Economics* 87, no. 4 (Nov. 1973): 546. In this seminal

article, Hirschman and Rothschild point out that people feel good about the prosperity of others only when they can reasonably expect to share in that prosperity.

4. Dana Canedy, "In Retailing, Biggest Gains Come from Big Spenders," *New York Times,* Dec. 26, 1996, p. 1.

5. Romesh Ratnesar, "The Axman Cometh," *Mother Jones,* Nov.-Dec. 1995, p. 2.

6. Alan Downs, *Corporate Executions* (New York: American Management Association, 1995), p. 31.

7. The much talked-about increase in family income in 1996 was insignificant, and all the real gains were in older, childless families. Overall, families with one or more children had a median income of $40,985 in 1996 compared with $42,335 in 1989. See U.S. Bureau of the Census, Current Population Survey, Historical Income Tables—Families, March 1997, Tables F8 and F10, www.census.gov. See also Associated Press, "Report: Incomes Fall for Parents Under 30," *Newsday,* Sept. 17, 1997, p. A46.

8. David M. Gordon, *Fat and Mean: The Corporate Squeeze of Working Americans and the Myth of Managerial "Downsizing"* (New York: Free Press, 1996), pp. 34, 42.

9. "Executive Pay," *Business Week,* Apr. 21, 1997, p. 59.

10. Gordon, *Fat and Mean,* pp. 18, 20.

11. Robert B. Reich, "The Unfinished Agenda," paper presented to the Council on Excellence in Government, Jan. 9, 1997, Technical Appendix, p. 2.

12. Alan B. Krueger, "The Truth About Wages," *New York Times,* July 23, 1997, p. 23. See also Alan B. Krueger, "What's Up with Wages?" paper prepared for Goldman, Sachs and Co., Oct. 21, 1997, and Alan B. Krueger and Jörn-Steffen Piscjke, "Observations and Conjectures on the U.S. Employment Miracle," Draft Working Paper #390, Industrial Relations Section, Princeton University, Aug. 14, 1997.

13. In 1995, 48 percent of all children under eighteen lived in households where family income was less than $35,000. Bureau of the Census, Feb. 19, 1997.

14. Edward M. Kennedy, "Can Workers Reclaim the American Dream?" *USA Today* (Magazine), Sept. 1996, p. 22.

15. Lester G. Thurow, *The Future of Capitalism: How Today's Economic Forces Shape Tomorrow's World* (New York: Morrow, 1996), p. 24.

16. Between 1950 and 1978, the inflation-adjusted family income of the bottom quintile grew by 138 percent, while the real income of the richest 20 percent of families grew by 99 percent. Reich, "The Unfinished Agenda," Technical Appendix, pp. 3–4.

17. John J. Sweeney, *America Needs a Raise: Fighting for Economic Security and Social Justice* (Boston: Houghton Mifflin, 1996), p. 32.

18. Gordon, *Fat and Mean,* p. 204.

19. Ibid., p. 208.

20. Sweeney, *America Needs a Raise,* pp. 81, 78.

21. Thomas Ferguson and Joel Rogers, *Right Turn: The Decline of the Demo-*

crats and the Future of American Politics (New York: Hill and Wang, 1986), Table 4.2.

22. Gordon, *Fat and Mean,* p. 211.

23. Sweeney, *America Needs a Raise,* p. 33.

24. Thurow, *The Future of Capitalism,* p. 23.

25. U.S. Bureau of the Census, Current Population Survey, Mar. 1997, Historical Income Tables—Persons, Table P34, www.census.gov. Figures refer to the median earnings of males working fifty to fifty-two weeks a year. See also Edward M. Kennedy, "The Rising Tide Must Lift More Boats," paper presented to the Center for National Policy, Washington, D.C., Feb. 8, 1996, p. 2.

26. Thurow, *The Future of Capitalism,* p. 23.

27. Ibid., p. 25.

28. Edward N. Wolff, "The Economic Status of Parents in Postwar America," paper prepared for the Task Force on Parent Empowerment, Sept. 20, 1996. See also interview with Edward N. Wolff, Sept. 20, 1996.

29. Jody Heymann and Alison Earle, "The Work-Family Balance: What Hurdles Are Parents Leaving Welfare Likely to Confront?" *Journal of Policy Analysis and Management* 17, no. 2 (1998): 7.

30. Drawn from Rachel L. Swarns, "4,000 Hearts Full of Hope Line Up for 700 Jobs," *New York Times,* Mar. 19, 1997, p. A1.

31. See Louis Uchitelle and N. R. Kleinfeld, "On the Battlefields of Business, Millions of Casualties," *New York Times,* Mar. 3, 1996, pp. 1, 26; N. R. Kleinfeld, "The Company: As Family, No More," *New York Times,* Mar. 4, 1996, p. A1; Rick Bragg, "Big Holes Where Dignity Used to Be," *New York Times,* Mar. 5, 1996, p. A1; Sara Rimer, "A Hometown Feels Less Like Home," *New York Times,* Mar. 6, 1996, p. A1; Kirk Johnson, "In the Class of '70, Wounded Winners," *New York Times,* Mar. 7, 1996, p. A1; Elizabeth Kolbert and Adam Cylmer, "The Politics of Layoffs: In Search of a Message," *New York Times,* Mar. 8, 1996, p. A1; David E. Sanger and Steve Lohr, "The Search for New Answers to Avoid the Layoff," Mar. 9, 1996, p. A1.

32. See Louis Uchitelle, "The New Buzz: Growth Is Good," *New York Times,* June 18, 1996, p. D1; Uchitelle and Kleinfeld, "On the Battlefields of Business."

33. Thurow, *The Future of Capitalism,* p. 27.

34. Ibid., p. 28.

35. Parent interview, Task Force on Parent Empowerment, Sept. 17, 1997.

36. John Stinson, economist, Bureau of Labor Statistics, telephone interview, Feb. 18, 1997.

37. Details taken from Lesley Alderman, "Here Comes the Four-Income Family," *Money,* Feb. 1995, p. 148.

38. Juliet B. Schor, *The Overworked American: The Unexpected Decline of Leisure* (New York: Basic, 1992), p. 29. Much of the data in the following paragraphs comes from this book.

39. Parent interview, Task Force on Parent Empowerment, Sept. 17, 1997.

40. Arlie Hochschild, *The Second Shift: Working Parents and the Revolution at Home* (New York: Viking, 1989), p. 272.
41. James Alan Fox and Sanford A. Newman, "After-School Crime or After-School Programs: Tuning In to the Prime Time for Violent Juvenile Crime and Implications for National Policy," A Report to the U.S. Attorney General, Sept. 1997, p. 6.
42. J. L. Richardson et al., "Substance Use Among Eighth Grade Students Who Take Care of Themselves After School," *Pediatrics*, 84, no. 3 (Sept. 1989): 556–66.
43. Michael D. Resnick et al., "Protecting Adolescents from Harm," *Journal of the American Medical Association* (Sept. 1997): 823–32.
44. Gordon, *Fat and Mean*, p. 28.
45. Sylvia Ann Hewlett, *Child Neglect in Rich Nations* (New York: UNICEF, 1993), p. 8.
46. Roger Cohen, "French Premier Proposes Cutting Workweek to Create Jobs," *New York Times*, Oct. 11, 1997, p. A3.
47. As of 1997, there were some fears, particularly in Germany, about pressure "for workers to put in more hours at less convivial times." But German workers have a long way to go before catching up with American-style hours. Allan Cowell, "Workers in Germany Fear the Miracle Is Over," *New York Times*, July 30, 1997, p. A1. See also Hewlett, *Child Neglect*, p. 8.
48. William Julius Wilson, *When Work Disappears: The World of the New Urban Poor* (New York: Knopf, 1996), p. xiii.
49. Center for the Study of Social Policy, *World Without Work: Causes and Consequences of Black Male Joblessness* (Washington, D.C.: Center for the Study of Social Policy, Dec. 1994), p. 1.
50. Ibid., p. 3.
51. Ibid., p. 15.
52. Ibid., p. 16.
53. The jury is still out on what proportion of fatherlessness in the black community is due to welfare policy (AFDC) and what is a function of joblessness and low earning power. However, the expert community agrees that both factors have important explanatory power. See Wilson, *When Work Disappears*, chap. 4.
54. Interview, Task Force on Parent Empowerment, Oct. 25, 1996.
55. Pam Belluck, "The Youngest Ex-Cons: Facing a Difficult Road Out of Crime," *New York Times*, Nov. 17, 1996, p. 1.
56. Marc Mauer and Tracy Huling, "Young Black Americans and the Criminal Justice System: Five Years Later," Sentencing Project, Oct. 1995, pp. 1, 4, Table 2.
57. Sweeney, *America Needs a Raise*, p. 59.
58. Gordon, *Fat and Mean*, pp. 81–83.
59. Ibid., pp. 81–83, 35.
60. Alex Markels, "Restructuring Alters Management Role but Leaves It Robust," *Wall Street Journal*, Sept. 25, 1995, p. A1.

61. Downs, *Corporate Executions*, p. 28.
62. Ibid., p. 14.
63. Gordon, *Fat and Mean*, p. 44.
64. Edward N. Wolff, *Top Heavy: A Study of the Increasing Inequality of Wealth in America* (New York: Twentieth Century Fund, 1995), pp. 7, 24, 22.
65. David E. Rosenbaum, "In Political Money Game, the Year of the Big Loopholes," *New York Times*, Dec. 26, 1996, p. 1.
66. Center for Responsive Politics, *Who's Paying for This Election? A Special Report on Fundraising Patterns in the 1996 Elections* (Washington, D.C.: Center for Responsive Politics, Oct. 1996), p. 6.
67. Leslie Wayne, "Business Is Biggest Political Donor, Dwarfing Labor's Contribution, Study Says," *New York Times*, Oct. 18, 1996, p. 27.
68. Robert Reich, *Locked in the Cabinet* (New York: Knopf, 1997), p. 91.
69. Wayne, "Business Is Biggest Political Donor."
70. Ibid.
71. Gordon, *Fat and Mean*, p. 82.
72. Krueger, "The Truth About Wages."
73. Derrick Bell, *Faces at the Bottom of the Well: The Permanence of Racism* (New York: Basic, 1993).
74. Steve Haugen, economist, Bureau of Labor Statistics, interview, Dec. 4, 1997.

4. Government Tilts Against Parents

1. Mark Zepezauer and Arthur Naiman, *Take the Rich Off Welfare* (Tucson: Odonian, 1996), p. 118.
2. Details taken from James Brooke, "Young Unwelcome in Retirees' Haven," *New York Times*, Feb. 16, 1997, p. 16.
3. Lester Thurow, *The Future of Capitalism: How Today's Economic Forces Shape Tomorrow's World* (New York: Morrow, 1996), p. 277.
4. See Shirley P. Burggraf, *The Feminine Economy and Economic Man* (Reading, Mass: Addison-Wesley, 1997), pp. 55–63, for a discussion of the additional social and parental-time costs. Burggraf estimates that when time and provision costs are combined, the cost of raising one child to age eighteen comes to $410,554, $811,997, and $1,502,231 for low-, medium-, and high-income families.
5. Brad Edmondson, Judith Waldrop, Diane Crispell, and Linda Jacobsen, "Married with Grown Children," *American Demographics* 15, no. 12 (Dec. 1993): 32.
6. The only policy we have in place is the 1993 Family and Medical Leave Act, which entitles eligible employees to take up to twelve weeks of unpaid, job-protected leave for specified family and medical reasons, including childbirth and adoption. More than a third (36.5 percent) of men and slightly less than a third (30.9 percent) of women are not covered by the FMLA. See U.S. Department of Labor, Commission on Leave, "A

Workable Balance: Report to Congress on Family and Medical Leave Policies" (Washington, D.C.: GPO, 1996), p. xvi.

7. David Popenoe pulls together the most recent scholarship in *Life Without Father* (New York: Free Press, 1996), pp. 52–56. See also Sara McLanahan and Gary Sandefur, *Growing Up with a Single Parent* (Cambridge, Mass.: Harvard University Press, 1994).

8. Judith S. Wallerstein and Sandra Blakeslee, *Second Chances: Men, Women and Children a Decade after Divorce* (New York: Ticknor & Fields, 1989), p. 12.

9. John Rawls, *A Theory of Justice* (Cambridge Mass.: Belknap Press, 1971), pp. 3–5.

10. Michael Lerner, *The Politics of Meaning: Restoring Hope and Possibility in an Age of Cynicism* (Reading, Mass.: Addison-Wesley, 1996), p. 93.

11. Ibid., p. 95.

12. David Guttmann, *Reclaimed Powers: Toward a New Psychology of Men and Women in Later Life* (New York: Basic, 1987), pp. 185–214.

13. Mirra Komarovsky, *Women in the Modern World* (Boston: Little, Brown, 1953), p. 258.

14. Allan Carlson, president, Rockford Institute, telephone interview, Feb. 10, 1998.

15. Cited in Allan Carlson, "Taxes and the Family," paper prepared for the Task Force on Parent Empowerment, Sept. 20, 1996. House Ways and Means Committee Report No. 1365, 78th Congress, 2nd Sess., p. 5; quoted in H. Seltzer, *The Personal Exemption in the Income Tax* (New York: National Bureau of Economic Research, 1968), p. 42.

16. Milton Greenberg, *The G.I. Bill: The Law That Changed America* (New York: Lickle, 1997), p. 9.

17. Theda Skocpol, "A Partnership with American Families," in Stanley B. Greenberg and Theda Skocpol, eds., *The New Majority: Toward a Popular Progressive Politics* (New Haven, Conn.: Yale University Press, 1997), pp. 114–15.

18. Greenberg, *The G.I. Bill*, p. 39.

19. Cited in Peter Winn, "Back to the Future: A GI Bill for the Nineties," paper prepared for the Task Force on Parent Empowerment, Jan. 1997, p. 7. See U.S. House of Representatives, Committee on Veteran's Affairs, *Hearings on Legislation to Provide G.I. Bill Benefits for Post-Korean Veterans,* 89th Congress, 1st Sess., 1965, p. 3091.

20. Greenberg, *The G.I. Bill*, pp. 61, 98.

21. Ibid., pp. 35–61.

22. "The Roots of Home," *Time,* June 20, 1960, p. 15.

23. Bruce Lambert, "At 50 Levittown Contends with Its Legacy of Bias," *New York Times,* Dec. 28, 1997, p. 23.

24. Barrington Moore, Jr., "Thoughts on the Future of the Family," in John Edwards, ed., *The Family and Change* (New York: Knopf, 1969), p. 456; Brigitte Berger and Peter Berger, *The War Over the Family: Capturing the Middle Ground* (London: Penguin, 1983), p. 27.

25. Carlson, "Taxes and the Family," p. 10.
26. Eugene Steuerle, "The Tax Treatment of Households of Different Size," in Rudolph G. Penner, ed., *Taxing the Family* (Washington, D.C.: American Enterprise Institute, 1983), p. 74.
27. Carlson, "Taxes and the Family," p. 13.
28. *The Economist,* Oct. 18, 1997, p. 28.
29. Jason DeParle, "Slamming the Door," *New York Times Magazine,* Oct. 20, 1996, p. 52.
30. Joint Center for Housing Studies, *The State of the Nation's Housing* (Cambridge, Mass.: Harvard University, 1997), pp. 20–23.
31. Parent interview, Task Force on Parent Empowerment, Nov. 22, 1997. In the fall of 1997, St. Paul was facing a new crisis in low-income housing. See Mike Kaszuba, "Higher Rents at Bloomington High-Rise," *Star Tribune,* Nov. 14, 1997, p. B1.
32. U.S. Department of Housing and Urban Development, Office of Policy Development and Research, *Rental Housing Assistance at a Crossroads: A Report to Congress on Worst-Case Housing Needs,* Mar. 1996, Table A3, p. A4.
33. Given a free choice, 33 percent of these women would work part-time and 51 percent would divide their time between home and volunteer work. See *Women: The New Providers: A Study of Women's Views on Family, Work, Society and the Future* (New York: Families and Work Institute, May 1995), p. 30. See also Children's Defense Fund, "Inadequate Child Care Strains America's Working Families," Fact Sheet, Nov. 4, 1997, www.childrensdefense.org.
34. National Association of Realtors, "Housing Affordability for the United States, 1970–1996," compiled from U.S. Bureau of the Census, Historical Income Tables, Nov. 1997, Table 1-7.
35. Parent interview, Task Force on Parent Empowerment, Oct. 28, 1997.
36. David Cay Johnston, "The Divine Write-Off," *New York Times,* Jan. 12, 1996, p. D1.
37. U.S. Bureau of the Census, *Money Income in the United States: 1995,* Current Population Reports, P60–193 (Washington, D.C.: GPO, 1996), Table 5; Shirley Smith, Census Bureau, telephone interviews, Jan. 31, 1997, and Feb. 3, 1997.
38. See discussion in Don Browning, BonnieJ. Miller-McLemore, Pamela D. Couture, K. Bryholf Lyon, and Robert M. Franklin, *From Culture Wars to Common Ground: Religion and the American Family Debate* (Louisville, Ky.: Westminster/John Knox, 1997), p. 192.
39. Youth interview, Task Force on Parent Empowerment, Feb. 13, 1997.
40. Conna Craig and Derek Herbert, "The State of the Children: An Examination of Government-Run Foster Care," National Center for Policy Analysis, Report No. 210, Aug. 1997, p. 2.
41. Details taken from K. L. Billingsley, "PC Kidnappers," *Heterodoxy,* Jan. 1993, pp. 4–6. For an in-depth account of this case and other examples of how the child welfare agencies victimize families, see Dana Mack,

The Assault on Parenthood (New York: Simon and Schuster, 1997), pp. 54–79.

42. Mack, *Assault on Parenthood,* pp. 59–60.
43. Richard Wexler, *Wounded Innocents: The Real Victims of the War Against Child Abuse* (New York: Prometheus, 1990), p. 17; Mack, *Assault on Parenthood,* p. 61.
44. Wexler, *Wounded Innocents,* pp. 14, 15, 18.
45. Ibid., p. 23.
46. Ibid., pp. 109–13.
47. See Mack, *Assault on Parenthood,* pp. 63–64.
48. Douglas Besharov, "How Child Abuse Programs Hurt Poor Children: The Misuse of Foster Care," *Clearinghouse Review* (July 1988): 222–23.
49. Details taken from Michael D'Antonio, "Catch-22: Working Dad Can't Live with His Kids," *Newsday,* Dec. 5, 1988, p. 5.
50. Wexler, *Wounded Innocents,* p. 48.
51. Mack, *The Assault on Parenthood,* p. 66.
52. Ibid., p. 67.
53. Craig and Herbert, "State of the Children," p. 6.
54. Mack, *The Assault on Parenthood,* pp. 71–72.
55. Ibid., p. 72.
56. Foster care stipends in 1995 were \$344, \$362, or \$416 per child, depending on age; American Public Welfare Association, *W-Memo Foster Care Maintenance Payments Rates: 1995 Survey* (Washington, D.C.: APWA, Oct. 1996), Table 1, p. 5. Note that most states and/or counties supplement these basic rates with additional payments. AFDC payments in 1995 were \$290.10 for one child; U.S. Department of Health and Human Services, Administration for Children and Families, "Characteristics and Financial Circumstances of AFDC Recipients, Fiscal Year 1995," Table 34. See also "Average Monthly AFDC Payment by Number of Recipient Children," p. 1, www.acf.dhhs.gov/programs.
57. Craig and Herbert, "State of the Children," p. 3.
58. See analysis in Edward N. Wolff, "The Economic Status of Parents in Postwar America," paper prepared for the Task Force on Parent Empowerment, Sept. 20, 1996, pp. 2–6.
59. Sylvia Ann Hewlett, *Child Neglect in Rich Nations* (New York: UNICEF, 1993), p. 3. See also Timothy M. Smeeding, "American Income Inequality in a Cross-National Perspective: Why Are We So Different?" draft paper prepared for the National Policy Association's Conference on "The Growth of Income Disparity," Apr. 10, 1997.
60. Office of Management and Budget, *Budget of the U.S. Government, FY 1998* (Washington, D.C.: GPO, 1997), Historical Tables, Table 3.1.
61. Ibid., Table 8.5.
62. Citizens for Tax Justice, "Brief Description of and Comments on the 1997 Tax Act," Aug. 1997, www.ctj.org.
63. Mary Ann Glendon, *Abortion and Divorce in Western Law* (Cambridge, Mass.: Harvard University Press, 1987), p. 142.
64. Ibid.

5. A Poisonous Popular Culture

1. From *Jerry Springer,* "I Stole My Twelve-Year-Old's Boyfriend!" July 30, 1997, Multimedia Entertainment; transcript produced by Burelle's Information Services.

2. Steven D. Stark, *Glued to the Set: The 60 Television Shows and Events That Made Us Who We Are Today* (New York: Free Press, 1997), p. 280, 277.

3. *Jerry Springer* is a syndicated, nationwide show watched by approximately 4 million people.

4. Megan Rosenfeld, "Father Knows Squat," *Washington Post,* Nov. 13, 1994, p. G1.

5. Parent interview, Task Force on Parent Empowerment, Nov. 4, 1997.

6. Details taken from Bill Reel, "Disney's 'Santa Clause' Is a Dad's Legal Nightmare," *Newsday,* Sept. 10, 1997, p. A43.

7. Nina C. Leibman, *Living Room Lectures: The Fifties Family in Film and Television* (Austin: University of Texas Press, 1995), p. 135.

8. Betty Friedan, *The Feminine Mystique* (New York: Dell, 1963), p. 52.

9. June Sochen, "The New Woman and Twenties America: Way Down East," in June E. O'Connor and Martin A. Jackson, eds., *American History/American Film* (New York: Ungar, 1979), p. 17.

10. Leibman, *Living Room Lectures,* p. 3.

11. Beth Austin, "Pretty Worthless: Whatever Happened to Making Movies That Make a Difference?" *Washington Monthly,* May 1991, p. 35.

12. Peter Ames Carlin, "Notes of Discord," *People,* Mar. 24, 1997, p. 56.

13. Kenneth Paul Rosenberg, "'Shine' Depicts False View of Mental Illness," letter, *New York Times,* Mar. 15, 1997, p. 22.

14. Michael Medved, *Hollywood vs. America: Popular Culture and the War on Traditional Values* (New York, HarperPerennial, 1993), p. 154.

15. Marilyn Manson, *Portrait of an American Family,* Marilyn Manson and Trent Reznor, Producers; Dinger & Ollie Music/Beat Up Your Mom Music, BMI, 1994.

16. Body Count, "Momma's Gotta Die Tonight," Body Count, Ice T/Ernie C., Producers; Rhyme Syndicate Music/Emkneesea Music, ASCAP, Sire Records Company, 1992.

17. Wu-Tang Clan, "A Better Tomorrow," Wu-Tang Forever, Wu-Tang Productions, New York, 1997. According to SoundScan, 1.5 million Wu-Tang albums had been sold as of Nov. 24, 1997.

18. Parent interview, Task Force on Parent Empowerment, June 1997.

19. See discussion in Don Browning, Bonnie J. Miller-McLemore, Pamela D. Couture, K. Bryhof Lyon, and Robert M. Franklin, From Culture Wars to Common Ground: Religion and the American Family Debate (Louisville, Ky.: Westminster/John Knox, 1997), pp. 190–98. In their survey of 1,035 therapists, Don Browning and his coauthors find a more complicated reality. Marital and family therapists, for example, have a less individualistic focus.

20. Ibid., p. 101.

21. Dr. Susan Forward, *Toxic Parents: Overcoming Their Hurtful Legacy and Reclaiming Your Life* (New York: Bantam, 1990), p. 175.

22. Ibid.

23. Ibid., p. 4.

24. Claudette Wassil-Grimm, *How to Avoid Your Parents' Mistakes When You Raise Your Children* (New York: Pocket Books, 1990), p. 11.

25. John Bradshaw, *Bradshaw on: The Family* (Deerfield Beach, Fla.: Health Communications, 1988), p. 20, cited in Dana Mack, *The Assault on Parenthood* (New York: Simon and Schuster, 1997), p. 45.

26. John Bradshaw, *Homecoming: Reclaiming and Championing Your Inner Child* (New York: Bantam, 1992), p. 209.

27. For a particularly lyrical and perceptive account of the Freudian view of childhood, see Anne Roiphe, *Fruitful: A Real Mother in the Modern World* (New York: Houghton Mifflin, 1996), pp. 84–85.

28. Ibid., p. 85.

29. See discussion in Mack, *Assault on Parenthood*, pp. 37–42.

30. Alice Miller, *For Your Own Good: Hidden Cruelty in Childrearing and the Roots of Violence* (New York: Noonday, 1990), p. 4.

31. Ibid., p. 97.

32. Ibid., p. 188.

33. Wendy Kaminer, *I'm Dysfunctional, You're Dysfunctional* (New York: Vintage, 1993), p. xvii.

34. Mary Pipher, *The Shelter of Each Other: Rebuilding Our Families* (New York: Grosset/Putnam, 1996), p. 76.

35. Ibid., pp. 26–27. Emphasis added.

36. Arlie Russell Hochschild, *The Time Bind: When Work Becomes Home and Home Becomes Work* (New York: Metropolitan/Holt, 1997), p. 200.

37. Barbara M. Jones, "Youth Violence and the Mass Media," paper prepared for the Task Force on Parent Empowerment, Oct. 13, 1995, pp. 4–7.

38. Robert Coles, "Safety Lessons for the Internet," *New York Times,* Oct. 11, 1997, p. A11.

39. Lynette Friedrich Cofer and Robin Smith Jacobvitz, "The Loss of Moral Turf: Mass Media and Family Values," in David Bankenhorn, Steven Bayme, and Jean Bethke Elshtain, eds., *Rebuilding the Nest: A New Commitment to the American Family* (Milwaukee: Family Service America, 1990), pp. 185, 188. Our analysis of the deregulation of the television industry relies substantially on Cofer and Jacobvitz.

40. Cited in Fred M. Hechinger, "About Education," *New York Times,* Feb. 28, 1990, p. 1.

41. Dorian Friedman, "The Politics of Children's TV," *Family Life,* Dec.–Jan. 1993–1994, p. 99.

42. Lawrie Mifflin, "Should Educational Programming for Children Be Left in the Hands of Broadcasters and Market Forces?" *New York Times,* Apr. 24, 1995, p. D9.

43. Paul Farhi, "Short-Circuiting Educational Television," *Washington Post,* Oct. 12, 1995, p. C3.

44. Bob Dole, "Giving Away the Airwaves," *New York Times,* Mar. 27, 1997, p. A29.
45. "Another Broadcast Giveaway," *New York Times,* June 25, 1997, p. A18.
46. David Sweet and Ram Singh, "TV Viewing and Parental Guidance," Education Consumer Guide, Office of Educational Research and Improvement, U.S. Department of Education, Oct. 1994, p. 2.
47. Lester Thurow, *The Future of Capitalism: How Today's Economic Forces Shape Tomorrow's World* (New York: Morrow, 1996), p. 85. In the average American household, children aged two to eleven spend twenty-three hours a week watching TV, while teenagers average twenty-two hours. These figures do not include time spent watching videocassettes or playing video games, so total TV time is actually significantly higher.
48. A. C. Huston et al., *Big World, Small Screen: The Role of Television in American Society* (Lincoln: University of Nebraska Press, 1992), pp. 53–54; Children's Defense Fund, *The State of America's Children Yearbook 1994* (Washington, D.C.: CDF, 1994), p. 64; Charles S. Clark, "TV Violence," *CQ Researcher,* Mar. 26, 1993, p. 176; Leonard D. Eron, testimony on violence and the media, U.S. Senate Judiciary Committee, June 8, 1993, p. 3.
49. Eron, testimony, p. 1.
50. "Violence on Television: What Can Technology Do?" *CRS Reports for Congress,* Congressional Research Service, Library of Congress, Washington, D.C., July 27, 1993, pp. 3–4.
51. Dan Oldenburg, "Tuning in the Future of Kids' TV," *Washington Post,* Sept. 12, 1995, p. B5.
52. Jones, "Youth Violence and Mass Media," p. 20.
53. Michael Shnayerson, "Natural Born Opponents," *Vanity Fair,* July 1996, p. 100.
54. Details taken from Shnayerson, "Natural Born Opponents," pp. 98–144. See also ABC News *Prime Time Live,* "Crime Spree," Sept. 18, 1996; Scott Parks, "Hard Questions," *Dallas Morning News,* Nov. 12, 1995, p. 1A; Frank Ahrens, "'You Have the Right to Remain Silent,'" *Los Angeles Times,* Sept. 25, 1995, p. E1; William C. Bayne, "Sarah Dosed Anxieties with Drugs, Say Parents," *Commercial Appeal* (Memphis), July 30, 1995, p. 1A.
55. See Thurow, *The Future of Capitalism,* p. 85.

6. The Disabling of Dads

1. Youth interview, Task Force on Parent Empowerment, Apr. 17, 1996.
2. David Blankenhorn, *Fatherless America* (New York: Basic, 1995), p. 49.
3. David Popenoe, *Life Without Father: Compelling New Evidence that Fatherhood and Marriage Are Indispensable for the Good of Children and Society* (New York: Free Press, 1996), p. 4.
4. George Gilder, *Men and Marriage* (Gretna, La.: Pelican, 1986), p. 8.
5. Blankenhorn, *Fatherless America,* p. 1.

6. Details taken from Sara Rimer, "For Old South Boston, Despair Replaces Hope," *New York Times,* Aug. 17, 1997, p.1; Brian MacQuarrie, "In South Boston, Residents Struggle to Cope with Social Decay," *Boston Globe,* May 4, 1997 p. A1; Brian MacQuarrie, "Mother Says Stop Led Son to Suicide," *Boston Globe,* Feb. 13, 1997, p. B1.

7. U.S. Bureau of the Census, *Studies in Marriage and the Family,* Current Population Reports Series P-23, No. 162 (Washington, D.C.: GPO, 1989), p. 5.

8. Quoted in Tamar Lewin, "Father's Vanishing Act Called Common Drama," *New York Times,* June 4, 1990, p. A18.

9. Daniel Patrick Moynihan, *Family and Nation* (New York: Harcourt Brace Jovanovich, 1986), p. 168.

10. Popenoe, *Life Without Father,* p. 8.

11. Sara McLanahan and Gary Sandefur, *Growing Up with a Single Parent: What Hurts, What Helps* (Cambridge, Mass.: Harvard University Press, 1994), p. 61.

12. Ibid., pp. 79–94.

13. National Center for Children in Poverty, "Map and Track: State Initiatives to Encourage Responsible Fatherhood," press release, July 1997; Wade F. Horn, *Father Facts* 2 (Lancaster, Pa.: National Fatherhood Initiative, 1996), p. 35; Jean Bethke Elshtain, "Family Matters: The Plight of America's Children," *Christian Century,* July 14–21, 1993, p. 710; ibid.; Allen Beck, Susan Kline, and Lawrence Greenfield, *Survey of Youth in Custody, 1987* (Washington, D.C.: U.S. Bureau of Justice Statistics, September 1988), p. 1.

14. Leslie Margolin, "Child Abuse by Mothers' Boyfriends: Why the Overrepresentation?" *Child Abuse and Neglect* 16, no. 4 (July/Aug. 1992): 545–46.

15. Ching-Tung Wang and Deborah Daro, "Current Trends in Child Abuse Reporting and Fatalities: The Results of the 1996 Annual Fifty State Survey," Working Paper No. 808, National Committee to Prevent Child Abuse, Apr. 1997, Table 1, p. 5; American Humane Association, "Child Abuse and Neglect Data," Fact Sheet 5/97, p. 2. Calulations ours.

16. Dewey Cornel et al., "Characteristics of Adolescents Charged with Homicide," *Behavioral Sciences and the Law* 5 (1987): 11–23; Beck, Kline, and Greenfield, p. 1.

17. David Guttmann, "In the Absence of Fathers," *First Things,* Feb. 1995, p. 16.

18. Moynihan, *Family and Nation,* p. 9.

19. Parent interview, Task Force on Parent Empowerment, May 20, 1996.

20. Blankenhorn, *Fatherless America,* pp. 161–162.

21. John Munder Ross, *The Male Paradox* (New York: Simon and Schuster, 1992), pp. 154, 157, as cited in Blankenhorn, *Fatherless America,* pp. 292–93n18.

22. Robert Wright, *The Moral Animal: Evolutionary Psychology and Everyday Life* (New York: Vintage, 1994), p. 100.

23. Some scholars claim that these facts merely reflect the difficulties a violent man may have in finding a mate. Despite these objections, recent epidemiologic studies show that "marriage has a protective effect for men independent of the marriage selection factor."

24. Details taken from Joe Sexton, "For Suspect, Days of Rage and Routine," *New York Times*, June 16, 1996, p. 23; N. R. Kleinfield, "Beating Suspect's Admission Eerily Echoes a Father's Life," *New York Times*, June 15, 1996, p. 1; Fred Kaplan, "As Suspect in NYC Arraigned, a Portrayal of Anger Emerges," *Boston Globe*, June 15, 1996, p. 3.

25. Kleinfield, "Beating Suspect's Admission."

26. Lester G. Thurow, *The Future of Capitalism: How Today's Economic Forces Shape Tomorrow's World* (New York: Morrow, 1996), p. 23.

27. Center for the Study of Social Policy, *World Without Work: Causes and Consequences of Black Male Joblessness* (Washington, DC: CSSP, Dec. 1994), p. 1.

28. Tom Wolfe, *The Bonfire of the Vanities* (New York: Bantam, 1988), p. 58.

29. Edward N. Wolff, *Top Heavy: A Study of the Increasing Inequality of Wealth in America* (New York: Twentieth Century Fund), pp. 10–13.

30. Blankenhorn, *Fatherless America*, p. 205.

31. Diana DiNitto, *Social Welfare: Politics and Public Policy* (New York: Allyn & Bacon, 1995), pp. 169–70; see also James Leiby, *A History of Social Welfare and Social Work in the United States* (New York: Columbia University Press, 1978), pp. 266–67.

32. C. R. Winegarden, "AFDC and Illegitimacy Rates: A Vector-Autoregressive Model," *Applied Economics* 20 (1988): 1589–1601.

33. Jodi R. Sandfort and Martha S. Hill, "Assisting Young, Unmarried Mothers to Become Self-Sufficient: The Effects of Different Types of Economic Support," *Journal of Marriage and the Family* 58 (May 1996): 311–26.

34. U.S. Bureau of the Census, *Child Support and Alimony: 1989*, Current Population Reports, Series P-60, No, 173 (Washington, D.C.: GPO, 1991), p. 1.

35. Jack Kammer, "What Do We Really Know About Child Support?" *Crisis*, Jan. 1994, p. 60; see also Jack Kammer, *Good Will Toward Men* (New York: St. Martin's, 1994).

36. Details taken from Kammer, "What Do We Really Know?" pp. 60–61.

37. Daniel R. Meyer and Steven Garasky, "Custodial Fathers: Myths, Realities, and Child Support Policy," *Journal of Marriage and the Family* 55 (Feb. 1993): 85–86.

38. Details taken from Kammer, "What Do We Really Know?" pp. 60–61.

39. From the 1995 movie *Boys on the Side*, directed by Herbert Ross, written by Don Roos; Hero Productions.

40. From the 1995 movie *Waiting to Exhale*, directed by Forrest Whitaker, screenplay by Terry McMillan and Ronald Bass, a Deborah Schindler/Ezra Swerdlow Production.

41. Quoted in Blankenthorn, *Fatherless America*, p. 76.

42. From the original version of Kammer, "What Do We Really Know?"

reprinted in full at www.flash.net/~badger/medial.html. Interestingly, this section of the article was cut from the version printed in *The Crisis*.
43. Ibid.

7. Escape Routes: Promise Keepers and the Nation of Islam

1. Interview, Sept. 20, 1996, Shea Stadium, New York.
2. Interview, Sept. 20, 1996, Shea Stadium, New York.
3. Interview, Sept. 20, 1996, Shea Stadium, New York.
4. Ron Stodghill II, "God of Our Fathers: The Promise Keepers Are Bringing Their Manly Crusade to Washington," *Time*, Oct. 6, 1997, p. 36.
5. William R. Mattox, Jr., "Christianity Goes to the Playoffs," *American Enterprise*, Nov./Dec. 1995, p. 39; Gustav Niebuhr, "Men Crowd Stadiums to Fulfill Their Souls," *New York Times*, Aug. 6, 1995, p. A1.
6. Laurie Goodstein, "Hundreds of Thousands Gather on the Mall in a Day of Prayers," *New York Times*, Oct. 5, 1997, pp. 1, 24.
7. Bill McCartney and Dave Diles, *From Ashes to Glory* (Nashville, Tenn.: Thomas Nelson, 1995), p. 293.
8. Mattox, "Christianity Goes to the Playoffs," p. 41.
9. Details taken from E. Glenn Wagner with Dietrich Gruen, *Strategies for a Successful Marriage: A Study Guide for Men* (Colorado Springs, Colo.: NavPress, 1994), pp. 65–75.
10. "Promise Keepers: All That Bonding Really Is No Cause for Alarm," *St. Paul Pioneer Press*, July 13, 1995, p. 2E.
11. Parent interview, Task Force on Parent Empowerment, Dec. 1995, Eugene, Oregon.
12. Kenneth Woodward, "The Gospel of Guyhood," *Newsweek*, Aug. 29, 1994, p. 61.
13. Roundtable discussion, Task Force on Parent Empowerment, Nov. 3, 1995, New York, New York.
14. Ibid.
15. John Stoltenberg, "Male Virgins, Blood Covenants & Family Values," *On the Issues* (Spring 1995): 26.
16. Laurie Goodstein, "Men Pack RFK on Promise of Religious Renewal," *Washington Post*, May 28, 1995, p. A7.
17. Roundtable discussion.
18. Goodstein, "Men Pack RFK," p. A7.
19. Niebuhr, "Men Crowd Stadiums," p. 30.
20. Goodstein, "Men Pack RFK," p. A1.
21. Quoted in Stoltenberg, "Male Virgins," p. 29.
22. Laura Ingraham, "Men Who Can Do Nothing Right," *New York Times*, July 10, 1997, p. A23. For a discussion of reactions from the women's movement, see also Laurie Goodstein, "Women and the Promise Keepers: Good for the Gander, But the Goose Isn't So Sure," *New York Times*, Oct. 5, 1997, p. WK4.
23. Roundtable discussion.

24. Stodghill, "God of Our Fathers," p. 7.
25. See discussion in Jane Flax, "The Family in Contemporary Feminist Thought: A Critical Review," in *The Family in Political Thought,* ed. Jean Bethke Elshtain (Amherst: University of Massachusetts Press, 1982).
26. See Don S. Browning, Bonnie J. Miller-McLemore, Pamela D. Couture, K. Brynolf, and Robert M. Franklin, *From Culture Wars to Common Ground* (Louisville, Ky.: Westminster John Knox Press, 1997), pp. 157–90, for a rich discussion of the interaction between feminism and religion.
27. Quoted in Mattox, "Christianity Goes to the Playoffs," p. 41.
28. Roundtable discussion.
29. Ibid.
30. Ibid.
31. Ian M. Rolland, "Inheriting the Earth: Louis Farrakhan and the Nation of Islam," speech to the Quest Club, Fort Wayne, Ind., Feb. 3, 1995; published in *Vital Speeches of the Day,* Spring 1995, p. 377.
32. Ibid, p. 378.
33. "From the Most Honorable Elijah Muhammad," *Final Call,* Aug. 30, 1995, p. 2.
34. The Honorable Elijah Muhammad, "The Muslim Program: What the Muslims Want," *Final Call,* Aug. 30, 1995, p. 39.
35. Glenn C. Loury, "One Man's March," *New Republic,* Nov. 6, 1995, p. 21.
36. Janet Hook, "Mfume Cuts Renewed Ties to Nation of Islam," *Congressional Quarterly,* Feb. 5, 1994, p. 219.
37. Fred X. Wyche, "New Trial for Mumia!" *Final Call,* Aug. 30, 1995, p. 2.
38. Don Terry, "In the End, Farrakhan Has His Day in the Sun," *New York Times,* Oct. 17, 1995, p. A19.
39. Jill Smolowe, "Marching Home," *Time,* Oct. 30, 1995, p. 41.
40. Mary McGrory, "Talking Race," *Washington Post,* Oct. 17, 1995, p. A2.
41. Minister Louis Farrakhan, "A Holy Day of Atonement and Reconciliation," *Final Call,* Aug. 30, 1995, p. 22.
42. Ibid.
43. Terry Neal, "Farrakhan's Message of Atonement," *Washington Post,* Oct. 17, 1995, p. A22.
44. Howard Schneider and Lonnae O'Neal Parker, "What Counted Most Were the Men Who Were There," *Washington Post,* Oct. 17, 1995, p. A19.
45. Ibid, p. A20.
46. Ibid., p. A19.
47. Harrison Rainie, "A New Awakening," *U.S. News & World Report,* Oct. 30, 1995, p. 38.
48. Loury, "One Man's March," p. 22.
49. Melinda Beck, "Beyond the Moment, What Can One Day Do?" *Newsweek,* Oct. 30, 1995, p. 39.
50. Rainie, "A New Awakening," p. 36.
51. Beck, "Beyond the Moment."

52. Rainie, "A New Awakening," p. 33.
53. Beck, "Beyond the Moment."
54. For a wickedly mocking account of the "Stand in the Gap" event, see Maureen Dowd, "Promises, Promises, Promises," *New York Times,* Oct. 4, 1997, p. A15.

8. What Do Parents Want?

1. Participant, middle-income fathers group, Fieldwork East, Fort Lee, N.J., Jan. 30, 1997.
2. Participant, middle-income working mothers group, Coudert Brothers, New York, N.Y., Feb. 6, 1996.
3. For more detail, see the appendix. See also National Parenting Association, *What Will Parents Vote For?: Findings of the First National Survey of Parent Priorities* (New York: NPA, 1996).
4. Charles R. Morris, *The AARP: America's Most Powerful Lobby and the Clash of Generations* (New York: Times, 1996), pp. 1–69.
5. Given an average life expectancy, the typical one-earner couple retiring in 1995 will get about $123,000 more from social security than the average earner and his or her employers ever paid into it, plus interest. See Peter G. Petersen, *Will America Grow Up Before It Grows Old?* (New York: Random House, 1996), p. 42.
6. Ruy Teixeira, "Political Trends among American Parents: The 1950s to 1996," paper prepared for the Task Force on Parent Empowerment, June 9, 1997, p. 3.
7. Theda Skocpol, "What It Will Take to Build a Family-Friendly America," paper prepared for the Task Force on Parent Empowerment, Oct. 24, 1997, p. 17.

9. A Parents' Bill of Rights

1. Sylvia Ann Hewlett, *When the Bough Breaks: The Cost of Neglecting Our Children* (New York: HarperPerennial, 1991), pp. 219–21.
2. Sylvia Ann Hewlett, *Child Neglect in Rich Nations* (New York: UNICEF, 1993), p. 34.
3. In 1993, First Tennessee Bank implemented flexible scheduling. Their family-friendly workplace options include work at home, job sharing, flextime, and compressed work weeks and benefits for part-time workers. "Following the introduction of a policy allowing full-time workers to switch to part-time without giving up their benefits, 85% of full-timers who were prepared to quit for family reasons decided to stay on instead. Total savings in replacement costs: $5,000 to $10,000 for each nonmanagerial employee and $30,000 to $50,000 per executive." See Julia Lawlor, "The Bottom Line on Work-Family Programs," *Working Woman,* July/Aug. 1996, p. 55. Hewlett Packard, one of the world's leading makers of computers, has been on *Working Mother*'s "100 Best Com-

panies" list for ten years. They now have 5,000 telecommuters, 450 job sharers, and 2,300 employees on compressed work weeks. Price Waterhouse has over 800 people on alternative work arrangements and three new partners working part-time. See Milton Moskowitz, "100 Best Companies for Working Mothers," *Working Mother*, Oct. 1997, pp. 53–54, 84.

4. Stanley I. Greenspan, "The Reasons Why We Need to Rely Less on Day Care," *Washington Post*, Nov. 5, 1997, Outlook, p. 3.

5. See discussion in James Q. Wilson, "Two Nations," 1997 Francis Boyer Lecture, delivered to American Enterprise Institute, Dec. 4, 1997, p. 5.

6. "Once their time limits are up, most recipients will lose all benefits and be on their own"; Alan Finder, "Welfare Clients Outnumber Jobs They Might Fill," *New York Times*, Aug. 25, 1996, p. A1. See also Robert Pear, "House Approves Shift on Welfare," *New York Times*, p. A12, and Francis X. Clines, "Clinton Signs Bill Cutting Welfare; States in New Role," *New York Times*, Aug. 23, 1996, p. A1.

7. Wilson, "Two Nations," p. 4.

8. A full-time worker earning $7 an hour would earn $14,560 a year, which in 1996 was 115 percent of the poverty threshold for a family of three (our calculation). Telephone interview, Janine Moss, Poverty and Health Statistics Branch, U.S. Bureau of the Census, Jan. 20, 1998.

9. At $4.00 an hour, the subsidy is $3.00; at $8.00 an hour, the subsidy is $0.71. See Edmund S. Phelps, *Rewarding Work: How to Restore Participation and Self-Support to Free Enterprise* (Cambridge, Mass: Harvard University Press, 1997).

10. Ibid., p. 3. Senator Edward Kennedy has proposed an alternative idea. He suggests that just as the United States rewards other countries with tariff benefits if they qualify for "most favored nation" status, we should reward companies that treat their employees well with "most favored company" status. Businesses would qualify on the basis of their quantifiable record over a rolling four-year period in creating jobs, avoiding layoffs designed simply to maximize profits, paying adequate wages, sharing gains, training and upgrading workers' skills, and providing decent health care and retirement benefits. "Most favored companies" would be taxed at a reduced rate (for example, 30 rather than 34 percent) or receive a 10 percent reduction if they are already taxed at a lower rate. To take advantage of the tax break, they would agree to allocate half of the resulting benefit to their workers. See Kennedy, "The Rising Tide Must Lift More Boats," address to the Center for National Policy, Washington, D.C., Feb. 8, 1996, pp. 5–7.

11. National School-to-Work Office, U.S. Department of Education and U.S. Department of Labor, "School-to-Work Opportunities Grants," Jan. 15, 1997; "The School to Work Opportunities Act: Learning and Earning" Fact Sheet; "Elements of the School-to-Work Opportunities Act: Connecting Activities" Fact Sheet; "School-to-Work Opportunities Act of 1994, Public Law 103-239, May 4, 1994": all at http://www.stw.ed.gov.

12. In a little-known provision of the Work Opportunity Tax Credit, hiring an ex-offender can reduce employer taxes by as much as $8,500 per hire. See U.S. Department of Labor, Employment and Training Administration, "Job Training Opportunities for Ex-Offenders," Fact Sheet, May 1991.

13. Bob Herbert, "Topsy-Turvy Tax Cut," *New York Times,* June 30, 1997, p. A11.

14. This concept, recently developed by a group of economists and bankers, is based on the idea that would-be homeowners exercise the option of owning just part of a house, selling off an equity stake to a financial institution for a portion of the sale price. This could cut in half the carrying charges on a family home and open up home ownership to many more working- and middle-class parents. See Andrew Caplin, Sewin Chan, Charles Freeman, and Joseph Tracy, *Housing Partnerships: A New Approach to a Market at a Crossroads* (Cambridge, Mass.: MIT Press, 1997), pp. 1–18.

15. Louis S. Richman, "Housing Policy Needs a Rehab," *Fortune,* Mar. 27, 1989, p. 92, and Paul A. Leonard, Cushing N. Dolbeare, and Edward B. Lazere, "A Place to Call Home: The Crisis in Housing for the Poor" (Washington, D.C.: Center on Budget and Policy Priorities and Low Income Housing, April 1989,) p. 29.

16. Estimates for homelessness and near homelessness are notoriously difficult to arrive at. The National Coalition for the Homeless estimates that about 6.6 million adults experienced homelessness between 1989 and 1994 and that several times that number lived close to the edge of homelessness (that is, they were living with friends or family). See National Coalition for the Homeless, Fact Sheet #2 (Washington, D.C., Jan. 1997), p. 3.

17. Raymond Seidelman, professor, Sarah Lawrence College, interview, Jan. 20, 1998. See also Bruce Miroff, Raymond Seidelman, and Todd Swanston, *The Democratic Debate: An Introduction to American Politics* (Boston: Houghton Mifflin, 1998), pp. 114–15.

18. Alexei Bayer, "Let's Give Parents an Extra Right to Vote," *New York Times,* May 4, 1997, p. F12.

19. Theda Skocpol, "A Partnership with American Families," in Stanley B. Greenberg and Theda Skocpol, eds., *The New Majority: Toward a Popular Progressive Politics* (New Haven, Conn.: Yale University Press, 1997), p. 123.

20. Andrew Cherlin, *Marriage, Divorce, Remarriage* (Cambridge, Mass.: Harvard University Press, 1982), pp. 47–48.

21. Kevin Sack, "Louisiana Approves Measure to Tighten Marriage Bonds," *New York Times,* June 24, 1997, p. A1. See also Amitai Etzioni, "Marriage with No Easy Outs," *New York Times,* Aug. 13, 1997, p. A23.

22. Michael Prowse, "When the Cornflake Bowl Is Empty," *Financial Times,* Aug. 8, 1990, p. 13.

23. For an in-depth analysis, see William A. Galston, "Observations on Some

Proposals to Assist Parents and Families," paper prepared for the Task Force on Parent Empowerment, Oct. 24, 1997, pp. 3–14.

24. See discussion in Allan Carlson and David Blankenhorn, "Marriage and Taxes," *Weekly Standard,* Nov. 17, 1997, pp. 24–27.

25. Conna Craig, "What I Need Is a Mom," *Policy Review* (Summer 1995): 48.

26. James Alan Fox and Sanford A. Newman, "After-School Crime or After-School Programs: Tuning In to the Prime Time for Violent Juvenile Crime and Implications for National Policy," A Report to the United States Attorney General, Sept. 1997.

27. Ralph Gardner Jr., "Protecting Children Going to School," *New York Times,* Dec. 15, 1994, p. C1.

28. "Men Against Destruction—Defending Against Drugs and Social-disorder" (MAD DADS), Omaha, Nebraska, Fact Sheet, pp. 1–3.

29. James Bennet, "Gun Makers Agree on Safety Locks," *New York Times,* Oct. 9, 1997, p. A1.

30. M. Edith Rasell and Lawrence Mishel, "Shortcoming Education: How U.S. Spending on Grades K-12 Lags Behind Other Industrial Nations," briefing paper (Washington, D.C.: Economic Policy Institute, 1989), pp. 1–2.

31. The French budget for child care and child health services expanded by 60 percent between 1989 and 1994. See Marise Simons, "Child Care Sacred as France Cuts Back the Welfare State," *New York Times,* Dec. 31, 1997, p. 1.

32. Lisbeth B. Schorr, *Within Our Reach: Breaking the Cycle of Disadvantage* (New York: Doubleday, 1988), pp. 192–200; see also Stanley I. Greenspan, *The Growth of the Mind: And the Endangered Origins of Intelligence* (New York: Addison-Wesley, 1996), p. 229.

33. Committee for Economic Development, *Investing in Our Children: Business and the Public Schools* (New York: CED, 1985).

34. Marian Wright Edelman, "Head Start Works," *CDF Reports* 18, No. 5 (April 1997): 3. The Clinton administration has proposed increasing Head Start funding by $324 million in fiscal year 1998 and plans to put Head Start on track to serve an additional one million children by the year 2002. This would still leave one million children unserved and represents a major step back from the administration's 1993 commitment to fund Head Start fully by FY 1999.

35. Nancy Rankin, "Highlights of Recently Enacted Education and Health Initiatives," paper prepared for the Task Force on Parent Empowerment, Oct. 24, 1997, pp. 1–3.

36. Ellen Galinsky, transcript of interview on "Bringing Up Baby," *Newshour* (PBS), Oct. 23, 1997, p. 1.

37. David Blankenhorn, "Shouldn't We Help Parents Be Parents?" *New York Times,* Dec. 19, 1997, p. A39.

38. Stanley Greenspan, transcript of interview on "Bringing Up Baby," *Newshour* (PBS), Oct. 23, 1997, p. 2.

39. Ellen Goodman, "Child Care Is a Measure of Our Values," *Newsday,* Jan. 18, 1998, p. B8.

40. Margaret O. Kirk, "Parents, the Ultimate Experts, Critique the Clinton Proposal," *New York Times,* Jan. 18, 1998, p. 4. Overall, Clinton is proposing a $21.7 billion package that includes an expanded child-care tax credit for middle-class families, block grants to states for poorer kids, and credits for businesses as well as monies for training workers.

41. See discussion in Blankenhorn, "Shouldn't We Help Parents?"

42. Telephone interview, Mary Crippen, family advocate, and Elizabeth Roe, child-care assistance specialist, Minnesota Department of Children, Families, and Learning, Feb. 13, 1998.

43. *School of the 21st Century,* Bush Center in Child Development and Social Policy, Yale University, Spring 1997.

44. Rankin, "Highlights," p. 4.

45. Ibid.

46. *National Survey Results on Drug Use from the Monitoring the Future Study, 1975–1996;* National Institute on Drug Abuse, "Facts About Teenagers and Drug Abuse," NIDA Capsule Series (C-83-07), 1996; "Monitoring the Future Study: Trends in Prevalence of Various Drugs for 8th Graders, 10th Graders and High School Seniors," NIDA Capsule Series (C-94-01), 1996.

47. Joseph A. Califano, chairman and president, National Center on Addiction and Substance Abuse at Columbia University, *Back to School 1997— CASA National Survey of American Attitudes on Substance Abuse III: Teens and Their Parents, Teachers, and Principals,* Press Release, Sept. 8, 1997, p. 1, www.casacolumbia.org.

48. National Center on Addiction and Substance Abuse at Columbia University (CASA), *CASA Adolescent Commission Report,* Part 4, Aug. 1997, p. 4, www.casacolumbia.org/pubs/aug97.

49. Join Together, "Drug-Free School Zones," Aug. 19, 1994, www.jointogether.org.

50. Barbara M. Jones, "Guns, Drugs and Juvenile Justice: Three Aspects of the Crisis in Youth Violence," paper prepared for the Task Force on Parent Empowerment, Apr. 17, 1996, p. 24.

51. Interview, Peggy Charren, founder, Action for Children's Television, Feb. 13, 1998.

52. Lynette Friedrich Cofer and Robin Smith Jacobvitz, "The Loss of Moral Turf: Mass Media and Family Values," in *Rebuilding the Nest: A New Commitment to the American Family,* ed. David Blankenhorn, Steven Bayme, and Jean Bethke Elshtain (Milwaukee: Family Service America, 1990), p. 198.

53. Broadcasters sometimes underestimate children's interest in educational shows. Nickelodeon, responding to "growing discontent among parents with other primetime offerings," has recently filled the eight-to-eight-thirty slot with children's shows like *The Secret World of Alex* and *Mack Hey Arnold!* and so far the rates for these shows have been surprisingly

strong. Lawrie Mifflin, "Nickelodeon Adds to Children's Hours," *New York Times,* Nov. 13, 1997, p. E8.

54. Telephone interview, David Walsh, president, National Institute on Media and the Family, Feb. 16, 1998.

55. Michelle Ganon, "Let's Have a Family Discount," *New York Times,* Jan. 20, 1998, p. A21.

56. See, for example, Fordham Institute for Innovation in Social Policy, *1997 Index of Social Health* (Tarrytown, N.Y.: FIISP, 1997).

57. CNN/USA Today/Gallup Poll, Dec. 16–18, 1994.

58. See George F. Will, "A G.I. Bill for Mothers," *Newsweek,* Dec. 22, 1997, p. 88.

59. Alison Mitchell, "Parties Rethink Their Core Goals as Deficit Shrinks," *New York Times,* Dec. 28, 1997, p. 1.

Appendix A

1. Participant, middle-income fathers group, Fieldwork East, Fort Lee, N.J., Jan. 30, 1997.

Index

men (cont.)
  185–211 (see also Nation of Islam; Promise Keepers)
Merchant family, 116–17
Messer, Alfred, 164
Metzger, Jeff, 197
Meyerson, Mitch, 137, 138
Miller, Alice, 139–41
Miller, Ellen, 84, 85
Miller, Thomas J., 209
Million Man March, 183, 185, 206–9. See also Nation of Islam
minimum wage, 67–68; need to raise, 236–37
Mondale, Walter, 114
Mondale Act, 113
Montel Williams (TV), 126
Moore, Barrington, 103
Morris, Jason, 91
mortgages: and decline of home ownership, 107–8; GI Bill providing, 101–2; need for family-friendly subsidies for, 239; tax deductions for, 99, 108–9
motherhood. See also single motherhood; feminist critique of, 95–96
mothers. See also parenting; changing roles for, 37–38; depicted in fifties culture, 129; noncustodial, 177–78; unpaid labor of, 36–39
movies: celebrating parents, in the fifties, 129; demeaning males, 180–81; denigrating parents, 127, 131–32
Moynihan, Daniel Patrick, 167
Muhammad, Elijah (Muhammad, W. D. Farad), 202–3, 204–5
Muhammed, Warith, 203
Mulammad, Khalid Abdul, 205–6
multiple-job families, 71–74
Murphy Brown (TV), 161, 181
music, popular: denigrating parents, 132–33

Naab, Jerry Lee, 91
NAACP, 206
National Assessment of Educational Progress, 46
National Association of Broadcasters, 149
National Association of Manufacturers, 64
National Association of Realtors, 107
National Bureau of Economic Research, 243

National Center on Child Abuse and Neglect, 114
National Coalition on Black Voter Participation, 209
National Commission on the Causes and Prevention of Violence, 147
National Labor Relations Act of 1935, 65
National Labor Relations Board (NLRB), 65
National Organization of Women (NOW), 198, 199
National Parenting Association, 215
National Parents' Day, 252–53
Nation of Islam, 40, 183–84, 185–89, 201–11; attributes shared with Promise Keepers, 185–89, 209–11; founding and evolution of, 202–6; and Million Man March, 182–83, 185, 206–9; self-discipline and, 189, 201–2, 207–9; separatism of, 202; teachings of, 204–6
Natural Born Killers (film), 151–53
Nelson, Michael, 206
Newberger, Eli, 115
New Darwinism, 166, 169
Newman, Sanford A., 245
New York Times, 86
Nixon, Richard, 103
Nobel Prize, 101
no-fault divorce, 94–95
noncustodial parents: child support by, 40
nursery schools, 246

obesity: increase of, 43
O'Donnell, Rosie, 34
on-line computer services, 145
Orlando Sentinel, 201
out-of-wedlock births. See also single motherhood; increase of, 162–63; welfare benefits and, 176
outside suppliers: replacing waged employees, 69
overtime: time off vs., 217–18
Ozzie and Harriet (TV), 129–30

Papathomas, Jim, 185–89, 195–96, 199, 200
parent(s): demands and expectations of, 215–29 (see also Parents' Bill of Rights); disabling and displacing of, 109–18; Freudian theory on, 139–41;

"Images of Mothers and Fathers"

The artwork on the front jacket of this book was contributed by students who participated in the art project called "Images of Mothers and Fathers." Credits for this work appear below, along with explanatory writings by the artists.

TOP ROW, LEFT: "My Angry/Sad Mother," by Su Li Zheng, 12th grade, Brooklyn. "When my mother is angry, she seems to develop two sides of her personality: one side sad and one side mad as hell."

TOP ROW, CENTER: "My Mother Now, Myself as a Mother (Images of Love)," by Jakia Bland, 7th grade, Bronx.

TOP ROW, RIGHT: "Sins," by Juan Padilla, 12th grade, Brooklyn.

Sins
Argument breaks out
Cry, scream, shout
Yells and sobs are heard
Chaos is the word
Displaying all fears
by a flood of tears
Stress builds up
Frustration piles on top
Empty is the feeling
staring at the ceiling
contemplating suicide
don't think I wanna die.
Striving to be strong
Things will not go wrong

Pray for better times
These thoughts are on my mind.

BOTTOM ROW LEFT: "Yearnings," by Diana Mercado, 8th grade, Bronx. "This picture is about my mother, father and me. It is about how I wish my father would live with my mother and I so that we could really take a walk in the park."

BOTTOM ROW, CENTER: "My Mother as a Clock Face (La Femme de Temps)," by Angela Williams, 9th grade, Brooklyn. "This picture expresses the life of my hardworking mother. Basically she is always busy. Her life is based on work and making money. She dreams of taking a long vacation from her busy days, but this may not happen so easily. My mother does not look like the average woman. She has very short hair and she doesn't wear jewelry or makeup. This picture describes her life in a nutshell."

BOTTOM ROW, RIGHT: "Maternal Love," by Dominique Theronier, 11th grade, Brooklyn. "This painting expresses the way I feel about my future with my child. I want my child to be happy and I want her to love me the same way I love her. In that way we will have a good relationship so that nobody will be able to take us apart. I wanted this picture to be alive; that is why I used a lot of bright colors."